The Dilemma of American Social Welfare

The Dilemma of American Social Welfare

William M. Epstein

Routledge
Taylor & Francis Group

LONDON AND NEW YORK

First published 1993 by Transaction Publishers

Published 2017 by Routledge
2 Park Square, Milton Park, Abingdon, Oxon OX14 4RN
711 Third Avenue, New York, NY 10017, USA

Routledge is an imprint of the Taylor & Francis Group, an informa business

Library of Congress Catalog Number: 92-29895

Library of Congress Cataloging-in-Publication Data

Epstein, William M., 1944-
  The dilemma of American social welfare / William M. Epstein
        p.   cm.
  Includes bibliographical references and indexes.
  ISBN   1-56000-088-0
     1. Social service—United States. 2. United States—Social
  policy—1980- I. Title.
HV91.E67
361.973—dc20

                                                    92-29895
                                                    CIP

ISBN-13: 978-1-4128-4586-1 (pbk)
ISBN-13: 978-1-56000-088-4 (hbk)

For my parents, Lillian and Harry

In memorium
Kiernan F. Stenson
1927–1991

Contents

Preface

This book tells the story of how science, social need and citizenship are betrayed in the contemporary culture of the United States. It speaks to the audience that listens with wonderment to professional claims for expertise in handling America's social problems while witnessing their steady growth.

The social sciences that are most germane to contemporary social policy—economics, psychology, the policy sciences, and sociology—have not provided credible information or impartial, objective advise. In their applied forms—psychiatry, psychology, social work, criminology, public administration, and so forth—they have largely avoided rigorous tests of their advice. Indeed, social science research and social service agencies have propagated the pleasing myth of social efficiency—that just a little bit, wisely spent, is enough to solve social problems in the United States. This myth of social efficiency dominates the discourse of social welfare. Superficial responses to serious deprivations will postpone a humane civic culture for the United States until some unforeseen economic event—perhaps cheap, accessible solar power—fortuitously coincides with a revolution in human consciousness to solve the nation's problems. Yet until the second coming of a compassionate technology, the United States is stuck with a dilemma.

The book's return to the critical tradition in the social services is made as an act of faith within the community of scholars concerned with the conditions of society. The utility of a scholarly role rests on its independent relationship to its culture, providing thoughtful interpretations of social policy. Its meanest role is played out as an apologist for that society's failures.

The task of depriving the human services of their scientific cachet is a political event with professional overtones. The issue of method, of the criteria for proving effectiveness, is an issue of social policy, the broad choice of strategy to resolve social problems. To mask failure as success behind pliable tests of effectiveness is knowingly to create misleading myths in both of its two senses: importantly as a decisive metaphor, that is, as propaganda, and less importantly as a fictional account of an event.

I am indebted to a number of colleagues and mentors for their valuable comments on earlier drafts: Robert Morris, Agnes Kwok, Al Bunting, Astrida Butners, Ngai Ngan-pun, Bernard Cooper, Mary Parent, Albert and Laverne Rodriguez, Tom Keenan, Brij Mohan, Lawrence Rubin, Marvin Bloom, Shirley Cox, Anthony J. Grasso, Roberta J. Warren, Joyce Lai Mah, Jonathan Reader, William P. Monahan, and Roy Deberry. Virginia Ng, my research assistant in Hong Kong, and Rachel Nielsen, my assistant at the University of Nevada, Las Vegas, saved me countless hours of labor by their careful work.

The superbly skilled and ever patient research librarians in the Humanities and Social Sciences Division of the Library of Congress, one of the nation's premier public institutions and one of the victims of its mindless penny-pinching, offered unique bibliographic assistance and research support.

Introduction

In the current—and probably characteristic—political climate of the United States, there are no feasible solutions to contemporary social problems. Even with modest budget increases, current strategies will still fail to handle serious social problems—poverty, unemployment, family dissolution, juvenile crime, drug abuse, and so forth. Only vastly greater expenditures to restore and improve the nation's basic social institutions—families, schools, work systems, and communities—have any reasonable chance of success.

But this unpopular course of action, anathema to the American ethos, is unlikely to be pursued in the current political climate of the United States, in spite of the fact that most Americans—probably 60 percent— are not doing well and are cut off from reasonable opportunities to either prevent or resolve their problems. Many Americans are afflicted by financial, employment, educational, psychological, legal, and health problems that are beyond their capacity to resolve. Many Americans lead third world lives.

Social problems tend to emerge and then to endure among those who can not or do not participate adequately in the customary and relatively permanent arrangements—social institutions—of their culture. The general strategy to address these problems would seem to lie along the line of providing more equivalent experiences in basic social institutions: family, work, education, community, and so forth. Presumably, people who go through similar beneficial experiences, by and large, end up behaving in similarly beneficial ways: abiding by law; accepting social restraints without coercion; contributing to the general good by fulfilling their roles as students, parents, and workers; and producing through their common behaviors a humane civic culture.

Many social problems are probably prevented in the first instance by adequate access to social institutions—whether this access occurs through the natural processes of private society or through the conscious provision of social welfare programs by government. Good schooling, caring families, safe communities, and productive work prevent problems. After they emerge, social problems tend to be resolved when surrogates can compensate for deficient prior participation in specific

1

social institutions. For example, children who are abused, neglected, or abandoned by their own families can be relocated with foster families that compensate for the prior harm by providing a culturally normal family environment.

Members of attentive social institutions tend to avoid drug addiction and delinquency. There may be a few bad seeds. But by and large, children become addicts and delinquents because of the failures of their families, schools, and communities. If crime and addiction are to be prevented or cured, then families must be present to guide their children, schools must shepherd them though a variety of learning experiences, and the community must provide them with a variety of opportunities and safeguards, notably today, a safe environment and the ability as adults to earn a living.

Contemporary American society denies large numbers of its citizens adequate participation in basic social institutions. Widespread need is destroying hopes for a buoyant civic culture, dragging Americans into a stultifying and predatory fifty-first state of the union in which fewer and fewer people can pursue the simple promises of modern life. This loss of a humane civic culture expresses a collective refusal among Americans to provide adequate resources for families, education, jobs, health and mental health care, social security, and public welfare.

Poverty is still a large problem in the world's wealthiest nation. Measured against a threshold of $10,563 per year (1987 dollars) for a four-person family, more than 13 percent of Americans have been poor every year since 1980. In 1990 the poverty rate grew for the first time since 1983. Since a low of 11.4 percent in 1978, the poverty rate has been gradually edging upward, with almost 32 million Americans living below this meager level in 1988. With a slightly higher threshold (25 percent more than the poverty line) 42.6 million Americans, almost 18 percent of the population, were poor in 1988.

Poverty is not distributed evenly. More than one in five children were brought up in poverty in 1990. Also in 1990, almost one-third of blacks and one-quarter of Hispanics were poor compared with only one-tenth of whites. Fully 44.5 percent of female headed households with children lived under the poverty line. These measures already reflect the impact of government and private welfare programs (data from the U.S. Bureau of the Census 1991).

Public welfare and retirement programs only removed a modest number of people from poverty. In 1986, the poverty rate would have been approximately 21 percent before government transfers. Social security payments (OASDHI), concentrated on the elderly, dropped the rate to 14.4 percent. The small cash assistance program (AFDC), a total net cost of only 17.1 billion in 1990, removed just a few more people from poverty, dropping the poverty rate to 13.5 percent. With the inclusion of food stamps, housing assistance and the value of Medicaid the poverty rate only drops to 11.6 percent (Statistical Abstract of the U.S., 1990, table 751).

The real value of welfare payments have decreased more than 26 percent since 1972, while the nation's wealth has grown (Committee on Ways and Means 1991, 1090). During these decades, social policy, reflecting social preferences, has approved a distribution of income and a redistributive role for government that favors the wealthiest Americans while increasing the burden on people who cannot afford to handle a variety of problems. Between 1967 and 1990, the share of aggregate family income declined for the poorer 60 percent of the population and increased for the top 20 percent. The share of income has fallen for the poorest 20 percent of Americans by 15 percent since 1967 and grown by 6 percent for the wealthiest 5 percent and 7 percent for the top 20 percent (Bureau of the Census 1991). Moreover, these measures of income actually understate the differences in wealth among Americans.

The threshold definition of American poverty itself has been set at bare subsistence while some states refuse to meet even this level. In 1991, Mississippi as one example capped off the combined total of AFDC and Food Stamp payments at $5,700 for a family of four. Even at subsistence levels, poverty was still a problem for as many as 20 percent of Americans in 1990. Moreover, another very large portion of Americans, perhaps a majority, live financially and, therefore, culturally precarious lives, one or two events away from desperation. Median family income before taxes has increased only slightly in the past two decades: $35,353 in 1990 and $31,226 (1990 dollars) in 1970. Income inequality, an imperfect but suggestive measure of cultural inequality (that again probably understates inequality measured by wealth), grew by almost 9 percent between 1970 and 1990.[1] In 1990, 61 percent of families earned less than $50,000 and 33.2 percent less than $25,000 (Bureau of the Census 1991). While there is a great turnover in the ranks of the poor, those who leave typically graduate only to slightly better conditions (Committee on Ways and Means 1991).

Consistent with income inequality, poorer families relative to wealthier families had fewer earners, the earners were less educated, and they were unemployed more often (Bureau of the Census 1991). In 1990, more than 15 percent of Americans—approximately 40 million people and largely the near poor and the working poor—were neither eligible for public health care nor could afford private health insurance.

The social problems of Americans are the manifestations of their culture's inadequacies, its refusal to provide access to common protections and opportunities for large numbers of its members. The conditions of children, in particular, have been deteriorating over the past three decades. While 87.7 percent of children lived with two parents in 1960, only 73.1 percent did so in 1989. For blacks the rate fell from 67 percent in 1960 to 38 percent in 1989. Of those living with one parent, only 4.2 percent of those parents had never married in 1960, in 1989 the figure was 30.9 percent (Committee on Ways and Means 1991). The sustained problems of children in the United States imply that the inadequacy of its institutions—its core of social arrangements—have been accepted if not actually endorsed by a decisive proportion of its population.

Among industrialized nations, the United States has the highest teenage pregnancy rates and some of the highest infant mortality rates. Substance abuse, crime ,and victimization rates are enormous (Committee on Ways and Means 1991, 969). In 1986, 1.8 percent of America's adult population—3,239,026 people—lived under "correctional supervision"; 65 percent on probation, 25 percent in prison or jail, and 17 percent on parole; 34 percent were black, 65 percent white (U.S. Department of Justice 1989). In 1985, 313 juveniles out of every 10,000 juveniles were in a correctional facility (Committee on Ways and Means 1991).

In 1989, the school dropout rate exceeded 10 percent. Only 83 percent of eighteen and nineteen year olds who were not in school had completed high school. Many graduates were not adequately prepared to earn a living. In 1988, 19.5 percent of children three to seventeen years of age had suffered "a delay in growth or development, a learning disability, or an emotional problem that lasted three months or more or required psychological help." Only 4.0 percent received any attention (Committee on Ways and Means 1991, 1002-3). The United States Department of

Education estimated that in 1988, 220,000 children were homeless at some point during the year. Estimates of the number of adults who are homeless run into the millions (Committee on Ways and Means 1991, 1068).

By and large, when the customary social institutions of American culture—family, school, medical care system, community, and labor market—fail, 60 percent of Americans, disproportionately female and overrepresenting ethnic minorities, have little recourse to alternative care or to alternative services.

In addressing the problems of American blacks, a committee of the National Academy of Sciences recently concluded that a new American challenge, emerging "after the civil rights era of the 1960's results from two aspirations of black Americans: equal opportunity—the removal of barriers to employment, housing, education, and political activities—and the actual attainment of equality in participation in those sectors of life" (Jaynes and Williams, 5).

But the attainment of greater equality requires the expenditure of much greater resources and not simply the removal of barriers, formal or informal. In this sense, the social problems of the U.S. have been color coded. The plight of blacks signal the persistent refusal of the American culture to correct its failed institutions. The conditions of blacks have traced the problems of poor people generally in the United States.[2]

An accurate and comprehensive social profile of the American people has been bitterly resisted, perhaps to maintain the comforting myth of a nation making progress against its problems. Both the economic and the social data of the large demographic surveys (conducted by Census Bureau, Bureau of Labor Statistics, Center for Health Statistics and others), in spite of their precision, still obscure the burden that any problem imposes on the poorer 60 percent of Americans. Indeed, measures of income are imperfect proxies for the more profound impacts of social institutions.

The drag of a social problem on poorer people is far greater than the same problem among people who can afford to purchase either cure or relief. Small emergencies wipe out gains and savings. The majority of American families cannot afford to supplement the inadequate public services of American life with educational tutoring, private counseling or residential programs, or vocational training and retraining. They have no financial cushion for extended illnesses, especially of breadwinners.

An enormous proportion of Americans must make do with inadequate institutions, living in a relatively permanent subculture of hardship. The achievement of true cultural citizenship for the majority of Americans— the ability to lead a decent life, to become decent people, to leave a social legacy of value—is blocked today not so much by racist barriers or strict class lines, although remnants of these still persist, but by the failure to pass through minimally acceptable families, schools, jobs, and communities.

The social services and the human services more broadly (which include health care and public health, and education in addition to the social services) are ostensibly designed to handle social problems either by preventing their occurrence or, once they have emerged, through rehabilitation and cure. The social services cover programs in mental health and hygiene, counseling, corrections, child care (foster, care, adoption, and others), residential and protective care, day care, vocational training and retraining, recreation and community centers, drug and alcohol rehabilitation, and a multitude of others designed to address specific problems such as spouse abuse and homelessness and specific populations such as the mentally retarded and the physically disabled. Social services also include the concrete provision of food, clothing, shelter, and the traditional cash transfer programs of the welfare system.[3]

The social service sector of the American economy is enormous. In 1990, 106,000 "firms" with revenues of almost $40 billion provided social services *outside of the mental health, health, and educational systems*. These revenues do not include cash benefits, food stamps, medical care, or housing subsidies. These firms employed more than 1.8 million people.[4]

Within the American workforce, a large number of people reported specialized social service occupations (including a variety of educational degrees): 603,000 social workers, 203,000 psychologists, 222,000 counselors, and 106,000 recreational workers.

In addition, a large number of people are employed outside of the social service occupational categories in tasks related to the delivery of social services: specialty training, evaluation, policy development, legislation, public administration, and so forth. A very conservative estimate of the total annual cost of the social services across the different sectors of the American economy, particularly including social services delivered through the medical care and education systems, probably exceeds $100 billion.[5] Nonetheless, the social services are still grossly inadequate to resolve America's social problems.

Social problems in the United States have been increasing along with a series of politically conservative administrations that took a mandate from their very large national victories and reduced the public commitment for social welfare. These policies have been very popular. The central tenets of this public philosophy deny the importance of greater social equality. In the rare instances when this philosophy acknowledges that greater social equality may be desirable, government—meaning the redistributive mechanisms of public policy—is cast for a small role in the expectation that an unencumbered private sector will secure social and economic justice. The failure of this role, resulting in widespread neglect, does not seem to carry severe political consequences.

The conflict between the resources needed to address contemporary social problems in the United States and the political unwillingness to come up with those resources defines the current dilemma of American social policy: solutions for social problems exist in principle but they are not politically feasible. The cost to repair the U.S. civic culture by providing surrogate social institutions to compensate for the failures of families, educational and vocational systems, labor markets, and communities is staggering. The majority of Americans are reluctant to restructure American society by relinquishing a large portion of their personal income either for the amorphous benefits of an improved civic culture or to subsidize their poorer fellow citizens. At the same time, the poor, the near poor, and other lower status groups have not effectively pressed their claims.

Juvenile crime and drug addiction in the United States are immense problems. They are being handled in typical ways that will not produce a solution. Yet psychotherapy, the core technique of many strategies to rehabilitate addicts and delinquents, remains stubbornly popular. New therapies become fashionable. New programs are funded. The professional literature periodically finds new grounds for optimistic reappraisals of its curative potency.

The public sector is not developing a strategy to handle social problems that has any reasonable chance to reduce crime and drug addiction, to rehabilitate criminals and addicts, or to prevent the abuse of alcohol, narcotics, and other drugs. The sustaining causes of crime and addiction are being ignored. Even the threat of widespread AIDS infection posed by intravenous drug use has not moved American social welfare policy off of its monotonic insistence upon parsimony.

This refusal to handle drug addiction and juvenile delinquency is emblematic of America's long-standing decision to endure the consequences of social problems and to preserve existing social arrangements. In recent decades, the United States has also made little if any progress against adult crime, poverty, unemployment, illiteracy and ignorance, family dissolution, mental disease, child neglect, and others. These failures are fracturing the culture. Even America's economic prosperity is threatened by its refusal to invest in its domestic welfare. Current social policy in the United States is aware of its inadequacy.

Plausible solutions, in terms of a more egalitarian social welfare agenda, will not be implemented without a deep political consensus. However, the public is not being fairly exposed to arguments for broad-based, that is, structural solutions to its problems. The community of human service scholars—largely composed of social scientists—tacitly accepts the implausibility of structural solutions and the intractability of current problems, being committed to one or another service technique, frequently some form of psychotherapy. These stakes have resulted in misleading and patently inaccurate claims of program effectiveness.

By denying the near uniform inability of America's network of social services to either prevent or to remedy social problems, the scholarly enterprise of the human services makes a Faustian bargain with political power and fails to fulfill its obligations to objective science. This distortion acts both against the immediate interests of people with problems who need an honest advocate and against the long-term ability of the United States to develop a humane civic culture. However, false claims for the effectiveness of questionable social welfare programs do endorse the value of socially efficient solutions.

The popularity of psychotherapeutic social rehabilitation programs is not surprising. They are far less expensive than programs designed to provide, as one example, delinquent youth, and the larger number of youth at risk of delinquency, with environments that are similar to those of their more successful peers. Social and political enthusiasms for low-cost cures, the characteristic responses of the United States to its social problems, maintain the belief that minimal interventions can be found that are effective in resolving deep social problems. Unfortunately, even at intensive levels, psychotherapy has failed to cure addiction and to rehabilitate young delinquents. It has failed to achieve any objectively measured behavioral change for any group of people. No other socially efficient cure has worked either. More intensive strategies and consequently more expensive ones have not been tried.

The American ethos has entrenched the belief that the circuit of social problems can be shorted without paying the huge costs and without making the institutional rearrangements that are required to resolve its social problems. This commitment to efficient solutions inspires the decisive metaphors of prevailing social myths. These myths reconcile the preservation of private income with the large amount of frank social need. If efficient solutions were possible, then no deep redistribution of resources and, consequently, no restructuring of American life would be needed.

The possibility of socially efficient solutions to social problems are based upon two assumptions that the social services claim to have realized in practice: first, that the cause of a social problem can be identified and controlled to engineer low-cost solutions, and second, that those solutions can be implemented within customary social arrangements. A pill is the classic metaphor for social efficiency, tiny costs relative to the disease and a form of treatment that is compatible with modern life.

Unfortunately, efficient solutions for the classic social problems facing contemporary America have rarely if ever been effective. Ironically, medicine and engineering, through the immense architecture of science and supportive social belief, have themselves transformed society. The true outcomes of America's social demonstrations, its experiments in preventing or resolving social problems, have been routinely distorted by pseudoscientific claims of effectiveness. Indeed, the pursuit of effective solutions to serious social problems has been warped by pressures to confirm the plausibility of socially efficient solutions. The social sciences, especially their applied clinical forms in psychology and social work have built professional standing on evidence that low-cost substitutes are plausible and that this evidence is scientifically credible.

The critical tradition in the human services has been small and ineffective. On the one side, human service practitioners, with large personal stakes in their particular techniques, have not tolerated demonstrations of their ineffectiveness. On the other side, conservatives, defined by their opposition to structural remedies for social problems, have been hostile to evidence that the meager current provisions for social welfare have been insufficient.

Caught between inadequacy and the impossibility of expansion, a ceremonial role—the justification of low public expenditures for social institutions—has emerged for the human services in the United States. Social service programs and the social science community are rewarded for propagating the myth of social efficiency through various rituals of modern professional life, most notably the invocation of science in justifying their treatment techniques and an unquestioning assurance of their value.

This ceremonial role supplants their production functions as purposive organizations to resolve social problems by delivering specific, measurable, controllable services to populations in need. Contemporary social services are *only* equipped to fulfill a ceremonial role; even under optimal "laboratory" conditions, they have been unable to demonstrate a production function in prevention and rehabilitation.

The acknowledged importance of scientific proof has not inspired credible tests of the effectiveness of human service programs. After decades of plangent admiration for objectivity and coherence in the caring professions and the social sciences, their many thousands of published investigations have neither tested program effectiveness with available techniques of methodological rigor nor reported their findings accurately. The shallow genuflections that most evaluations of human services make to rational accountability preserve the tenets of social efficiency: that low-cost human service programs are at least partially *effective*, that *progress* is being made, that social problems are novel infectious diseases that will eventually be cured when *a dedicated subcommunity of social scientists invents the appropriate social pill.*

Reality is quite different. The basic technologies of the social services are misguided. At their current levels of funding they cannot replace failed social institutions nor compensate for prior deprivation. They are misdirecting their pitifully scarce resources into unproductive channels. Psychotherapy is not effective in correcting deviant behaviors. Contemporary solutions based upon modern incentive theories and more traditional attempts to resolve these problems also fail.

Reliable and valid methods of investigation have not been commonly applied to the either the social services nor more generally to the human services. An enormous gap separates the capacity to evaluate the effects of human services, especially when they are delivered in settings that are analogous to medical clinics, from the reality of outcome research. Studies of human services have been routinely disciplined by the stakes of professionals, not by the dictates of objectivity and coherence. Indeed, subjective tests of effectiveness, quickly responsive to these stakes, are being resurrected from the bleak scholarship that predated modern science's concern with credible information.

Recent American experiences that nurtured the immense growth of the social sciences provide no hopeful leads. Among the experiments that were unable to produce *credible* findings that testify to the effectiveness of any social service program are: Mobilization for Youth, which inspired the early programs of the War on Poverty; the programs that eventually comprised the War on Poverty; the income maintenance experiments of the 1970s that informed the public debate over a guaranteed wage; the work incentive experiments that fed into the welfare reform debates of the 1980s; and the thousands of far smaller policy investigations and program evaluations that comprise the core professional literature of the human services.

The literature that grew around the income maintenance studies, notable in economics and statistics, probably represent the most sophisticated level that the social sciences have ever reached in any applied area. Yet the most astute analysts of these experiments doubt their usefulness especially when the quality of the information that they produced is weighed against their dollar costs.

The failure to provide credible information is even more marked in the voluminous literature of the personal social services designed to reduce alcohol, cigarette, and drug abuse, to prevent teen pregnancy, to treat chronic mental disease as well as less severe mental disorders, to reduce crime and criminal recidivism, to reduce poverty through work incentives, and so forth.

Most studies, however, produced *positive* findings. Yet these studies were grievously flawed and grossly distorted attempts to confirm the effectiveness of relatively inexpensive social service programs. Even the recent fashion of using randomized controls, a necessary condition of credible research in the human services, has not been sufficient to guard the integrity and accuracy of findings against experimenter biases, demonstration effects, reactive measures, theoretical irrelevance, and other serious pitfalls in establishing claims to effectiveness.

Bogus proofs of effectiveness mislead the discussion of social problems. They censor the public's knowledge of its own problems. They also restrict the range of possible solutions by reinforcing the myth of efficiency at the price of more helpful and realistic principles of social welfare, namely greater social equality.

The enduring depth to which the ideology of social efficiency has been accepted and institutionalized within American culture has curtailed challenges to its tenets. It has silenced the scholars who study the human services. Social service research, dominated by the federal government, has limited the purposes and targets of evaluative research. Research has largely become propaganda for federal policy. The universities, perhaps because of their own financial problems, have compromised their independence—their role as social critics and their corollary role in creating new ideas—by allowing prevailing political tastes to set their research agendas and to dictate their interests. The censored have willingly become the censors.

Yet the social services and the social sciences are strangling in the ties of their Faustian bargains. Their doctrinal rigidities are producing pseudoscientific proofs of effectiveness that carry no more authority than faith healing, scientology, phrenology, and teleportion.

No programmatic or rational reason exists to deny the provision of greater equality. Unfortunately there is also no credible empirical proof that structural solutions will resolve deep-seated social problems. The viability of broad-based solutions is arrived at by default and made plausible by the failure of alternative strategies: neglect is unacceptable while socially efficient human services do not have any demonstrable impact on social problems. But even by default, the failure of a strategy based upon social efficiency does not compel a structural approach.

Need and dissatisfaction also dictate the requirements of proof. At a time of political tranquillity, the burden to prove effectiveness seems to rest with the proposed change. In contrast, when political pressures demand solutions for problems then the burden shifts to those who would deny the popular will for trying something new. In these terms the political argument for structural solutions waits for widespread discontent to discredit current arrangements.

Social disturbances—riots, intense criminality, rebellions, and terrorism—customarily expand political tolerances. Contemporary American society is the wealthiest culture that the world has ever seen. It is wealthier than it has ever been. But wealth does not assure wisdom, the capacity of the American people to act in humane forethought.

The conspiracy of an American elite does not account for the perseverance of terrible social problems in the United States. Cabals of social class, commercial interest, or ethnicity, such as that implicit in a number of popular critiques of American social policy, notably Cloward and Piven's *Regulating the Poor*, seem farfetched and conveniently paranoid, relying on the terrifying unknown for proof.

Conspiracy theories are also overly neat, suggesting that solutions for problems lie in simple acts of social purification. But the success of social efficiency does not rely on a conspiracy of the elite but on its great popularity with a majority of Americans, the perverse observation that the victims seem to accept the system that penalizes them.

Culture itself is the grandest conspirator, hugely effective in a society as centralized and communicative as the United States. The American people elected their current social policy. They are not being defrauded or hoodwinked. They have gotten what they said they wanted. The popularity of a conservative public policy for the past twenty years deeply perfuses the institutions of American life. It is probably unwise. It is certainly cruel. But its tenets express the will of the American people.

The literature of the human services is vast, virtually infinite. In order to make a more general comment about the way in which the United States fails to handle its social problems, this book analyzes an essential portion of that vast literature: psychotherapy, which has been the quintessential technique of social efficiency; welfare initiatives; the programs designed to handle juvenile delinquency and drug abuse, which metaphorically if not actually are the nation's most deeply felt current problem; and a variety of social work interventions that span the range of the social services.

The book traces the implications of the myths of social efficiency through the claims of the social services to effectiveness. Therefore the discussion of each area is structured around its outcome studies—the evidence of effectiveness—and around systematic discussions of those proofs. The most rigorous research and the most comprehensive and systematic reviews—not the typical offerings of the literature—are analyzed.

In the same way, the areas selected for scrutiny encompass the dominant techniques of the social services and the central claims for professional effectiveness. Chapter 1 discusses standards of proof in social science research, setting the basis for the subsequent discussion of the different social services. For decades, psychotherapy (chapter 2) has been a pillar of social care and of training for the emergent professions of the welfare state—social work, counseling, psychology, and even home economics.

The social services associated with social work are analyzed in chapter 3. Chapter 4 evaluates two of the largest social experiments ever undertaken—one tested the feasibility of an incomes guarantee, the other a variety of programs to stimulate welfare recipients to find jobs. The more rational social science approaches to social problems, dominating economics and operations research, have inspired claims to public policy expertise and to the public's trust in their superior handling of data and their probity in research. Economics has emerged as the favored social policy discipline. But rational technique is no assurance of either a rational product or objectivity in research.

Chapter 5 analyzes approaches to two of the nation's most pressing and related problems, juvenile delinquency and drug addiction. The conclusion, chapter 6, could be bleaker, an argument that the persistence of social problems through good times and bad is evidence that they are insoluble. The dilemma of American social welfare will probably perpetuate their failure: only vastly greater resources have any chance at resolving social problems but these expenditures are not politically feasible. Yet a dilemma is a trade-off and always holds out hope for greater wisdom and compassion in making choices.

Notes

1. The Gini coefficient was .394 in 1970 and .428 in 1990.
2. Jaynes and Williams tend to equate economic progress with cultural or social progress. This is a common fallacy. But the conditions of culture go beyond material wealth per se. During these past five decades, crime, juvenile delinquency, and substance abuse rates have increased dramatically. For the past few decades income equality has declined even while incomes have risen; it is unclear that those increases have purchased superior social participation or social outcomes. Effective education, that is, education that equips a child with the ability to make a living, has

probably declined even while literacy has risen. Divorce rates and child dislocation rates have shot up.

It may also be appropriate to speculate that the United States may be a more balkanized, hostile, and predatory place in 1992 than it was even during the 1930s. It is clear that more blacks vote than in years past and that there are now apparently more blacks in the middle class. It is not clear, however, that the aggregate condition of blacks has improved proportionate to its middle-class gains. Chances for blacks (and whites) who are born into the lower strata of American society may be as poor and perhaps worse than they were fifty years ago. The lives these people will lead, while perhaps better fed and better clothed and more frequently in touch with a physician, may also be less meaningful to themselves and far more desperate. Social expectations, perhaps the decisive consideration in culture, have risen far faster than income or the opportunities provided to poorer people generally.

3. There is no conventional or systematic definition of social services. There is no systematic survey of occupations that specifies professionals by the services they provide. Budgets, revenues, expenditures, and so forth are estimates. But in any event the fact remains that social services and the human services generally are enormous enterprises by any measure.

4. Mental health is counted frequently as health care although most mental health services are nonmedical. The vast majority of mental health care is provided by psychologists and social workers, outside of the hospital. Revenue figures and the number of firms come from the most recent Bureau of the Census (1987) *Census of Service Industries*. Manpower estimates are reported from the most recent Bureau of Labor Statistics (1991) *Manpower and Earnings* January.

5. Adding health services, public health and mental health care, and education together with social services, the human services probably account for more than one trillion dollars annually, and employ the largest portion of the American work force. The total of one trillion is probably a very conservative estimate of the total budgets of social services, all schools and universities, and all mental health, public health, and health care organizations.

1

Science and Scholarship
in the Human Services

Science is not at issue here, social service effectiveness is. Major social services have failed to conduct credible tests of their effectiveness.[1] The viability of the human services, generally, in producing a socially valuable product hinges on the quality of their proofs that they do so. While the social sciences have gone far in perfecting methods of research, their applied disciplines—the base of the human services—have gone further in subverting their application. No study in the following chapters—not one—critically tests a social service program.

As a consequence, none of the claims of psychotherapy, of welfare reform programs, of juvenile delinquency and rehabilitation programs, of drug treatment and prevention programs, and of social work programs in general stand up to scrutiny, in spite of the fact that their findings are as consistently positive as their methods are flawed. The best of the studies underwrite skepticism to effectiveness.

The evaluations could have been far less flawed or, failing the resources to provide credible tests, the researchers could have refused to conduct research that even at the outset promised to result in misleading findings. But the community of scholars refuses to take a stand for scientific standards. To the contrary, it nourishes the mythmakers of contemporary life. The social services themselves are the dramas of social myth that are scripted by the social sciences.

The concern with method and science is practical and political, not only aesthetic. Scientific standards erect obstacles that a proposition must overcome in order to achieve certification as scientific truth. The current "truths" of the social services have not answered these challenges but they have still been institutionalized. Yet contemporary social services

are patently inadequate to achieve their goals while belief in their
effectiveness impedes the search for true remedies.

Scientific procedures are the epitome of human rationality but the
decision to adhere to them by a community of scholars is political,
stemming from the particular social circumstances of its tasks and goals
that are themselves decisively shaped by the broader culture. Scientific
credibility confers social prestige and more material rewards. The appearance of scientific credibility may also. In this way, the social value
of the social services, acting through the communal ambitions of its
scholars, greatly influences its scientific enterprise.

The historic effectiveness of the scientific process in achieving social
goals of great value (e.g., longer life, improved health, material plenty)
has created an immense social belief in its benign powers and a near
mystical susceptibility to its symbols. Science is a social value in its own
right. With some considerable justification, the scientific process and
industrial productivity, both golden fruit of the Enlightenment, have
come to symbolize democracy and advanced, humane civilization.

Science offers specific rational alternatives to other methods: religious
proofs through personal faith in the accuracy of revelations, social proofs
through tradition, political proofs through the authority of leadership,
individual proofs through personal experience, and proofs through unquestioning blind adherence to doctrine. At least on the level of ideology,
that is, avowed practice or proscriptive standards, accountability in the
human services has installed a belief in the scientific evaluation of the
human services. At least formally, modern American society has rejected
religious proofs, personal proofs, sectarian testimonials, political convenience, and other spectral evidence as the arbiters of social service
effectiveness. *Satisfaction* with the outcomes is quite a different matter,
for which a tally of individual preferences may be adequate.

As certain as its formal preference for scientific over subjective
values, social service research has inverted them in practice. Important
portions of the social service community have even rejected scientific
standards of proof in the belief that "practical" methods of research—
subjective, professional, and reputational outcome criteria— are more
appropriate for the social services.

The *popularity* of a reinvigorated subjectivism in the research community is a greater threat to the quality of social services than leaky
methods for testing outcomes. By reducing the rigor of its research and

releasing researchers from the binding discipline of objective proof, implicit and self-serving certification pushes the tattered credibility of the social services even further toward the cult fringes of the human potential movement—EST, Rolfing, Past Life Therapy, biofeedback, meditation (transcendental and otherwise), pain management, sleep learning, parapsychology, jogging, dianetics, positive thinking, astrology, stress management, split brains effects, and the rest.

The Scientific Enterprise

Science functions through a communal process that creates plausible conjectures and then tests their accuracy through a gauntlet of challenges. The credibility of surviving propositions depends upon the rigor of the challenges and the quality of their defenses. The particular circumstances of the human services have defined a series of specific challenges that must be successfully met if a proof is to carry the cachet of scientific truth.

The consciousness of subjects in human service research, not just researchers, distinguishes the methodological requirements for human subject research from the hard sciences and the natural sciences. The principles of research—randomized placebo controlled trials (RPCT), prospective experimentation, blinding, objective measures, and unbiased measurement—may be compromised in astronomy and paleontology, as two examples, whose conditions defy direct experimental manipulation, yet still produce precise and reliable findings that are useful, replicable, reliable, and precise. But in human service research, the same compromises with methodological rigor directly and severely compromise the credibility of its outcomes. If nothing else, the pervasive possibility of researcher and subject biases has been the stellar demonstration of the laboratory research of social psychology. Atoms may have inert quarks, but humans have active egos. As a consequence, human services research requires greater methodological rigor, even if less precision, than research in physics. Pitfalls of research are flaws in its methodological seal. If a petri dish is not covered, then the mold that grows may not be the product of the experimental specimen but the air. Similarly, if psychotherapists are allowed to evaluate the outcomes of their own patients, then the reported positive outcomes may reflect their own stakes more than actual patient changes. The whole baroque intellectual architecture of a scientific community is built precisely to shelter research techniques that exclude alternative, contaminated interpretations of the outcomes of its critical tests.

The scientific enterprise depends on the accumulated, specific research of many different individuals. In a crucial way, it depends upon the mood and ethos of its particular subcommunity of researchers, their respect for skeptical consecutive argumentation, and their collective commitment to impose rigorous standards on their own research. More than any other human activity, science nurtures criticism. Through its peer review processes, journals, forums, laboratories, research teams, schools, and professional societies, a scientific subcommunity institutionalizes freedom of expression in recognition of the unique role that skepticism and doubt play in clearing out the underbrush of weak, misleading information.

A variety of cultural institutions need to be in place—freedom of expression, broad-based and nondoctrinaire education, political tolerance, a skeptical, nonconformist tradition, plurality of thought, and so forth—for scientific inquiry to flourish. The scientific enterprise has typically failed to be grafted onto developing nations, with China as the largest and most notable example, where the social institutions in support of scientific inquiry are absent. Science has also failed in more economically advanced authoritarian nations. Russia was unable to develop a productive scientific community in political isolation from its society.[2]

The scientific enterprise taken broadly as a pattern of scholarship is not simply the activity of a specialized community of researchers but also an intimate product, an institution, of a culture. In turn, the vigorous practice of science reinforces these institutions. The scientific community may be a pure form of both democracy and meritocracy.

When the scientific institution works well, it stays open to new ideas, tying the social and material ambitions of scientists to their scientific productivity. However, this tie is frequently broken, and scientists act organizationally out of a narrow self-interest to protect their work and prestige from new challenges. In this regard Max Planck noted that "A new scientific truth does not triumph by convincing its opponents and making them see the light, but rather because its opponents eventually die, and a new generation grows up that is familiar with it" (Meinert 1986, 15).

Max Planck had an optimistic view of mortality. Unfortunately, when the old truth enjoys a powerful political constituency, the old generation of intransigents may be replaced by a new generation of intransigents. Underlying social stakes and the cultural ethos shape the scientific enterprise at all of its stages (Ravetz 1971). Almost as an axiom of sociology, the prolonged failure of a scientific enterprise to fulfill its tasks of proof—what would appear to be its scientific obligations—suggests that it fulfills a role distinct from that of a scientist.

The social services *have* been accountable, except not to service effectiveness. Their profound and prolonged failure as a scientific enterprise has been sustained by the fictions of their research—that weak, inexpensive, and socially compatible strategies are effective in handling grievous social problems. Porous research methods have nurtured these compliant findings.

However, depression cured by psychotherapy, as one example, occupies the same niche in the logic of science as headaches resolved through biofeedback and learning while asleep. What distinguishes the psi research community from the psychotherapy research community is the social utility of the symbols of their scholarship and their social role as mythmakers. The actual outcomes, the production functions, of these human enhancement techniques are the same: indeterminate at best, and usually ineffective.

Yet the process for debunking fringe science is frequently easier than the process for refuting established social science doctrine. In a rebuke to the gullible, an experienced magician can replicate the miraculous. But the demonstration that the preferences of a researcher consistently distort patient reports of psychotherapeutic cures requires a cost at least equal to the initial research for each instance of proof. Moneys are rarely available for these chores of replicating social science research. Social preferences tend to side with established research, setting funding agendas in the National Institute of Mental Health, the Office of Substance Abuse Prevention, the Ford Foundation, and the Russell Sage Foundation, as four examples among many, that deny support for rigorous tests of orthodox services.

At the same time, researchers themselves are loath to make a bad career move by challenging the authority of people who influence their well-being or by impeding their competitiveness for research funds. Researchers tend to hold their skeptical tongues when they sense opposition within their fields and the absence of support within either the broader scientific community or the culture itself. Universities frequently view successful grantsmanship as an important criteria in promotions and hiring.

There are many penalties for disputing politically successful ideas. Personal responsibilities to feed a family and ambitions to stay alive in the marketplace of ideas temper a passion for truth. The freedom of academic tenure is balanced by the threat of obscurity. In this regard, it is worth noting that neither the Army nor the National Academy of Sciences (NAS) took on the effectiveness of "ordinary" psychotherapeutic techniques but only the claims of the "extraordinary" performance enhancement techniques that sit on the fringes of scientific acceptance (Druckman and Bjork 1991).

The NAS review was purchased by the United States Army to evaluate the potential utility of fringe techniques for personnel training and national defense. Most importantly, the NAS standards for evaluating evidence of effectiveness involved the application of science's prudent skepticism to the research *methods* that were employed to test whether any technique had actually enhanced performance. Biofeedback, sleep learning, extrasensory perception, and the other techniques were marginal in two senses. First, they had not yet become socially established even while evidence was accumulating that suggested their effectiveness, and second, their claims to effectiveness were not clearly credible. The NAS found little evidence for the effectiveness of any technique. The large issue of expectancy biases crippled their proofs.

The same critical intelligence has only rarely been applied to the human services whose redemption from the fringes of science is more a result of social custom and comfort than any scientific superiority. Indeed, social expectations for the human services, perhaps apart from medicine and formal education, tend more to endorse their ceremonial roles than their true production functions in relieving social problems.

The Pitfalls of Human Service Research

Because the human services typically promise to change particular conditions, human service research takes on the obligation to establish the causal relationship, not simply the association, between a specific outcome of social value and a specific service intervention. Two types of research pitfalls impede proof of causality in human service research: first, systemic pitfalls in establishing the fact of change that are related to the nature of the research and to the service problems being investigated; and second, human bias pitfalls caused by the motivations of subjects, of researchers, and of service providers that are external to the research situation itself.

At the outset, the research has the task of isolating its experimental conditions—its independent variables—from all other factors that can influence the outcomes of the study. Prospective experimentation, in which the researcher selects subjects and then administers the experimental conditions to them, avoids the many pitfalls of retrospective experimentation, in which those conditions are reconstructed. Retrospective studies cannot control biases; their environment is not adequately protected from outside influences; the experimental condition cannot be uniformly or adequately administered. Prospective experimentation is broadly accepted as a fundamental requirement for outcome research that seeks to attribute specific outcomes to specific causal events.

The seasonality of the conditions being investigated (e.g., depression, work habits, drug addiction) threatens the credibility of human service outcome research. The work patterns of welfare recipients, and the acuteness of mental disease and social distress vary over time. Many studies that do not adjust for the "spontaneous" remission of these conditions, the natural tendency for some of those in a group of the unemployed to return to work during the study period or for the rate at which depressed people feel better without therapy, falsely attribute natural cure to the experimental condition.

The epidemiological characteristics of most mental health conditions and social problems have not been established. As a result, uncontrolled studies of these problems cannot credibly tie their interventions to their discovered outcomes. The absence of accurate epidemiological information also exacerbates problems of sampling. Without information that describes the incidence and prevalence of a condition, it is difficult to establish the representativeness of a sample, particularly a small sample, that is not drawn randomly from the underlying population of concern. Convenience samples—accepting those who are available for study, usually existing patients or solicited subjects—are probably *not* representative of the research concern.

Attrition and censoring have also bedeviled many studies. The tendency to lose patients and information grows along with the duration of an experiment and the time distance of its follow-up measurements. Attrition and censoring circumscribe the representativeness of samples, diminishing the relevance of the findings for the underlying populations of concern. Particularly when the samples are small and contain distressed people, attrition and censoring cannot be ignored as random events simply on the grounds that those who finish treatment or who do provide information are statistically indistinguishable from those who do not.

Follow-up measures and replications of the research are necessary to establish the persistence of any effect. Replications—of the original research, at other sites and at different periods of time—are particularly pertinent when an outcome is established in an optimal "laboratory" but is intended for a far more complex "field" situation.

Studies that address customary treatment situations need to incorporate those situations into their experiments. Unfortunately, a demonstration or test of a treatment creates an atypical situation. Hawthorne effects have come to stand for all unpredicted effects that emerge from subject participation in a test situation, not only the unexpected benefits of worker participation that emerged from the original Hawthorne studies. Controls by themselves will not respond to this problem. Replications—across time, in the same site and in other sites —together with accurate epidemiological information (as a caution in viewing the behavior of the control group) and the definition of a standardized test environment, such as "sea level conditions", begin to avoid the demonstration pitfall. Still, the act of measuring performance itself may distort behavior in *unpredictable* ways.[3]

Frequent systemic pitfalls have severely diminished the credibility of human service research. Research that employs small, and inappropriately controlled or uncontrolled convenience samples, that applies unreliable measures in laboratory situations without follow-up, and that suffers high rates of censoring and attrition have become the common currency of human service research. However, the pitfalls of uncontrolled biases emerging from the extraneous stakes of research participants have done even greater damage to the credibility of the scholarly enterprise of the human services. Placebo nontreatments are only a partial solution to the problems of patient motivation.

The expectancies (of the researchers and the care givers) that are unrelated to the treatment or therapeutic intervention itself can distort the *reported* outcomes of a study. Practitioners and researchers usually have enormous stakes in demonstrating positive outcomes, not simply in conducting true tests. Researcher expectancies can induce research subjects to report that they feel better and that their behaviors have changed in the desired direction. These expectancies can induce researchers and care givers to exaggerate their own assessments of the therapeutic outcomes. Expectancies can also bias research design toward positive outcomes—for example, selection of subjects with a high probability of cure, acceptance of outcome measures that are susceptible to clinician influence, and application of assessments that favor the intervention's curative power.

Rosenthal and Rubin (1978) "showed that the probability that there is no relationship between experimenter's expectations and their subject's subsequent behavior is less than .0000001." The mean effect size of the expectancy effect across the 345 studies included in their meta-analysis was large (.33) and related only to what Rosenthal and Rubin consider to be "unintended" effects of expectancies. Some research may not be this innocent. Harris and Rosenthal (1988) pointed out a variety of mechanisms by which expectancies can be transmitted to subjects: encouragement, eye contact, praise, and so forth.

Blinding procedures and independent, nonreactive, objective measurement are designed to address expectancy biases. Patients can be blinded through placebo nontreatments but researchers, judges, and care givers should also be blind to a subject's status. These conditions are not always possible. However, it *is* frequently possible to objectify measures and it is always possible to employ blind or neutral judges to assess patient outcomes who are professionally and organizationally independent of the experiment's researchers and care givers. Audio-and videotaping have been attempts at independent outcome assessment in psychotherapy research; they have been largely unsuccessful.

But these steps still do not solve the problem of exaggerated patient reports or temporary patient conformity with desired behaviors. Even the protections of placebo controls may be inadequate since professionals, especially psychotherapists, may be better at transmitting their biases than the nonprofessionals or others who provide the placebo nontreatment. Through their self-reports or temporary behavioral accommodations (especially during videotaped outcome assessment sessions), patients may seek to protect and reward their therapists.

Particularly in psychotherapy, but in many other social services as well, patients may feel that their success is more than simply a sign of solving a particular problem; it is also certification of their general human superiority. This provides an immense incentive for subjects to report improvements where none may objectively exist. The felt needs of patients to achieve insight in psychotherapy and "clear" in dianetics are two of the many quiet avenues that transport expectancy biases from care givers to patients.

In addition to the customary precautions of careful research, Rosenthal and Rosnow (1984) listed a number of strategies to avoid the expectancy pitfall: experimenter blinding, increasing the number of experimenters, minimizing experimenter-subject contact, observing experimenter behaviors, and developing training manuals. They also suggested that the expectancies of researchers be made a conscious independent variable in the studies themselves. Yet in the end, their "expectancy control design" has problems of its own, including increased research costs.

Sample Size, Randomization, and Trials

Large, randomly selected samples improve representativeness, increase the power of a study and inhibit expectancy biases. Small convenience samples invite expectancy biases. It is more difficult to influence 100 subjects or know their cues than it is to know and influence fifteen subjects. The random assignment of randomly selected subjects to experimental groups and to placebo controls are the essential characteristics of randomized placebo-controlled trials (RPCT).

RPCTs are costly, complicated, and organizationally disruptive. They are difficult to administer. Yet without them the human services will be locked into ceremonial roles, failing to reach intellectual coherence by failing to credibly establish their value in resolving social problems. Only RPCTs can avoid many of the pitfalls of human service research by providing greater assurances than other types of procedures that samples of experimental subjects are equivalent to samples of control subjects. RPCTs are feasible, ethical, and legal. They supplement customary research procedures. The stakes in maintaining the fiction of service effectiveness are the largest obstacles to their widespread use.

Types of Controls

In any experiment, four types of controls are possible: randomized controls, nonrandomized controls, historical controls, which are a form of nonrandomized control, and crossover designs of one sort or another through which an experimental group acts as its own control.

Nonrandomized comparison groups do not avoid the pitfall of producing spurious differences that emerge as a function of the pretest differences between groups instead of the effects of the experimental condition itself. Nonrandomized selection procedures fail as safeguards against the many *unknown* factors that may predict outcomes.

Meinert (1986) simply discards the value of historical "controls" in the belief that any reconstruction of experience after the fact will necessarily produce biased results.

Crossover controls fall into a class of experimental designs in which an experimental group acts as its own control. They are not appropriate when the experimental condition has a sustained effect (that is, when the experimental condition is withdrawn, its effects do not decrease or disappear). As quasiexperiments (in which there is no control group per se), single subject designs (a quasiexperiment with a sample size of one), or experiments in which alternative treatments are applied, a crossover design is typically inappropriate for the human services in which the assumption of sustained effects is reasonable.

Types of Randomized Controls

A pool of research subjects can be randomized to two types of control conditions: treatment controls and nontreatment controls. Treatment controls, in which one form of treatment is compared with another, are valuable when the efficacy of one of them has been established. They avoid the ethical problem, particularly acute when mortality or serious morbidity are possible outcomes, of withholding a cure from a group of patients. However, when the efficacy of a standard treatment is itself questionable—the pervasive case of the human services —then comparisons with alternative interventions obscure the basic issue of effectiveness. Only comparisons with a group that has not received the experimental treatment can establish the degree of its effectiveness.

A variety of nontreatment controls are possible: strict nontreatment, in which one group of subjects are simply denied treatment, placebo controls, and deferred treatment controls (commonly, wait-list controls). The fact of placebo effects, that is, positive effects related to the experimental situation apart from the experimental intervention, has been long established. Placebo effects are distinct from demonstration effects. Placebo effects may be replicable, true effects, perhaps stemming out of the patient's motivation for cure. Demonstration effects are evanescent, the result perhaps of extraordinary experimental conditions. No test of a drug is credible without some form of placebo condition that masks the patient from his or her membership in the experimental or control condition.

Perfect equivalence of all conditions between experimental and control groups, except for the receipt of the experimental condition, is violated when extraneous factors differentially motivate the control group members and experimental group members. The selection for membership in a nontreatment control may affect the moods, motivations, and behaviors of those subjects differently than membership in an experimental condition may affect experimental subjects. This is obviously true of those denied treatment and those who are told they have to wait longer for treatment. This differential effect is particularly pertinent when motivational change is itself an import research outcome, the frequent condition of human service research. This bias may be especially severe in mental health research. The different motivations may create the appearance of positive treatment effects by causing deterioration or by suppressing natural remission in control subjects, thus increasing the differences between control and experimental groups.

Only patients randomized to a placebo condition can avoid the pitfall of nonequivalence. The construction of a true placebo for human services is a work of art in which the placebo patients feel that they are receiving service. Ideal placebos, in the sense of a placebo pill, may be impossible for some human services. Yet even imperfect conditions of any placebo treatment set standards against which intervention effectiveness is measured. In this way, structured group recreation as a nontreatment placebo is also a benchmark for the outcomes of professional psychotherapy.

The Optimal Design

Without other protections against bias, the RPCT is *not* a classical experiment. Indeed randomization between research groups has become the vulgarization of scientific credibility in the human services, not its substance. Optimal outcome research in the human services, at least in the form in which it is dispensed through a "clinical" environment, entails: the RPCT *and* random patient recruitment from the underlying problem population; large samples; blinding and other expectancy controls; objective, multiple, nonreactive measures and measurement; and replications. In short, the pitfalls of human service outcome research are not avoided simply by incorporating a randomized prospective procedure. The other safeguards of scientific experimentation are also required to establish cause. Each departure from optimal requirements raises additional doubts that a study's interventions are related to its reported outcomes.

Barriers to the Use of Optimal Designs

Legal arguments against placebo and other nontreatment controls focus on violations of an implicit contract caused by withholding services. Patients who pay for a particular service must be provided with that service. For this reason standard treatment controls and wait-lists are employed. Yet these controls are inadequate. The solution may be to offer services gratis and obtain informed consent from participants or to repay those who do not receive treatment, securing an agreement first from the appropriate legal authorities. Yet these steps increase the cost of a study while making the research situation less representative of the live field situation.

Ethical barriers to the use of placebos and nontreatments relate to the harm caused by withholding services and to subjects' rights to balance these risks for themselves in deciding whether to participate in an experiment. But again, the amount of potential harm is itself a product of credible research that establishes the outcomes of those services, including the various risks of deterioration.

The ethical problem increases when people specifically solicit a particular treatment. It is not so severe when people present themselves with a problem and the service organization is willing to acknowledge the plausible equivalence of a nontreatment placebo and their services. In this case, informed consent entails advising subjects that they will be assigned to one of two treatment conditions of presumed equivalence. This presumption sticks in the throat of many committed practitioners. But it is frequently sustained by a literature that cannot credibly demonstrate effectiveness of its standard treatments. Research deception itself—that is, not obtaining informed consent—might be conscionable in these circumstances.

Indeed, there is considerable weight to the argument that all patients who enter psychotherapy of any type ought to be informed that they are participating in an experimental procedure of still questionable value. The failure to obtain informed consent in the standard treatment condition thus justifies avoiding informed consent in the experimental procedure, too.

The barriers of cost and disruption need to be balanced against the costs and harm caused by continuing questionable services. Solid outcome research disciplines a whole field; its benefits can be enormous if it simply results in the termination of ineffective, wasteful, or actually harmful services.

Yet the largest impediment to the use of placebo controls is the belief that the standard treatment is effective and therefore cannot be withheld to test true effectiveness. This is a vital lie of the human service professions. It creates a curious circularity in which methodologically corrupted studies produce a fiction of effectiveness, which is then squeezed through a strainer of ethics and law as testimony against the use of rigorous designs to test effectiveness. However, there is no credible evidence of the effectiveness of a variety of important social services. If nothing else, the following chapters remove objections to placebo nontreatment controls based on the presumed effectiveness of standard treatments.

The Residual Category

The use of RPCTs can be justified in many more fields than medical care: psychotherapy, substance abuse, health education and health services delivery, psychotherapy, foster care, institutional care, community mental health, education, and so forth. Nevertheless, some human services are not amenable to RPCT designs. These exceptional services are sanctioned to provide material care (e.g. food, clothing, shelter, protective services) and access to the "normal" conditions of family (adoption services), education, and so forth. Yet when the central claim of a service is that it cures, rehabilitates, or prevents, then RPCTs are feasible, ethical, and highly desirable.

The Scientific Literature and the Communal Process of Science

The scientific process works through its literature, the fundamental medium for accumulating, transmitting, discussing, and analyzing experience. Publication is crucial, signaling the maturation of a private idea into a common, public, professional property. Publication is scientific life. Without an audience findings have no social influence. Careers in science rise and fall on the single issue of publication. While the individual study is the basic unit of the scientific enterprise, the journal is the basic unit of its literature, involving a peer selection of what is to be published and the form it should take.

In many disciplines publication is not routine but faces rigorous screening by a committee of the field's standard bearers. If the application of those standards stays true to the scientific commitments of the field, then the field's enterprise stays on a scientific course by rewarding credible studies with publication and by denying the field's cachet to inadequate work. If, however, the journal review process flavors the consideration of submitted research with its nonscientific ambitions for status and material rewards, then it provides back alleys that subvert its scientific value. Accumulated biases in published research distort the field's pool of information, discourage the production of contrary evidence, and corrupt its basic authority. Censorship in science is not an office for a bureaucrat in a tyrant's regime. It is a structural distortion of the communal enterprise that is eventually expressed in its journals, its research, and its social meaning.

A scientific literature contains different levels of information. Yet critical tests discipline all of the different activities of a scientific enterprise and provide the single most important unifying theme for its literature. Critical tests are credible demonstrations of causal relationships between a field's defining interventions and its defining tasks.

Service effectiveness is the crucial outcome of the human services. Professional expertise is the preferred causal factor in socially efficient explanations to predict service success. In contrast, ideologies based upon some notion of greater equality predict that more equivalent participation in the institutions of culture, not the shortcuts of professional intervention, is the dominant cause of socially valuable outcomes.

A scientific enterprise collects information that permits it to tool up for its investigations and to select priority areas for research. These priorities affect the tooling process and the standards for their acceptance. Priorities are keyed rationally to the theoretical reach of a particular line of inquiry; they are also affected by its potential social value. A field's priorities sometimes emerge as the summation of the widely blown interests of many scientists, each separately assessing theoretical reach, social value, and personal preference. But more commonly, because the scientific enterprise is costly, research priorities are arrived at more systematically in practical deference to the social and political needs of the broader culture. These social and political preferences are introduced to the scientific community through competitive funding and frequently through government research itself (e.g., the National Institutes of Heath, NASA, the U.S. Department of Defense).

When the step was simple, inexpensive, and short between curiosity and investigation, a community of scholars could more easily operate outside of a broad social mandate. But today, the successful scientific enterprise is also a successful political enterprise that draws on the organized base of its discipline to convince taxpayers of its social value. This is probably wise in a democratic society, exposing its intellectual elite to public debate and accountability. However, the process of lobbying the public is necessarily partisan, selectively invoking powerful symbols of loyalty to cultural myths in a competition for scarce resources.

The danger is always present that a subcommunity of scientists in shaping its meaning for the factional political conflict will also enforce a harmful silence on its own members in pursuit of funding and social approval. An unacknowledged sensitivity to its professional image may explain why criticisms within the human service literature are so qualified and convoluted and why practitioners have typically succeeded in blocking credible investigations of their effectiveness.

Levels of Information

The task for human service research on the descriptive level is to engineer reliable and accurate methods to obtain information. Because of pressures to establish priorities of social importance, the task is a difficult one. The tools for human service research are frequently survey instruments and scales that describe human needs and the conditions for satisfying those needs, including the immense complexity of personal and social systems. The literature created at this fundamental level of description relates to the engineering of these instruments.

At the next level, preliminary investigations are conducted of likely relations between promising causal variables and important social outcomes. These pilot tests of relationships establish a plausible basis for either conducting full blown critical tests, the next level, or for abandoning a line of inquiry as unproductive. An immense range of techniques is appropriate at this level to sort through initial observations, to begin tests of intuitions and insights, and to stimulate imagination. Case studies, hermeneutics, uncontrolled and retrospective studies, regression analyses, quasiexperiments, and so forth are practical and extremely valuable for these purposes.

Methodological rigor increases from pilot tests to critical tests. The insights, hunches, inspirations, and guesses of small experiments at the pilot level are given full blown trials at the level of definitive tests in order to separate the plausible from the profound, possible effectiveness from proven effectiveness, and laboratory experiments from techniques for general practice.

There is a tendency in any scientific field, especially when its practice community is dominant, to substitute information at the descriptive and pilot levels for information at the level of definitive tests. The ability to resist these pressures is one of the important tests of a field's scientific maturity and integrity.

The literature of definitive tests is the production gold of a scientific enterprise. It measures the weight of a field's scientific value, comprising proofs that its interventions can achieve important social goals. Definitive tests in the human services entail RPCTs.

The intelligence of a field perfuses all of its literature, accumulating a reflective tradition as its highest level of information that analyzes, interprets, weighs, imagines, and defines the standards of research and the standards of conduct for its members. A field's sense of itself has important implications for all of a field's other activities. Its reflective literature contains summary assessments of its activities, interpretations of its definitive tests, redefinitions of its standards, and statements of its value. The scientific enterprise acts simultaneously through all levels. Insight and imagination are present at all levels, as are compromises with rigor and false starts. A single study usually has meaning on more than one level, although its principal task is to fulfill a relatively small number of research purposes. However, as information is accepted at succeeding strategic levels, its grasp on the field increases. Information that is assumed to have the weight of a definitive test will naturally influence a field more than a pilot test.

The Burden of Proof

Definitive tests inhibit the ambitions of a scientific community to conform with cultural values. They are a reluctant custom of self-regulation. The profound sense of science in the human services—its rules and methods—implies that the burden for proving the effectiveness of any human service is carried by its proponents, especially when their claims are amenable to scientific testing. The burden is not on the shoulders of the skeptic. This burden of proof implies credible testing at a definitive level, not a pilot test. The test implies the use of credible methods—RPCTs and the other protections of scientific procedures.

The burden of proof is considerably relieved when proponents of a human service do not make objective claims for effectiveness or deny the relevance of science. But this lighter burden of proof also implies a less important social role for the field.

While critical tests have been accepted as a formal goal for human services research, they have not been widely implemented. Rigorous outcome research has not disciplined the different levels of human service research. A growing portion of the human service community is denigrating objective evaluation, insisting upon more "practical" techniques. However, if this rejuvenated subjectivism is successful, it will drive the human services, particularly the social services, back to cult status, depriving neglected populations of a rational advocacy by confusing the self-interests of their caretakers with the preferences of those in need.

"Practical" Research in the Human Services

The "practical" approaches to research in the human services—"ecology, phenomenology, ethnomethodology, structuralism, hermeneutics, and functionalism" along with quasiexperiments and single subject designs—deny that rigorous science is applicable to their special conditions (Heineman-Pieper 1985). The denial is made on two grounds: either the tactical barriers to implementing trials are insurmountable or science itself is an inappropriate discipline, an outmoded method to study the human services. All of the "practical" approaches justify large compromises with optimal scientific designs; none of them acknowledge the proportionate penalties paid in the coin of credibility and social authority. "Practical" methodologies in the human services tend to promote the importance of pilot tests to the level of critical tests.

The "practical" approaches taken together make a number of curious assumptions about the environment and philosophy of research. The research community is assumed to harbor benign ambitions that do not intrude on the objectivity of their outcomes. Services are provided by people whose altruism outweighs their ambitions for status, power, or income. The central role of the human service community generally continues to be in heroic opposition to the dominant social and political values of the United States. The position of skepticism must prove its own worth; that is, human services are effective unless proven to be ineffective.

The "practical" position evaluates research against the standard of whether it "promises to be more helpful than current research" (Heineman-Pieper 1985, 4). Helpfulness is bounded by the view that scientific methods have constrained professional expertise, depriving the field of the "judgement and common sense of (its) researchers, practitioners and administrators (denying) the fruits of human perceptiveness, experience, introspection and judgement" (Heineman-Pieper 1985). Indeed, "each program has the *right* to be evaluated in relation to the goals *it* chooses . . . " (emphasis added, Heineman-Pieper 1985, 8). Susceptible to their own legends of charity and altruism, "practical" researchers have conveniently built professional roles on their own myths.

This mood of self-certification is carried over from the social service agencies themselves. Many agencies, like religious sects, develop through an inspirational style. A community leader or service worker hears a calling to service, makes a personal commitment, receives a higher sanction (divine, social, personal, or ethnic) for the ensuing struggles and presses on to funding for services. These agencies are frequently framed in initial conflicts with funding sources, other provider organizations and other methods or schools for delivering services.

Outcome evaluation is perceived as a threat to agency continuity. A constant portion of the practice literature is devoted to the reconciliation of evaluation with practice. Within this climate, resistance to evaluation is an act of faith and loyalty.

The literature of the human services is the long-accumulated product of the inspirational style, not science. "Practical" research has been refuted by a portion of the human service community even while it is realized in their work. Geismar (1982) and Hudson (1982) are probably correct in pointing out that the human service literature is not simply threatened by a rebarbative subjectivity; it is "already like this," that is, heuristic, subjective, and phenomenological.

The "practical" position has spawned a great variety of widely employed, methodological alternatives to rigorous tests.[4] As prominent examples, Bloom and Fischer (1982) popularize for social work the social sciences' renewed interest in case studies. In presenting a very compromised process for evaluating practice, they acknowledge, however reluctantly, that "*clear* evidence of effectiveness *generally* requires the traditional type of research—experimental, control group designs" (emphasis added, 15). Witkin (1991) goes one step further than Bloom and Fischer, fusing single subject designs with social services in proposing an "empirical clinical practice." He rejects both the logic of optimal requirements and the consequences—lack of credibility—for doing so in asserting the superiority of questionable research designs over scientific rigor.

The problem with these methods does not emerge from their methodological weaknesses per se, but from their use as if they were rigorous, the confusion of their preliminary information with credible information that can only emerge from definitive tests. Nevertheless, the dispute over practical research methods is not particularly rational. The stakes in that argument relate to the ambitions of human service workers for professional status, social power, and material rewards.

The denial of science by the "practical" position is staged as though the nobility of a calling to the human services were sufficient protection against its pitfalls. The fervor of the dispute over methodology and the readiness to abandon rigorous accountability recall cultish claims to special powers and special insights. Indeed, humanistic psychology, the popular psychologies, and even the more standard psychotherapies are breeding grounds of true belief.

"Practical" research is a romantic style of science that defers to the decisive power of a personal reality, a "striving for immediacy, of contact with the living things themselves rather than with book-learned descriptions" (Ravetz 1990, 319). "Practical" research is marred by a "chaos of form and corruption of content" that quickly exposes its inability to achieve rational ends. Yet the persistence of this romantic form suggests that its meaning lies less in classically scientific tasks and more in immediate political service.

Discussion

Science is a conservative bulwark against true belief and the fashionable fanaticisms that, like the spectral proofs of the Salem witchcraft trials and the race tests of Naziism and apartheid, have often had terrifying political consequences. Rigorous science in the human services means the use of RPCTs together with the canons of objectivity and accurate measurement. There are many benefits—effective services, lower costs in the long run, efficiency, informed public debate —to offset the inconvenience of a scientifically tested social policy. Scientific skepticism is itself an expression of political freedom and a buttress of a democratic civic culture.

The convergence of findings from a multitude of studies testifying to the effectiveness of a social intervention, even in the absence of contrary evidence, still does not constitute scientifically credible evidence of effectiveness. One credible disconfirming study carries more logical weight than many methodologically questionable studies that confirm effectiveness. Culture, especially one as powerful and nationally homogeneous as the culture of the United States, is a grand conductor, operating through personal ambitions and social rewards—funding and fame—to consistently orchestrate the outcomes of susceptible research.

"Practical" research opens the door to research bias. These methods may be helpful and efficient for preliminary investigations; they are also an unavoidable recourse for intractable problems of research in many fields. But by the time that they are telephoned down the line to the applied professions of the social sciences, they are too warped and removed from their initial inspirations to credibly test service effectiveness.

Convergent findings from weak, "practical" studies create the appearance of credibility. A subcommunity of scholars that consistently begs off rigorous tests of its effectiveness invites damaging comparisons with the sideshows of American pseudoscience: quackery and bogus cures, bhagwans and maharishis, teleportion, bent spoons, liver pills, and laudanum. Science protects the public. Yet it cannot satisfy a neurotic thirst for certitude nor create the strength of will to resist premature belief. In the twentieth century, presumably the age of scientific rationality, superstition still flourishes, perhaps to a greater extent than in the nineteenth century (Gardner 1988).

Scientific safeguards—the optimal design—are necessary precautions against the very human biases of human services research. These standards were explicitly adopted by the National Academy of Sciences in their review of performance enhancement techniques at the fringes of scientific respectability.

Science's communal process of doubt and challenge has not extended to the social services. Even in medical research, trials for clinical procedures are not yet routine although they are far more prevalent than in the other human services. The decisive portion of the critical literature of the human services—its summary critiques—fails as a responsible skeptic. Yet in claiming scientific credibility, the field implicitly also claims that the proofs of its benefits could survive an NAS-type scrutiny.

The health of both science and culture is nurtured by criticism of established practice, perhaps even more than by scrutiny of novelties on the fringe. Skepticism toward established practice maintains an openness for new ideas; it nurtures modesty; it maintains efforts to pursue socially valuable goals; it reduces superstition; it promotes intellectual honesty by protecting unpopular but defensible ideas; and it controls the population of prophets.

Notes

1. The discussion of research methodology in this chapter and its relationship to the social environment of the researcher is selective, focusing on the most pertinent issues. It is not intended to fulfill the functions of a textbook nor to be an exhaustive

treatment of human service research methodology. Indeed, it relies upon arguments and techniques worked out in that literature: Johnson and Johnson (1977), Friedman (1985), Spriet and Simon (1985), Iber (1987), The Association for Clinical Research (1988), Meinert (1986), Fleiss (1986), Shapiro and Louis (1983), and Schwartz (1980). Meinert is the most thorough and detailed, Fleiss contains the most comprehensive statistical treatment. All agree on the basic value of trials.

2. See the discussion of Soviet science in Graham 1987 and Rabkin 1988.

3. There is a true and probably severe Heisenberg problem in all human service research. Even integrating outcome measures within the normal flow of business does not escape this pitfall, since the claim would be tenable that the positive effects emerged from administrative accountability, not from the experimental intervention itself.

4. Piele (1988) offers three largely phenomenological methods; Brekke(1980) scolds the field for avoiding a new metaphysic. Zimmerman's (1989) moderation in method results in a preference for greater contextual description, presumably a step forward in establishing the "pertinent variables" of service effectiveness.

Proctor (1990) endorses case studies and uncontrolled methods to assess clients, change, and effectiveness: "purpose not design should drive evaluation." Proctor does not consider RPCTs necessary to establishing causal relations, stating that only "some degree of experimental control" is necessary (37). With this weak criterion, Proctor claims that proving the effectiveness of psychotherapy is old hat: "psychotherapy researchers now agree that simply showing that therapy works is relatively uninteresting . . . " (3).

Mullen applauds a diversity of weak research methods, as though convergence from weakness were a proof of strength. Ruckdeschel (1985): "Qualitative research and the qualitative perspective offer a methodology that is consonant with these contexts and concerns (of human services) and that has the potential to narrow the gap between researchers (in Heineman's sense) and practitioners." Haworth (1984): "The element needed to make practice more scientific is not the direct quantitative pursuit of generalization, but publicizing and sharing the qualitative uniqueness of encounters of whatever size and purpose."

2

The Myth of Psychotherapeutics

Psychotherapy is the quintessential program of social efficiency, promising not only to change (cure, prevent, and rehabilitate) problem behaviors but to do so cheaply and without disrupting the comfortable flow of society. In a few short sessions that do not entail large public expenditures or taxes, that do not imply dislocations of populations, social conflicts, family disruptions, or violence, that do not require major initiatives of planning and implementation, psychotherapy promises to resolve social problems on schedule, in the comfort of an office, and largely by talking. Family therapy and group therapy even offer the benefits of scale.

But on scientific grounds, the value of psychotherapy remains indeterminate at best. Scrutiny of the best outcome studies of psychotherapy either before or after the 1980 benchmark of Smith et al. does not substantiate its effectiveness. Although the field's research methods appear to have improved over the past few decades, outcome studies are still grievously flawed and appear to be incapable of screening out researcher biases and of protecting the integrity of the research from other serious threats to its credibility. Definitive tests of psychotherapy have yet to be conducted with the result that definitive summaries of the field's effectiveness, however technically profound, are still premature.

Yet the field continues to publish pseudoscientific testimonials that may have the perverse effect of provoking skepticism about its motives and true impacts rather than cultivating respect for its authority. Social discourse and political decisions have been fueled by these inconclusive and frequently misleading studies. The apparent comfort of the American culture with flawed claims for the effectiveness of psychotherapy indicates a far less innocent interpretation of its indeterminacy. As long as cheap, nondisruptive solutions appear to be possible—keeping hope alive for social efficiency—there will be little impetus to consider more effective cures.

The summary reviews of the basic clinical tests have distilled the many reported successes into potent claims that psychotherapy provides efficient solutions for social problems. A contaminated mash of studies has produced intoxicating evidence for the ability of psychotherapy to engineer highly desirable social outcomes. These claims, shaped into the dramatic myths of treatment, have been promising even greater efficiency over the past decade of federal fiscal crises as brief treatment is coming to supplant extended treatment as the intervention of choice. The critical tradition, providing only occasional voices of skepticism, has been shouted down by the field's self-serving research.

The psychic healing business is not in recession. Large institutional incentives, not the least of which is government funding of research, guide the field's scientific enterprise. They also seem to nurture the pursuit of "clinical" as opposed to social solutions. Commercial firms make a considerable profit from a variety of packaged programs for substance abuse and delinquency prevention, alcohol and drug treatment, employee assistance, and others.

Clinicians who gain a reputation for healing enjoy profitable consultantships. They occupy important academic positions. They enjoy lucrative opportunities to publish articles, books, and newspaper columns. They provide advice through television and radio. Some even achieve celebrity.

The Smith et al. Citation

The critical literature of psychotherapy has defined the specific methodological requirements to assure the credibility of a test of outcomes. The basic clinical studies of its effectiveness and the discussion of that body of research—the intuitive reviews, box scores, and meta-analyses—have led to generally optimistic and frequently enthusiastic endorsements of psychotherapy's effectiveness.

For much of the field, the issue of its effectiveness has been settled by the more prominent of these reviews, in particular the Smith et al. (1980) "citation classic" that provided the field with a comprehensive meta-analytic benchmark of its outcomes. Yet their procedures and even their data can not support their optimism.

Smith et al. (1980) identified 475 reliable, controlled outcomes studies that they felt adhered to "the acknowledged canons of experimental science" (8).

All controlled studies of the effectiveness of any form of psychotherapy formed the population of interest for this project. . . . No form of psychotherapy was excluded if the therapy (1) involved clients identified by themselves or others; (2) if the clients sought or were referred for treatment . . . ; (3) if the treatment or intervention was psychological or behavioral; and (4) if the person delivering the treatment was identified as a psychotherapist by virtue of training or professional interest. (Smith et al., 55–56)

Studies were compared across eighteen variables: the date of the study and its form of publication; the experimenter's professional affiliation, allegiance, and experience; the degree of blinding; the client's diagnosis, similarity to the therapist, and intelligence; whether clients were analogues or real patients; the process of assignment to research groups (i.e., randomization); attrition; internal validity; type and duration of therapy; modality; and the type and reactivity of the outcome measures.

Smith et al. found that psychotherapy was basically effective: "the average person who would score at the 50th percentile of the untreated control population, could expect to rise to the 80th percentile with respect to that population after receiving psychotherapy." In addition, "little evidence was found for the alleged existence of negative effects of psychotherapy. . . . Only 9 percent of the effect sizes were negative. . . . Nor was there convincing evidence in the dispersion of the treated groups that some members became better and some worse as a result of psychotherapy" (88).

Some of the therapies, cognitive therapies in particular, appeared to be very effective. Patients given some form of cognitive therapy would be better off then 99 percent of the control group subjects after therapy. Yet other interventions such as "reality therapy" produced only small but still positive results.

When possible, Smith et al. (1980) compared the published outcomes of therapy to groups that had received no treatment at all (wait-list controls) and to controls that had received placebo treatment (usually time structured, nontherapeutic activities given in a group).

Smith et al. argued that the appropriate comparison was with the nontreatment controls, not the placebo controls. Indeed Bergin and Lambert's (1978) later conversion to belief in the effectiveness of the field generally stemmed from their contention that placebos are actually the essential ingredient of therapy.

Smith et al.'s analysis was provocative. The reactivity of measurement was the only variable that showed a large relationship with effect size. In other words, the degree to which measures were susceptible to the biases of the researchers and other evaluators of outcomes accounted for a large portion of the positive effects. Moreover, when patients were evaluated at follow-up points after treatment, their therapeutic gains fell as much as 50 percent. The duration of the therapy itself did not seem to be associated with its benefits.

> The characteristics of a therapy . . . bore surprisingly little relation to the size of effect. Individual therapy and group therapy and combinations of them were equally effective . . . [however] the characteristics of the clients involved in the therapy evaluation influenced the size of the effects eventually produced. Depressed clients and clients with simple, monosymptomatic phobias were associated with the largest effects; psychotics, neurotics, and handicapped clients with the smallest. (125)

The problems with Smith et al. and the critical literature are considerable. Their most serious flaws flow out of a self-serving gullibility.

The summaries—the studies of studies—repeat the distortions of the base of primary outcome research, carrying through their near uniform enthusiasm for the value of psychotherapy. These reviews are important ideological statements. They package the collective judgments of the field, a sense of its social value, for public policy and social approval. They are the fields' attempts to speak broadly to its political constituency.

Yet the basic requirement—adequate research methodologies—for reaching any scientifically credible judgment on the effectiveness of treatment is missing. The claims for effectiveness themselves provide an estimate of the problem. The meta-analyses have come up with only small estimates of the superiority of psychotherapy over any controls. Indeed a reanalysis of Smith et al. (1980) suggests a wild-west of therapeutic outcomes and the persistent likelihood, reflecting the tyranny of grouped data, that many patients deteriorate during the course of therapy. Moreover, even its slight meta-analytic edge is lost by the consistent pitfalls of psychotherapy research and the expectancy biases of its researchers and practitioners.

First, Smith et al. prefer comparisons with nontreatment groups. But following the logic of rigorous science, the true effect of an intervention is measured by the benefits it confers above a placebo. The fact that their reported placebo effects are so large in comparison with their treatment effects (effects sizes of .56 vs. .86) suggests that the added value of psychotherapy above nonprofessional time structured activities is very small, on the order of 10 percent.

Second, even this small increment is doubtful in light of their own evidence that measurement reactivity accounted for at least 10 percent of the effect size variance. Furthermore, contrary to their initial claims that they only included rigorous studies, their meta-analysis contained both analog studies, (studies that were not controlled), and, more importantly, studies whose outcomes did not reach statistical significance (in other words, differences that could be due to chance itself). They actually contradict their avowed commitment to science by condemning rigorous standards as a "device for cutting" the outcome literature. They criticize previous reviews, especially those that questioned the efficacy of psychotherapy for arbitrarily imposing

> "textbook" standards; these methodological rules, learned as dicta in graduate school and regarded as the touchstone of publishable articles in prestigious journals, were applied arbitrarily; for example, note again Rachman's high-handed dismissal on methodological grounds of study after study of psychotherapy outcome. (38)

Third, the issue of patient deterioration in psychotherapy is persistent. The frequent rejections of the possibility of patient deterioration (May 1971, Mays and Franks 1980, Bergin and Lambert 1978, Lambert et al. 1986) occupy a curious position, hiding behind the methodological weaknesses of the field by insisting that the burden to prove harm is on the shoulders of the critic and not that the burden to prove effectiveness and safety is on the shoulders of the therapist. They argue that because the research fails to *credibly* demonstrate harm, the charge of deterioration is still indeterminate and probably false. However, they fail to extend their argument to the observation that the outcome literature fails also to credibly test *any* effect of psychotherapy, not just its deterioration effects. In contrast, Smith et al. (1980), in a long discussion of the obligations of research, set the burden of proof firmly on the shoulders of the interventionist.

While the Smith et al. data seem to refute the challenge of deterioration, a reanalysis of their data support it. These recomputations imply that a huge proportion of the effect sizes of a normal distribution of effect sizes would fall below the "0" score, that is, the score for nontreatment.[1]

These huge variations suggest that the benefits of psychotherapy are wildly unpredictable.

Moreover, these data may underestimate the gravity of the actual situation since the recomputations make no adjustment for reactivity, expectancy biases, and misreporting nor do they subtract the placebo effects from the reported effect sizes.

In addition, many of the studies were conducted under optimal conditions of therapy, by highly regarded and responsible therapists in research situations. For all their problems and uncertain outcomes, these studies may yet be very high estimates of psychotherapy's benefits. The actual conditions of psychotherapy for the typical patient may be far more uncaring, abusive, and unprofessional. The data invite a host of speculations. Deterioration may be common for patients whose failures to improve challenge the curative pretensions of their therapists or disappoint them in other ways.

Finally, Smith and Glass (1977), in their early version of the Smith et al. (1980) study, commented on the curiosity that the benefit rate for psychotherapy measured by their analysis was the same that Eysenck, an early and reviled critic, had reported in his "tendentious diatribes in which he claimed to prove that 75 percent of neurotics got better regardless of whether or not they were in therapy" (Smith and Glass, 752). Yet their study seems to corroborate Eysenck's skepticism if not actually his work.

Subsequent to Smith et al. (1980), summaries of outcome studies— intuitive discussions, box scores, and meta-analyses—have usually been even more encouraging in pointing to the benefits of separate treatments and treatment conditions. On the basis of a meta-analysis of 163 treatment-control comparisons of psychotherapy outcomes for children, Weisz et al. (1987) found that treated groups were 29 percent better off than controls. Casey and Berman (1985) found that treated children were 26 percent better off than controls. Howard et al. (1986) analyzed "15 diverse sets of data from their own research and from research previously reported in the literature" over the past thirty years; they concluded that "by 8 sessions approximately 50 percent of patients are measurably improved, and approximately 75% are improved by 26 sessions" (159). Patterson (1984) found that even Bergin's reviews were too cautious and biased:

Considering the obstacles to research on the relationship between therapist variables and therapy outcomes, the magnitude of the evidence is nothing short of amazing. There are few things in the field of psychology for which the evidence is so strong. The evidence for the necessity, if not the sufficiency, of the therapist conditions of accurate empathy, respect, or warmth, and therapeutic genuineness is incontrovertible. (437)

Miller and Berman (1983) concluded on the basis of forty-eight studies that "cognitive behavior therapies were superior to no treatment; however there was no firm evidence that these therapies were superior to other psychotherapies" (39). In the same manner, a variety of different summaries of outcome studies found consistent grounds for the effectiveness of psychotherapy of one form or another in the treatment of fear (Glaister 1982), headache (Blanchard and Andrasik 1982, Blanchard et al. 1980), insomnia (Borkovec 1982), and anorexia nervosa (Hsu 1980). Moreover, the basic Smith et al. (1980) meta-analysis has been corroborated and extended by a number of studies (Landman and Dawes 1982, Shapiro 1985, Andrews and Harvey 1981, Shapiro and Shapiro 1982a, Giblin and Sprenkle 1985, Steinbrueck et al. 1983, Dush et al. 1983).

But these interpretative summaries, meta-analytic and others, are not credible; their base of primary research does not contain even one credible test of outcome. The buoyant optimism of these summaries has overwhelmed the field's few critical voices that call attention to the inherent weakness of the research (e.g., Strube and Hartmann 1982, Shapiro and Shapiro 1982b, Prioleau et al. 1983). While others acknowledge the methodological weakness of research in the field, they do not allow these cautions to inhibit their finding some positive, and by implication, redeeming benefit for psychotherapy.

The clear but infrequent voice of the critical tradition in psychotherapy has been largely ignored. Prioleau et al. (1983) reanalyzed the most credible portion of the Smith et al. (1980) data set, the thirty-two studies in which psychotherapy was compared with a *placebo control.* They found that their net median effect size was very small (only .15), representing an improvement over placebo controls of only 6 percent. Yet even these studies, presumably the cream of the crop, are so lax in protecting against researcher and therapist biases, that the possibility cannot be ignored that psychotherapy may actually be consistently harmful. The fact that the field has flourished in spite of Prioleau et al. strongly suggests that its meaning does not lie in its explicit function as a rational method for curing, preventing, or rehabilitating those who suffer from mental health problems.

The Base of Outcome Studies

Good research opportunities in mental health are relatively scarce. This is an ongoing problem. Many programs refuse to open themselves to rigorous, independent evaluation or research. Cook and Shadish have noted with some force that the community health centers, as one example, were not prepared to describe their activities even on rudimentary levels, let alone engage in sophisticated outcome evaluations. It is difficult to reconcile the posturing of concern in many programs to "protect our patients" from the harm of bad research with their own failure to conform to minimal rules of professional accountability.

The field is very shy of independent investigation while funding sources, notably the federal government, have not insisted upon rigorous outcome research. Clinicians exercise extraordinary control over their own assessments. Access to a mental health service or a psychotherapy program for purposes of evaluation frequently requires a researcher to relinquish control over its design and interpretation to partisans of the outcomes.

The researcher must frequently demonstrate a commitment to psychotherapy that satisfies the program's staff. This is the implication to be drawn from Hollister et al. (1985) whose research required the approval of the agency they set out to evaluate. In the end, the concessions they were required to make to the agency vitiated its value.

More than any other factor, the assumption of effectiveness that is implicit in allowing mental health programs to control their own accountability limits the possibilities for studying the effectiveness of psychotherapy. As a result, questionable standard treatments take on the force of proven value, limiting the use of any nontreatment control—placebo, wait-list, or no treatment at all—in evaluative research. The self-regulation of psychotherapy generally is at odds with the essentially experimental nature of its interventions and tends to reduce pressure on the field for credible research.

It is difficult to assess whether the researchers themselves consciously distort the research process or simply accommodate to hostile program environments. But it is hard to avoid the impression that the system in which their work is supported, interpreted, published, and funded as well as the broader social system that influences these processes are neither neutral nor inhibited in protecting their perceived stakes in psychotherapy's effectiveness.

The best of the recent outcome studies taken together present the scientifically robed judgment that relatively inexpensive treatments are effective in securing or making material progress in resolving important social problems. But a search through the basic outcome literature of psychotherapy subsequent to Smith et al. fails to reveal any recent credible evidence of effectiveness.[2] Neither the methodologies of the outcome studies nor their territory of concern (their theoretical importance) permits conclusions of effectiveness. Not one study stands as a critical test of psychotherapy; every study seriously departs from the requirements for methodological rigor. At the very least, the outcomes are indeterminate while strong suspicions remain that: (1) positive outcomes if they occur at all may not be substantial or relevant to the true populations of concern; (2) positive reports of outcomes may not reflect true behavior changes but only the accommodations of patients to the expectations of their therapists and to the research environment; (3) many patients may have deteriorated as a result of therapy; and (4) the community of researchers are not systematically pursuing the issue of effectiveness; instead they are creating the cultural myths that nurture support for the process of psychotherapy.

Two examples of the best recent outcome research in psychotherapy illustrate the field's persistent failure to provide credible evidence of effectiveness.

Miller et al. (1989) tested three treatments for depressed inpatients. The first, standard treatment, consisted of hospital "milieu" therapy, pharmacotherapy, and medication management sessions with a psychiatrist. These twenty minute medication sessions occurred once per day while patients were in the hospital and six to eight times during the twenty week outpatient period. The second treatment condition, cognitive therapy, was provided on top of the standard treatment. It began "after the second week of hospitalization and continued on a once-a-day basis while the patient was in the hospital and for 20 weeks after discharge . . . typically on a weekly basis. . . . All sessions were 50 minutes in length" (29). The third treatment, social skills training, was also provided in addition to the standard treatment but as an alternative to cognitive therapy, lasting the same amount of time with the same intensity.

Miller et al. found that each of their "treatment conditions produced significant improvements at discharge from the hospital and the end of treatment 4 months later . . . " (41). However, by the end of treatment the groups receiving cognitive therapy and social skills therapy in addition to the standard treatment contained patients with fewer and less severe psychiatric symptoms and contained higher percentages of patients who made complete recoveries than did groups of subjects who received the standard treatment alone. With unusual candor, the authors identify four methodological problems with their study: small sample sizes (less than twenty and often less than fifteen), pretreatment differences between samples (e.g., the social skills group contained patients with "a greater degree of personality difficulties"), the use of "only one therapist per psychotherapy" and a lack of uniformity in administering medications.

In addition, the authors might have gone on to point out that their study suffered a high rate of attrition (30 percent), the raters "were not blind to the treatment condition nor assessment period," and the measures were subject to patient and researcher biases. A nontherapy control was not employed, which limits the degree to which experimental outcomes, if they existed, could have been attributed to the two therapeutic conditions. Finally, the authors' own stakes, possibly in cognitive therapy and possibly the unintended source of the positive outcomes themselves, were not considered in the research.

Yet in spite of these large methodological problems, the authors still insist that "the results of this study suggest that cognitive-behavioral treatments can produce additional benefits 4 months after discharge for depressed patients who required hospitalization. . . . " Neither the study itself nor the authors' discussion of their findings put to rest the very live possibility that patients did not improve from "therapy." Improvements, if they occurred at all and if they were sustained, were perhaps the result of the simple benefits of periodic surveillance or the cessation of their abusive conditions attendant on the patients' decisions to seek therapy.

A less complimentary conclusion for psychotherapy keeps intruding itself: the key to treating depressed patients may lie in a nonabusive environment, not in the elegant constructs, rare insights, and skills of trained psychotherapists.

Kazdin et al. (1989) randomly assigned antisocial children to one of five therapists and one of three treatments: "problem-solving skills training, problem-solving skills training with in vivo practice, which included therapeutically planned activities to extend training to settings outside of treatment, or client-centered relationship therapy" (523). All three treatments were completed in twenty-five sessions, each lasting fifty minutes and administered individually to each child as outpatients and inpatients.

> The bulk of (problem-solving skills training) was devoted to enacting interpersonal situations through role play, where the child applied [steps that had been taught. In vivo practice consisted of] therapeutically planned activities outside of the sessions. . . . The focus of the [relationship therapy] was on developing a close relationship with the child and providing empathy, unconditional positive regard, and warmth . . . helping the child to express feelings. (527–28)

The Kazdin et al. (1989) study is theoretically important, speaking generally to the broader problem of juvenile delinquency. They report that their

> results are consistent with other studies on the effectiveness of problem-solving skills in altering behavior in aggressive, antisocial, and impulsive children. The literature is relatively sparse in demonstrations of the effects of cognitive-behavioral treatment with children clinically referred for antisocial behavior. Studies showing effects with clinic samples have reported limitations in the extent to which effects generalize to nontreatment settings, are sustained over time, and place individuals within the normative levels of functions. . . . In the present study, changes in behavior at home and at school were evident, and the effects were sustained through a 1-year follow-up assessment. However, after treatment, the majority of children remained outside the normative range of functioning on measures of deviance at home and at school. (The skills training treatments) tended to place a greater proportion of children within normative levels than relationship training. . . . Yet, with one exception, the differences among the three treatment conditions were not significant. (533)

However, the study did not utilize a nontreatment control and cannot account for the amount of remission that might naturally be due to seasonality or to the aging process itself. The measures, all self-reports of parents, teachers, and children, were potentially reactive to the experimental conditions and the therapists' expectancies. The study, replicating many of the characteristics of the second phase of the California Youth Authority experiments of the 1960s and 1970s curiously fell into many of the same methodological pitfalls that invalidated those experiments (see chapter 5).

The minimal interventions of the Kazdin et al. study were again insufficient to change antisocial behavior. During the study, that is, while the antisocial children were being supervised to some degree, there was a significant but minor change in their behavior. But when the minimal surveillance provided by the therapies—its surrogate power—was withdrawn, the children largely reverted to the prestudy patterns of antisocial behavior. Problem solving skills training, even with in vivo experience and relationship training, and especially in the short-term mode of the experiment, are unpromising avenues for treating antisocial behaviors, presumably the precursors if not actually the substance of juvenile delinquency. If this social problem is to be handled, normal conditions of childhood probably need to be provided over extended periods of time to all children. The substitution of relatively inexpensive therapies for the provision of these "normative" conditions does not appear to be effective. Renaming the provision of common, nonabusive, family experiences in the terms of specialized psychotherapy simply clouds the issue of care.

The drift of Kazdin et al.'s discussion is that more *therapy*, perhaps involving multiple influences, is needed. But the force of the accumulated research in psychotherapy, especially when passed before a skeptical eye, is that other approaches—especially social approaches that replicate customary conditions of participation in important cultural institutions, particularly school and the family—need to be embraced. Talk is not much of a substitute for substance and the institutional conditions of psychotherapy seem quite inadequate to handle the social nature of personal problems. Therapists are poor social advocates; their professional interests lie elsewhere.

The General State of Psychotherapy Research

These two studies are not characteristic of the field's general outcome research. Notwithstanding their many invalidating flaws, they are among the best. The theoretical value of the base of outcome studies is circumscribed by their subject samples, by their therapists, by their interventions, and by their settings. Moreover, the extant body of research is probably an inaccurate reflection of the practice of psychotherapy in the United States, overrepresenting both psychiatric research centers on the one hand and commercial interests on the other.

Few of the studies were the work of researchers who were independent of the outcomes. Most researchers were staff clinicians, usually psychiatrists, in large hospitals with large outpatient programs, who took the opportunity of their positions to publish their experiences. They embodied the stakes of their institution's and professions. On the other hand, some of the studies were conducted by psychotherapists with an entrepreneurial interest in selling their therapy packages.

Many studies still utilized analogue subjects (students, community recruits) instead of people with the defined condition. Many others sampled patients who were not clearly representative of the problem that was being studied thus limiting the relevance of their findings to the underlying populations of interest. Although more representative of the underlying problem than analogues, patients in the study samples were frequently self-selected volunteers, and thus probably highly motivated to change. Moreover, the psychological problems represented by the outcome studies since 1980 does not adequately represent the true dimensions of social problems nor the demographics of mental disease. The interests of research have not coincided with the extent of psychological problems.

Very few studies conducted multicenter trials or had the freedom to draw stratified samples of patients from a variety of settings. No study started with a concern about a social problem (prevalent dysfunctional behavior) and then sampled the problem directly, going through the process of testing the efficacy of psychotherapy against live social conditions. Rather, the studies utilized active patients or analogues.

The therapists who provided care in the studies were not representative of the level of community care. They were not drawn randomly from the active pool of therapists but were usually attached to the teaching institution that conducted the research as students, instructors, or staff therapists. Community therapists were infrequently utilized but in these cases they were often selected for their reputations as superior care givers. Moreover, therapy was carefully supervised and controlled during the research period.

In these ways, the studies represent conditions that exaggerate the report of psychotherapy's effectiveness. Therefore, much of the research tends to be laboratory tests of prototypes, not field tests or quality assurance tests of a standardized product. But even under these optimal conditions, few if any benefits accrued to psychotherapy.

The implicit assumption in going from the laboratory to the field—that the controlled conditions of the laboratory that impinge on outcomes can be replicated in the field—may not be viable for psychotherapy. The more customary conditions of day to day psychotherapy in the United States are probably very different than the conditions of the research laboratories. The general pool of therapists probably contains less well trained and motivated personnel than the therapists in the studies. Their patients are probably sicker and are under the duress of complicating social problems such as poverty. And most notably, psychotherapy outside of research centers is customarily provided in unsupervised settings.

The problem of generalizing the findings from the research samples to populations of concern is also frequently increased by large rates of patient attrition and censoring (loss of data). The initial measures of patients are decidedly not sufficiently sensitive to the patients' mental disorders to assure that 20 percent attrition rates are random even where no differences seem to discriminate dropouts from finishers. Especially where the patients are very disturbed, volatile, and in need of care, high attrition rates tend to vitiate any findings of group improvement.

Measuring the outcomes is a problem. The studies frequently report findings as changes on a variety of scales. But changes on the scales, even if reliable and statistically significant, are not necessarily associated with commensurate changes in the disease. A 20 percent improvement on, for example, the Beck Depression Inventory may or may not indicate an important clinical change in depression. Many studies employ multiple criteria, frequently applied by different judges (patients, therapists, significant others, independent assessors) who often report consistently positive change. But these changes are rarely large while the clinical importance of the change is frequently uncertain. Moreover, judges frequently disagree with each other.

Even when claiming that measures are made independently, the studies employ personnel who are not neutral on the issue of outcomes. Students and colleagues of the researchers and others drawn from the psychotherapeutic community have an implicit bias. Lecturing them on the dignity of science does not protect against their biased assessments.

Video- and audiotapes of patient behaviors have not solved the problem of independent ratings, reliability, or accuracy. Cure may not be indicated by changed behaviors during the therapy session or behaviors may have changed only as an adaptation to the therapy environment. Moreover, by often containing subtle clues to those who have gone through psychotherapy and those who have not, the tapes compromise the objectivity of the judges.

However, the heart of the criticism of the studies, and the major reason that they are not credible statements or true tests, is that they failed to protect against the possibility of customary biases, threats to internal validity. Their small sample sizes, frequently under twenty, are a problem in terms of the range of experience that they include—their representativeness. But the larger problem of small samples is that they are more amenable to subtle distortion than larger samples in which the biased responses of a few subjects will be outweighed by many accurate reports. The problems of bias are even more acute in view of the usually small and ambiguous changes that the research typically reports.

The measures employed, the raters, and the ways in which ratings are made are all easily susceptible to bias. In the first instance, the essence of psychotherapy depends upon the patient-therapist relationship, characterized by "trust, warmth, acceptance, and human wisdom." Patients are typically protective of their therapists. Self-reports of their progress in therapy may therefore distort their objective disease conditions. It is simply fanciful to rely upon patient reports as indicators of their objective state in any way in which the relationship with their therapist may impinge upon their judgments.

Furthermore, the nature of therapy for many patients is such that achieving improvement is a signal of their human superiority, of a higher level of human consciousness, and of a greater maturity and insight. Their admission of failed therapy would be an admission of their own inferiority. Patients customarily pay for therapy and have a financial incentive in reporting improvement. In these ways, patients may be induced to report improvement where no improvement actually takes place.

In many of the studies the therapists themselves or the study's principal investigators rated patients or made judgments of outcomes. These are simply not independent and should not constitute an important portion of any serious research activity. Frequently their students or those they trained made ratings. Again, these are not independent judges. "Significant others" are also open to a variety of subtle biases precisely because they are deeply involved and may be motivated to reward the patient with more enthusiastic reports of improvement than is warranted.

These threats to internal validity that may mediate the expectancies of the psychotherapeutic community exist because blinding procedures are not or can not be maintained for the patient, the therapist, and the raters. In this regard, control groups composed of patients on wait-lists or of nontreatment patients do not offer appropriate comparisons for treated groups because members of these controls are presumably aware that they are not receiving therapy. Only placebo treatment groups could answer this challenge.

Furthermore, the studies did not establish the persistence of positive outcomes. Follow-up measures were not routine. They were frequently made shortly after therapy (three months). Attrition and censoring problems increased with time. The follow-up interviews were frequently conducted by partial judges, sometimes even the therapists.

The credibility of the body of research is also constrained by a number of more technical issues. Hardly any negative results are reported. One can expect a certain amount of negative findings, perhaps 5 percent, to be produced by simple sampling error, predictably unfavorable samples, even when a truly positive effect exists. In addition, few of the studies adjust significance levels for their multiple comparisons. Hardly any study reports anomalous findings or spurious correlations; again these are statistically predictable occurrences. Some researchers report their findings selectively and in their most favorable context, pushing at the boundary of scientific propriety.

But more importantly, despite their patently weak designs, very few researchers challenge their own findings. Especially in studies whose small experimental samples contain large, although not statistically significant differences with control groups, the researchers customarily refuse to discuss the degree to which these differences might account for their results. Moreover, the community of researchers rarely challenges these findings.

The body of outcome research subsequent to Smith et al. (1980) has not avoided earlier pitfalls, failing in its turn to prove the effectiveness of psychotherapeutic interventions. The consistent use of randomized controls in recent years is little more than the vulgarization of science by studies that typically avoid blinding procedures, objective ratings, large samples, follow-up measures, meaningful subjects, and other procedures to assure credibility. The enterprise of psychotherapy continues its war with the enterprise of science.

Yet in spite of their many methodological flaws, the findings of many different studies—conducted by different researchers, in different institutions, and with different patients—seem to converge on at least a modest level of effectiveness for psychotherapy. But the power of the American culture is immense. It orchestrates the behaviors of its members (e.g., traffic flow, food tastes, and social motives). Without this conductor, civilization, even on a rudimentary level, would be impossible.

Culture itself distorts the studies. It takes a very strong act of will to step outside of its socializing force to fulfill the objective dictates of science. Since the culture's force is to reward conformity, there are typically penalties for defiance—penalties in the instance itself (the loss of respect and affection from peers) and penalties in general for upsetting the comforting pattern of social assumptions.

The subcommunity of scholars that conducts the outcome scrutiny of psychotherapy is also a subcommunity of practitioners, which itself is a highly integrated expression of the broader culture. The best subcommunities of scholars have negotiated amnesty from the broader culture to pursue important social questions relatively unhampered by transitory political preferences. But this mandate is itself temporary and the independence of any field is usually short-lived.

The utility of independent scholarship is at the heart of the issue of freedom of expression and rests in large part on its social value for the rest of the culture. The problems of the social sciences, psychotherapy, and the helping professions, in this instance, emerge out of the conditions of independent research. The critical analysis of outcome research is, in this sense, part of the argument over the social utility of the interventions themselves and therefore resonates directly with the classic political question: to whose benefit?

This analysis follows much of the logic of the NAS scrutiny of human enhancement techniques. It certainly comes to similar conclusions. There are few grounds on which to separate the "popular" psychotherapies from the more mainstream types. Quacks, charlatans, and psychotherapists may have much in common.

The Nature of the Therapeutic Process

It is not surprising that psychotherapy fails. It would be surprising if it succeeded, especially in its abbreviated current forms. The notion itself is odd. Persistently deviant behaviors, many of them cherished by the patients and reinforced within their abusive environments, are expected to change as a result of what would appear to be superficial interventions, usually a series of discussions with a wise and skilled therapist. Freud's later despair, and perhaps one of his few insights to withstand time and scrutiny, was based upon the persistence of his patients' sickness in spite of all his efforts. Psychotherapy's faith in rational induction may itself be a neurotic optimism, blind to its own failures. A cultlike devotion to its methods belies a commitment to science, depriving its patients of a just advocacy. Dysfunctional behaviors may not be amenable to psychotherapy's gentle persuasiveness. They may require far more expensive, material, and commonplace solutions.

In spite of the many problems with method and bias that undermine the outcome research of psychotherapy, it may still produce a beneficial effect although probably far less than the outcome studies suggest and perhaps not frequently related to important behaviors. However, even acknowledging the *possibility* of some positive outcomes that can be attributed to the therapeutic interventions themselves, there still remain alternative, nontherapeutic explanations for the gains of the treated groups. One possibility, discussed at considerable length in regards to family therapy, is that the patient population is not very distressed to begin with and indeed their pursuit of therapy is itself a strong signal that they have already gone far to resolve their problems. In these situations the therapist performs a ceremonial affirmation of the patient's inherent human value, a ritual endorsement of the patient's own unassisted choice of appropriate behavior.

A second nontherapeutic explanation, and the one with far greater theoretical and ideological force, is that the power of therapy, if it exists at all, lies in its simple ability to fill deprivations and to prevent deprivations by providing surrogates for common cultural institutions, notably the family and community, when they are not present. Yet the body of outcome research suggests that psychotherapy may be a relatively ineffective way to handle these deprivations; each nurturing session of psychotherapy may not be able to compensate for much more than a relatively equivalent amount of previous psychic or social suffering. The benefits of psychotherapy for patients may derive not from its elegant, specialized, and rare techniques but from its far more common provision of simple decent human interaction. This sort of common human decency may lie at the heart of the placebo effect, the large relative gains that controls made from nontherapeutic, structured activities. The small additional gains for therapy, approximately 10 percent over the controls in the Smith et al.'s study, can probably be explained away by expectancy biases alone.

When deprivations are slight, the weak interventions of the typical therapeutic regimen may be sufficient to restore appropriate behavior, to calm psychic pain, and to create patient satisfaction with the process. But in these cases, the patient may not be in serious need. Far less expensive alternatives, perhaps time itself, may be just as effective. Nonhelp alternatives may even be more effective for the mildly deprived and the forlorn. Their own miseries may prod them to an adjustment for which they can take a personal credit and that may build more confidence in their own problem solving skills. It would certainly decrease the amount of unnecessary dependence on psychotherapy, one of its iatrogenic costs. Indeed, the deterioration effects of "time therapy" may be less than for psychotherapy since the probability of suffering from unskilled or incautious practitioners is reduced.

On the other hand, for the severely deprived, psychotherapeutic interventions appear to be patently inadequate to fill their needs. Psychotherapy does not offer society an inexpensive or effective way to comfort the severely distressed or to change socially problematic behaviors. Psychotherapy cannot compensate for the prior deprivations that may be at the root of severe distress and, by extension, of deep-seated social problems.

The denial of these conclusions in creating an illusion of effectiveness is the field's vital lie. The few beneficial outcomes of psychotherapy—if they exist at all—may emerge from ceremonies of affirmation performed by psychic priests of modern society on relatively well-adjusted but superstitious people who have already solved their own problems.

The larger impact of psychotherapy, and perhaps the one that explains its persistence, may lie outside of the therapeutic session itself, in its extrinsic contribution to social stability, its role in constructing the myth of social efficiency. Yet there is a price for playing out this role. Patients are not cured. Distressed people are also denied the search for solutions to their problems. The possibility is pushed aside that imperfections in the culture, not simply unusual personal circumstances, have caused their distress. Alternatives to socially efficient interventions—particularly those that provide greater social and economic equality—are ignored in the belief that therapy is sufficient or will become sufficient. Some people deteriorate in therapy. Some become addicted to therapy. The culture is allowed another superstition. Social progress is thwarted.

Social Efficiency: Explaining the Persistence of Psychotherapy

Modern American culture adores psychotherapy. In spite of a body of research that recalls fringe science, psychotherapy occupies center stage in the drama of social prevention, cure, and rehabilitation. The difference between the condemned fringe and the unscientific center lies in the social and political utility of psychotherapy, not in its effectiveness against mental illness.

It seems intuitively reasonable for the weak interventions of psychotherapy to fail, lacking a powerful ability to substitute for the effects of great deprivation. Yet the marvel is that psychotherapy and the many extensions of clinical psychology have enjoyed such a prolonged popularity, becoming culturally institutionalized as favored responses to personal and social problems, without offering any credible proof of an ability to modify dysfunctional personal behavior. American society apparently believes in the production function of psychotherapy—its power to cure, to prevent, and to rehabilitate. Its persistence, however, may not lie in its production function but in its ability to create the decisive metaphors of myth that affect social attitudes.

Psychotherapy's inherent promise of social efficiency reconciles important portions of the culture to the implausibility of more thoroughgoing social change, which in contemporary American society implies the repugnant strategy of taxing wealthy groups on behalf of populations in need. But the enterprise of psychotherapy, in failing science, also fails to realize a true production function of service.

What then is psychotherapy? Psychotherapy may be little more than an indulgence for the superstitious, self-centered, bored, and neurotic who take refuge in a chain hotel personality. It competes in the open market of personal improvement regimens with numerology, body building, religion, and bowling.

Ernest Becker may possibly have it just right. The process of introspection, of questioning personal behavior and trying to understand one's personal existence, is an exquisite and perhaps fulfilling episode in the passage through life. It is probably an important philosophic experience that all people should go through. But Becker makes no claim that this process is associated with important behavioral changes or indeed that this process is therapeutic. Psychotherapy, in this sense, may enrich life but it does not solve problems. Perhaps those most likely to benefit from it are those least in need of modifying their behaviors. But even on this basis, current training in psychiatry, psychology, social work, and counseling is quite incapable of producing adequate guides for Becker's philosophic journey. The sage business has yet to be successfully professionalized, nor has the business of resolving social problems.

Social work directly focuses on a broad range of social problems. It accepts psychotherapy as its "nuclear" skill along with a number of weak social interventions, in justifying an expertise in resolving and preventing social problems. Yet social work's combination of social and psychological interventions has been as ineffective as psychotherapy alone. Social work, imitating the psychotherapeutic community, also refuses to acknowledge its failures, denying standing to its small critical tradition while fulfilling a role not in curing its "clients" but in maintaining the fiction of social efficiency. Social work's retreat from the intractable enormity of social need to a comforting psychic world of attitudes, satisfactions, and preferences expresses the culture's institutionalized concession to social efficiency over the need for greater equality.

Notes

1. For example, 8 percent of the effect sizes for psychodynamic therapy would fall below "0," 36 percent for reality therapy, 14 percent for behavior therapy, 27 percent for systematic desensitization. (See Epstein 1984a for a complete listing of the recomputed effect sizes.) Throughout their analysis, Smith et al.(1980) presented effect sizes of the different therapies as though they were populations of outcomes instead of samples drawn from the underlying populations. Following the more tenable assumption that the grouped effect sizes are actually a distribution of sample means, the underlying distributions of the population of effect sizes increase dramatically. Their assumed standard deviations are really standard errors. As a result, the revised estimates of the standard deviations of the underlying populations increase dramatically. As the assumed sample sizes increase, variations become so

large that in every case almost 50 percent of the outcomes fall below zero effect size, that is, into the area of negative effects relative to nontreatment controls.

2. The indeterminate condition of psychotherapeutic outcomes seems to be a permanent condition of the field. There is no credible research that testifies to the effectiveness of psychotherapy. This judgment is based upon a critical analysis of Smith et al. and the largest portion and the most sophisticated of the subsequent studies: Alden, Alexander et al., Andrews and Harvey, Azrin et al., Bagarozzi and Rauen, Baggs and Spence, Barlow et al., Baucom et al., Baucom and Lester, Beach and O'Leary, Beck, Behrens et al., Bellack et al., Bergin, Berman et al., Bland and Hallam, Blanchard et al., Blanchard and Andrasik, Boelens et al., Borkovec, Botvin et al., Brock and Joanning, Brom et al., Butler et al., Casey and Berman, Cobb et al., Cooper and Clum, Cooper, Cross et al., DeRubeis et al., DeWitt, Dush et al., Emmelkamp, Emmelkamp and deLange, Falloon, Fleischman and Szykula, Giblin and Sprenkle, Girodo et al., Glaister, Gurman et al., Hafner et al., Hahlweg, Hahlweg and Markman Hall and Crisp, Hill et al., Hoberman et al., Hollister et al., Holroyd and Andrasik, Holtzworth-Munroe et al., Howard et al., Hsu, Imber et al., Iverson and Baucom, Jacobson, Jacobson et al., Jarrett and Nelson, Joanning, Johnson and Greenberg, Kane and Kendall, Kazdin et al., Keane et al., Kloslo et al., Lambert et al., Landman and Dawes, Leff et al., Lester and Doherty, Lewinsohn et al., Mann et al., Manne et al., Marchine, Mattick and Peters, McClean and Hakstian, Mehlman et al., Miller et al., Miller and Berman, Miller , Morris, Nezu and Perri, O'Farrell et al., O'Leary, O'Leary and Beach, Patterson, Pilkonis, Piper et al., Pisterman et al., Prioleau et al., Raz-Duvshani, Rehm et al., Rehm et al., Rounsaville et al., Russell et al., Russell et al., Scogin et al., Shapiro et al., Shapiro, Shapiro and Shapiro, Shipley and Boudewyns, Silverman et al., Simons et al., Snyder and Wills, Snyder et al., Sokol, Sprenkle and Storm, Stanton et al., Steinbrueck et al., Strube and Hartmann, Swift, Szapocznik et al., Telch et al., Wampler, Weisz et al., Wellisch and Ro-Trock, Williams et al., Woody et al., Yohman et al.

3

Science and Benevolence in Social Work

More than any other field, social work is associated with the social services. Social work practice cuts across programs in mental health, public health and medical services, education, public welfare, foster and protective care, counseling, day care, recreation and community centers, corrections, drug and alcohol rehabilitation, residential care, mental retardation and others. Social workers are neither the mandarins of human service practice—the physicians, psychiatrists, clinical psychologists—nor its dirty workers, the paraprofessionals. They occupy middle management and middle service positions, receiving a salary commensurate with school teachers, counselors, firemen, police and military officers.

The field's ambitions for professional status have been tied largely to psychotherapy, its "nuclear" technique. Many students seek an advanced degree in social work motivated to become psychotherapists, preferably practicing in a private clinic that serves a middle-class clientele. Nevertheless, they customarily end up working in departments of welfare (providing foster care, protective and "prevention" services, and less frequently, cash benefits themselves), public residential care facilities (such as hospitals for the chronically ill, half-way houses, and "deinstitutionalized" community care facilities for the developmentally disabled and physically disabled), and the multitude of counseling agencies (e.g., family service agencies, and sectarian charities such as Catholic Charities, Episcopal Charities, and Jewish Philanthropies) that operate in tandem with the public sector and receive much of their funding from public budgets. Social work's intellectual efforts, especially those of its university-based faculties, have concentrated on this core of social services. These services handle, almost exclusively, problems of individual adjustment. The auspices of these agencies constitute the core of social work's constituency.

In contrast to this focus on personal pathology and individual adaptation, a persistent but decidedly minor theme in the field has addressed the imperfections of society that are associated with poverty and the needs of poorer, low-status groups. This tradition, drawing breath from the essential similarities between problem groups and privileged groups, has argued that social problems are frequently the result of inequitable social deprivations and that remedies should therefore conform to a theme of greater social and economic parity. This "structural" orientation had a much bigger play in England than in the United States, especially after World War II, when a uniquely English socialism won at the polls and then set about instituting broad-based changes in health, education, welfare, and social services.[1]

In the United States, structural solutions have failed in the contest with approaches to need dictated by social efficiency. Social work has perpetuated the fallacy that efficient solutions, usually based in some form of psychotherapeutic or personal change strategy, have been effective.

Reluctantly at times, many of the field's researchers have accepted at least the formal terms of a credible science as their criteria of proof. Yet the failure of the field to ever achieve this goal of proof and its continuing abandonment of the poor and other lower-status groups in serving its ambitions for greater professional status have not seemed to harm its institutional success. Indeed, the explanation of the field's persistence despite credible proofs of its effectiveness and without commitment to its traditional target populations is paradoxical. Yet the clue to unraveling the puzzle lies along the line of the distortions of its research—"proofs" that low-cost, socially nondisruptive interventions are effective. More than simply molding itself to the image of psychotherapy, social work has been driven by the practical rewards of social efficiency. It has thrived as one of the principal guardians of the myth.

The critical tradition in social work has usually been the disciple of a "small band of prophets" secure in the occasional arms of political gains on the left. For a few brief moments, recollected in the 1970s and muffled again in the 1980s, the field confronted its failure to cure, rehabilitate, or prevent social problems. But it quickly recognized that grants, social position, professional status, growth, standing within the university, and the other rewards of professional status and organizational health would be threatened by the perception that social work practice was ineffective *and* antagonistic to popular preferences. The research of the field can be read as an accommodation to political reality, the triumph of power over social need in the practice of the social services.

Ironically, Fischer, one of the field's severest critics, produced the statement that most clearly justifies the modern accommodations of the field with political orthodoxy. Scarcely eight years after taking the field to task for its weak and bogus research and for the ineffectiveness of its interventions, Fischer (1981) discovered a new "scientific revolution" in social work research. The field followed along, dutifully producing new findings testifying to effectiveness.

Yet neither the social reality nor the quality of the field's scholarship have changed in any way to explain Fischer's conversion. Indeed, between the early 1970s and the early 1990s, conditions have deteriorated for poor and lower-status Americans even while the social work scholarship itself has become more certain of its value. Nonetheless, the state of social work has been largely the same throughout. Only its style of adaptation has changed, tamely acknowledging the harsh political penalties that are exacted for skepticism and for an advocacy that promotes expensive social remedies.

Prior to 1981 and the Scientific Revolution in Social Work

Wootton (1959) laid out the social science terrain of programmatic effectiveness in perhaps the single most penetrating analysis of the social services and social work. Wootton claimed to have reviewed the entire modern literature of the social sciences relevant to social pathology, that is, mental disease and criminality. She concluded that the conditions of research into social pathology were "barren" and "fruitless" and that the practice of social work, based upon that research, was "unfortunate."

The tacit subplot of her work indicated the poor quality of the research as the principal obstacle to progress: selection bias in studying problems, "insufficiency of factual information," subjectivity of the data, "dubious reliability," "clumsiness of tools," absence of appropriate criteria, absence of appropriate controls, and what she termed research "prejudice," a concept more broadly thought of today as a expectancy bias.

> No elaborate argument is necessary to show that, in the investigation of human affairs, prejudice is likely to be a more dangerous threat to scientific integrity than it is in, say, the study of crystalline structures. In the natural sciences integrity may be threatened by love of one's own hypothesis, or by the desire to discredit a rival or to maintain an intellectual position which has in effect become a vested interest. In the

social sciences we have all this to cope with and more beside; for the social scientist has constantly to extricate himself from a tangle of social and ethical value-judgments. (317)

Wootton argued that the effect of the research was to endorse services that treated "the infected individual rather than to eliminate the infection from the environment" (328). Her preference was to attack income poverty itself which she felt lay at the root of most other social problems of individual deviance. Her analysis pointed to the failure of study after study to establish credible causes of deviance in class, family, or genetic factors. As a result "the chief effect of precise investigation into questions of social pathology has been to undermine the credibility of virtually all the current myths" (326).

But Wootton's belief in the Pygmalion myth, laying at the hearts of both her commitment to Fabian socialism as well as to modern American liberalism, is also a fatality of social science debunking. The elimination of poverty and thereby social pathology is probably not, as this myth of generosity and good will suggests, a relatively easy and inexpensive task. Perhaps the weakness in her work is the belief that the elimination of economic poverty would lead inevitably to an elimination of social problems, the idea that economic poverty and cultural poverty are amenable to the same solution.

Nevertheless, her most powerful conclusion is not practical at all, for the destruction of the Pygmalion myth leaves no feasible recourse for social policy:

By tracing the springs of anti-social behavior to the individual rather than to his social environment, we are, after all, only following what has long proved itself to be the path of least resistance; for, difficult as it is to cope with the mishaps of individual men and women, the institutions in which they enchain themselves are even more obdurate still. Conditions which favor pathological developments, either in the medical or in the social sense, are notoriously awkward to deal with. In medical research . . . 'the cynic may ask what, having shown that a disease is closely correlated with adverse living conditions, we propose to do about it, for it is admittedly beyond the ordinary powers of doctors to transfer their patients from (a low social class to a high social class) and so to relieve them of some of their bronchitis, tuberculosis, and myocardial degeneration'. . . . So also in social affairs, to treat an individual is a very different matter from converting the underprivileged into the privileged. Always it is easier to put up a clinic than to pull down a slum, and always it is tempting to treat the unequal opportunities of the slum and of the privileged neighborhoods as part of the order of nature. If only for these reasons, theories which direct attention away form social conditions towards the deficiencies of individual personality are bound to enjoy a considerable practical advantage. They are very comfortable. (329)

But her practical conclusions—the humanizing effects of psychiatry and the exaggerated importance of medical remedies for sociological problems—are futile against the enormity of her own analysis. Indeed, Wootton's despair that little if any progress is possible against social problems has been borne out by the thirty years of English experience subsequent to the publication of her work. Problems are obdurate because they are embedded in the culture. Social science research and social services have been unable to escape the same encrustation, failing to transcend their own professional, political, organizational, and personal stakes to speak to the objective reality of social conditions.

The literature had failed to identify causes of deviancy and Wootton was too modest to concoct one. Yet in the assumptions implicit throughout her analysis, Wootton overestimated economic parity as a cure for cultural problems. Then and now, money, at least at the very meager levels being discussed as welfare reform, cannot buy cultural equality even while it may close the economic gap between the rich and the poor.

In an unusually well-informed essay, Segal (1972) attempted to assess social work's experience with therapeutic interventions. Again, because psychotherapy is so central to social casework, that body of research figured prominently in his discussion of social work. He uncovered a pool of insubstantial and biased research that frequently reported harmful effects. Moreover he noted that many of the studies, especially those assessing new programs, were "token attempts" at research. Segal concluded:

> One might be most pessimistic about traditional preventive therapeutic interventions with delinquent populations. . . . [A]nalyses are not done to enable the evaluator to detect effects of the magnitude he thinks are important. The evidence with respect to the effectiveness of social work therapeutic interventions remains equivocal. The trends in the data, however, point strongly in the negative direction. (15)

His impression that the stronger studies produced more negative findings may have been true at the time but perhaps only as an accommodation to the times itself. The last decade covered by Segal (the 1960s) seemed to nurture both randomized designs and a skepticism (if not an actual hostility) toward social work's traditional outcomes. Yet this inverse relationship between method and outcome, repeated often through the years, has not been borne out in more recent research in which randomization is seemingly no protection against the expectancy biases of researchers.

Segal knew "of no study of outcome with respect to social work therapeutic interventions with both an adequate control group design and positive results" (3). In 1992, this conclusion still holds true for social work, psychotherapeutics and probably the remainder of the social services if "adequate" is taken to imply methodological protections (particularly blinding) in addition to randomization that guard reliability and validity.

The totality of the studies that Segal reviewed expressed the field's preoccupation with socially efficient solutions. Except possibly for one study (Irgens 1936), the range of interventions represented by the social work literature was narrowly conceived with a self-absorbed tendency to focus on the characteristics of the therapist (warmth, genuineness, and empathy), ignoring a broader range of possible interventions that provided more material supports.

Fischer (1973a), supporting both Wootton and Segal, concluded that "at present, lack of evidence of the effectiveness of professional casework is the rule rather than the exception" (19). He even found evidence that casework may have actually harmed many of its clients. Yet his conclusions resulted from an analysis of only eleven studies, the only ones that passed his minimal screen for methodological rigor to emerge as credible statements of social work practice.

Fischer surveyed social work journals, dissertation abstracts, and even agency reports, finally identifying seventy studies from the 1930s to the early 1970s of social work effectiveness. He excluded from this group studies that lacked a control group, that did not focus on professional social workers (those with a master's degree in social work), and that were conducted outside of the United States. Of the eleven studies that met his inclusion criteria, not one established the effectiveness of social work intervention. "In slightly under 50 percent of (Fischer's eleven) studies, clients receiving services in the experimental group were shown either to deteriorate to a greater degree than clients in the control group or to demonstrate improved functioning at a lesser rate than control subjects" (Fischer 1973a, 15–16). Indeed Blenkner et al. (1971) reported serious deterioration and mortality among the treated group.

Yet the porous quality of the research itself could not sustain any conclusion except perhaps that the research inadvertently expressed the spirit of the times more than their social reality. Ten of the eleven studies were published after 1961. These studies, presumably the most credible and relevant of the social work literature, may have done little more than conform with their age of petulance, doubt, and challenge to authority— the latter 1960s and early 1970s. The unpopularity of traditional social work at that time—the image was of intrusive case workers snooping on behalf of racist welfare bureaucracies to enforce the "man in the house rule"— may have nurtured professional ambitions to oppose the field's orthodoxy. This mood, not the reality of social conditions, may have generated a number of negative findings in the research. But these findings, perhaps satisfying to the rebellious soul, were not scientifically credible.

Without the protection of credible methodologies, these findings simply represented another political accommodation and one failing to provide an institutionalized voice on behalf of effective services. Uniformly negative, those studies were still not credible statements of program outcomes: weak instrumentation and frequently subjective out-come ratings, inappropriate statistical analysis, biased and frequently small samples, lack of blinding, inappropriate criteria, high rates of attrition and censoring, lack of randomization, demonstration effects, and so forth. None replicated earlier research. None were replicated.

Perhaps suggesting a general satisfaction with social work, only eleven outcome studies were conducted in a period of almost forty years that conformed with Fischer's minimal criteria of credible research. Yet scientific credibility is quite distinct from social utility. If the Fischer conclusions were accurate or even plausible, they suggested that the value of social work lay outside of its social service function. In address-ing his critics, Fischer pointed out that:

> A technical research corollary to this conclusion [ineffectiveness], and a comment frequently appearing in the social work literature, is that "we also lack good scientific proof of ineffectiveness." This assertion, however, taken alone, would appear to be rather insubstantial grounds on which to support a profession. (19)

But Fischer may have ignored the usefulness, at least from the perspec-tive of the social service community, of a belief in a flat, socially efficient Earth. Scientifically based professions employ scientific demonstrations of their effectiveness; social professions only need proofs that they are compatible.

Wood (1978) continued the skeptical tradition in social work but refused to embrace its implications. She reviewed the casework literature from 1956 to 1975, and identified twenty-two outcome studies, including Fischer's eleven and many of Segal's stronger studies, that met her inclusion criteria. In contrast to Fischer, Wood also included interventions conducted by any level of social work practitioner and research that employed any kind of control or comparison group. Wood's studies covered corrections, services for the aged, for the poor and for children, and the conditions of interventions per se (e.g., short-term versus long-term care). Her findings closely paralleled those of Wootton, Segal, and Fischer. Only six of her twenty-two studies reported positive outcomes; five reported mixed and trivial outcomes; six studies showed no differences between experimental and comparison groups; and five studies actually reported significantly greater deterioration among the treated clients than among control clients.

Anticipating the later call for "appropriate treatment", Wood concluded with a hope for a more scientific and differentiated practice of social work:

> What can be learned from these studies . . . ? Unfortunately, the answer seems to be, with a few exceptions, not a great deal. It is difficult to draw prescriptive conclusions from the group of studies as a body for a number of reasons. A lack of standardization among outcome measures . . . weakness in design, in implementation of the design or in analysis of the data. However, the evidence of the studies does lead to the not-so-startling conclusion that poor practice is indeed ineffective. . . . Studies that reported positive outcomes—that demonstrated effectiveness of the casework or group work interventions applied—appear to have involved a better quality of practice. (451)

Wood claimed that the studies that produced positive client outcomes, representing "quality practice," conformed with a more rational process of accurate problem definition, analysis, and treatment. In relation to services for the poor, as one example, Wood pointed out that the principal tasks of the social workers were to "accurately define the problems in the case, what is causing them, and what can realistically be done about them within the limits of available time and service; to see that what can be done is done; and to evaluate the effects of the intervention in terms of the original problem and goals" (446).

Not surprisingly, this primarily entailed providing money, housing, and medical care for poor people. Wood reported, but only as a *speculation*, that "projects which focused on poor clients' economic and other instrumental needs, rather than on their expressive needs, were more likely to be successful" (443). Indeed, this stage whisper should have been the climactic soliloquy of her research. It seems strange, and a tribute to the depressing effects of psychotherapy on the imagination of the field, that social work could be so quaintly out of touch with social reality as to require the drama of empirical research and the delicacy of a "speculation" to raise this theme.

It seems far more reasonable to argue that resources to provide greater cultural parity and not the elegance of psychological diagnosis and technique determine the outcomes of social work practice. Wood's twenty-two interventions typically failed when they addressed the emotional problems of people who were in need of material supports and when their emotional problems entailed an intensity of care beyond levels that social workers could provide (e.g., a nonabusive and caring home for emotionally disturbed children).

Yet even in the six instances when Wood's studies reported social work's success, it is far from certain that the outcomes were credibly tied to the social work interventions or signified hopeful steps against serious social problems. As two examples of these positive studies, Schwartz and Sample (1967) and Wilson (1967) were both greatly flawed, undercutting Wood's attempts to salvage some benefit for "quality practice." Schwartz and Sample tested the effect of small caseloads and various forms of management on the functioning of public welfare clients. They found that small caseloads and professional social work supervision improved client functioning. The finding had considerable importance for the field since the experimental conditions were closely identified with the prevailing theories of social casework. The experimental conditions entailed longer amounts of time spent by clients with professionally trained caseworkers and an administrative structure that placed master's level supervisors in strategic management positions.

Yet the Schwartz and Sample findings—the net benefits that accrued to experimental groups in comparison with controls —were very small; they occasionally favored controls, and they were not particularly meaningful in terms of the general social problem of family conditions and services. If, for example, the welfare families that received intensive casework also received more dental care, then in light of the limited amount of charity dental care available at that time, some other welfare family did not receive services or clients were simply shifted onto existing waiting lists. But more troubling is the fact that none of the study's measures of client outcomes were either verified or objective. The outcome assessments depended upon client self-reports and the global assessments by raters who were not blind to the subjects' status. These raters were "highly experienced social workers" with "backgrounds either in child welfare or psychiatric social work" (Schwartz and Sample).

This research design was more a prescription for expectancy bias than objective research. The raters had an ostensible commitment to the experimental conditions and had to have been frequently aware of which clients were in the experimental groups and which were in control groups. In the end, experimental subjects appeared to be at most 18 percent better off than controls. But this 18 percent was a subjective global rating that could not be translated into concrete improvements—more money, fewer problems, and greater opportunity. By itself, the fact that Segal had earlier considered this study to be among the three best in its area of interest indicts research in social work.

The second example of Wood's six positive studies, Wilson (1967), is even weaker than Schwartz and Sample. Wilson also applied a form of intensive casework to a welfare caseload. In the end, Wilson only produced occasional and small positive findings. The principal finding was that more families on welfare who saw social workers with small caseloads were independent of public assistance after two years than families on welfare who saw social workers with larger caseloads. The difference was only 12 percent.

Yet no differences were found in terms of family functioning and other social measures. This would seem to argue against the effectiveness of intensive casework, a treatment strategy that employs a variety of techniques to improve social and familial dysfunctions:

> Family-oriented casework, including a concentrated effort to involve absent fathers. Group meetings with persons having common problems. Intensive contact with individuals during periods of personal crisis, including daily sessions when necessary. Special efforts to attain optimum use of community health and welfare resources through a carefully structured referral and follow-up process. (302)

The fact that intensive casework had little effect, if any, suggests that treatment integrity was not maintained, or that the caseworkers were incompetent, or that intensive casework is inadequate. Wilson could not distinguish between these factors. Yet as Wilson points out, "the duration of time in which intensive casework was administered did not seem to affect financial independence." This further strengthens a skeptical view of casework's value while underscoring its inadequacy for the problems of poor people.

Yet even Wilson's mixed and modest findings are not credible. The study employed an "'approximated' control group" while failing to provide evidence of its equivalence with the intensive casework group. As he points out, "marginally afflicted AFDC families" are easily amenable to improvements, so much so that his small findings could easily be accounted for by small initial differences between his groups.

Contrary to Wood's characterization of these two studies, neither one actually provided clear or credible positive outcomes nor did they endorse her sense of "quality practice." Both deprive her of even glimmers of credible evidence for social work's effectiveness.

Wood's recommendations, manifesting a deep acceptance of the myth of social efficiency, called for technical refinements within the confines of existing practice—intensive casework. Yet the more appropriate conclusion to be drawn from her base of studies, flowing logically and naturally out of her own observations and criticisms, was that more resources were needed and that the research in the field was not focused on this problem, failing to provide a just advocacy for the existing caseload of need. Intensive casework is decidedly not the equivalent of intensive social services.

The few outposts of skepticism in social work began to be disassembled by one of their architects. In 1978, Fischer attempted a general statement about the social services by updating his earlier coverage of social work while extending his analysis to psychotherapy, corrections, psychiatric hospitalization, and educational services. "The facts are that it does appear that very little 'works.'" But *something* does.

He claimed to have identified two classes of "positive exceptions" to the barren conclusion of uniform ineffectiveness. The first were "inconsistent positive findings" and he put little confidence in them. However, the second class of positive findings, those that "show up with some consistency" even though "few and far between," provided Fischer with substantial grounds to believe that practice was occasionally but consistently effective. "Perhaps the most striking of these is the research on behavior modification" with humans.

Four out of five of the areas reviewed here (with the exception of social work practice which, despite some interest in this area, has yet to produce controlled research documenting positive results for professional social work practitioners using behavior modification) contain a number of studies showing the positive, significant effects of the application of behavior modification procedures. In fact, in the aggregate, there are over 200 controlled studies showing effective results using behavior modification, studies spanning the areas of psychotherapy and counseling, psychiatric hospitalization, and education. . . . This conclusion is bolstered by the results of over 150 published, rigorous single case studies using the A-B-A-B reversal design. . . . (233)

But 350 supportive, consistent, high-quality studies would not simply constitute evidence that is "few and far between." They would establish an overwhelmingly conclusive basis for declaring the effectiveness of behavioral treatment. This would have been important news if it were true, but it wasn't.

These studies were neither credible nor definitive. They were frequently distorted and trivial. They suffered from many of the invalidating pitfalls that Fischer identified among the social work literature. It is worth adding that none of them approached the rigor of operant conditioning experiments with animals and in going from animal tests to human tests, research standards generally need to *rise*. None of them have been as extensively replicated.

Fischer gleaned these 200 controlled and 150 single case studies from reviews and textbooks on behavior modification. These weak works frequently provided far more conflicting data about behavior modification than Fischer acknowledged. Robin's (1976) summary analysis of thirty-nine outcome studies of behavioral instruction in colleges reported "a highly consistent 8 percent to 11 percent achievement gain across instructional disciplines" (measured by grades). Yet "certain common methodological weaknesses permeate (this) literature": only twelve of the thirty-nine studies employed randomized controls; many lacked any controls at all; attrition rates were different for comparison and experimental groups and high; many studies provided insufficient data to properly assess outcomes; and many failed to apply appropriate reliability checks while employing questionably valid measures. Samples were frequently tiny.

Robin acknowledged the probability of expectancy biases: "in the majority of studies teacher-made, self report questionnaires have served as the primary measure of student attitudes" suggesting that the teacher's "social influence" may have affected their satisfaction with "behavioral instruction." Behavioral instruction interventions seemed typically to provide both more intense and more personal tutoring but the studies did not control for these factors. As a result any improvements that may have occurred could well have been the simple products of additional instruction and not the elegant technological results of behavior modification.

In a manner similar to Robin, Fischer's cited textbooks and reviews failed to identify credible tests of the effectiveness of behavioral treatments (Bergin and Suinn 1975, Craighead 1976, Gambrill 1977, Kazdin 1977, O'Leary and Wilson 1980, Rimm and Masters 1974). The research they reported contained a weak cohort of studies while they failed to acknowledge that many of the studies they relied on violated their own methodological standards, usually set out in a chapter on research (e.g., Kazdin 1977).

Even in possibly its most effective form—the token economy—behavior modification provides an ambiguous benefit with little evidence to suggest that it improves upon the simple rules of institutional management. Moreover, the transfer of modified behaviors to settings outside of the conditioning situation has typically failed. Conditioned behavior, when it occurs, seems transient and dependent upon the continued presence of the conditioning contingencies (Kazdin 1977, 282).

The small samples, the lack of controls, the conceptual ambiguities (especially treatment integrity—the issue of what is being done), problems with measurement and reliability, and selection biases have permitted the convergence of findings that affirm the preferences of the researchers. But little if any behavior change has been credibly induced. Without the prudence of skepticism, the behavior modification textbooks have become the ideological tracts of partisan therapists, stringing shreds of empirical evidence along the frayed lines of their preferred behavioral theories.

All of Fischer's 150 supportive studies that employed single system designs would have failed to pass the minimal and inadequate inclusion criteria that Fischer employed in his 1973 review. They lacked controls. They also opened many of the other methodological backdoors that introduce the expectancy biases of the researchers to their findings.

As a concession to the skepticism of his earlier paper, Fischer reluctantly acknowledged that these problems "mitigat(e) against the helping professions becoming unduly enamored with the field of behavior modification":

Frequently, the effectiveness research on behavior modification falls short of really demonstrating effectiveness—at least on the target variables of most concern. In many studies [but presumably not his (350)], there is clear evidence that behavior modification can change behavior, but the behavior may not be the most socially significant outcome behavior, or the positive results do not generalize to the natural environment . . . [Nevertheless] behaviorists have conducted a score of controlled studies showing effective use of behavior modification to change selected behaviors in the field of corrections; but, of these, only a handful actually address recidivism. (234)

Nevertheless, Fischer labored on to identify other approaches of proven effectiveness besides behavior modification:

in four or five areas of professional endeavor . . . [again, with social work practice as the exception], illustrating the significant and positive effects of the communication of the interpersonal skills of empathy, warmth, and genuineness on a range of client and student behaviors. Further, these interpersonal skills demonstrably can be learned in special training courses and workshops. . . . In fact, there is an increasing body of research showing that individuals who communicate high levels of empathy, warmth, and genuineness are also more effective in applying behavior modification, an interesting and potentially very important combination of interpersonal skills. . . . (235)

However, once again his proof, the base of the supposedly credible research he cited in support of these contentions, was not credible at all. Two of his citations were not available, drawn from the field's fugitive literature (Harris and Lichenstein [1971] was a conference speech, Cairns [1968] was an unpublished master's thesis). All of his other citations utilized analog patients and analog therapists who were college undergraduates (Dowling and Frantz 1975, Mickelson and Stevic 1971, Morris and Suckerman 1974, Namenek and Schuldt 1971, Vitalo 1970). Moreover, Namenek and Schuldt actually provided evidence that behavioral therapy was ineffective.

Effectiveness is very enticing for contemporary social argumentation, suggesting that important social goals—the reduction of crime and mental illness, the enhancement of learning—can be realized simply through the technique and the affability of therapists. The cult of the miraculous—an audience perched on the advent of such wondrous news—does not withhold their belief on technical quibbles over proof. But this body of research, weak even within the body of psychotherapeutic outcome studies, is neither consistent nor in any way credible.

Behavioral treatments even augmented with empathy, warmth, and genuineness were not proved to be effective against social problems. The literature did not even appreciate the dry irony of training for genuineness (like practicing spontaneity). Single subject designs, Fischer's new enthusiasm for rigorous methods, are not rigorous at all. They defy the essence of rigor—large randomly drawn samples and placebo controls. Moreover the host of Fischer's controlled studies frequently vulgarized science, testifying only to the continuing need for neutrality, objectivity, and relevance in outcome research. Without methodological protections, the convergence of his 350 studies is testimony to little more than the field's consistent ability to distort findings in support of its institutional needs. Fischer put practical research to practical use.

His curious paper, torn between the remnants of a commitment to critical analysis and the social services' insistence on hopeful leads, marks the transition between the short-lived skeptical mood in social work and its return to self-aggrandizing orthodoxy. It signals both Fischer's later, 1981, benediction of social work for achieving the communal standards of science as well as the subsequent research reviews that consistently affirmed social work's effectiveness. Unfortunately Fischer and the other optimists achieved their proofs by cheapening science, not by demonstrating the ability of efficient solutions to handle social problems.

Yet, by their continuing service to the myth of social efficiency, Segal, Wood, and Fischer confirmed Wootton's far deeper indictment of the social sciences as blind to social reality. Social work was unwilling to consider that its own weak interventions were the root cause of the field's failures. Social work's intellectuals explored only a narrow range of responses to social problems, those focused on the individual's pathology and those that employed its rare skills, (e.g., behavior modification and genuineness). They pointedly ignored far more extensive "structural" interventions, such as the provision of true surrogates for failed families, communities, schools, labor markets, and so forth. By 1981, this stubborn dogmatism led Fischer to certify the emerging quality of social work research, the "new spirit of science in social work," arguing for the patient support of social work's continuing search for effective programs.

The False Dawn of Fischer's Scientific Revolution

Fischer (1981) reached his Kuhnian epiphany of a scientific revolution in social work on the basis of "material presented at social work conferences, from the literature and from less concrete sources of evidence such as the new 'spirit' or 'world view' that seems to be emerging among many social workers" (199). Although in 1973 he was able to identify only eleven credible studies of social work practice—presumably from among many tens of thousands of research reports in the social work literature—scarcely eight years later he was confident that the field was utilizing "procedures of demonstrated effectiveness" and "new processes of knowledge development" that constituted a paradigm shift in social work (Fischer 1981).

> In essence the practice of social work appears to be moving away from the use of vaguely defined, invalidated and haphazardly or uncritically derived knowledge for practice. In its most salient characteristics, the paradigm shift appears to involve a movement toward more systematic, rational, empirically oriented development and use of knowledge for practice. For want of a better phrase, this could be termed a movement toward *scientifically based practice* in social work. . . . [S]ocial workers are increasingly explicating new approaches that are systematic, clear, and oriented to both the rigors of research evidence and the realities of practice. (Fischer 1981)

The key to the revolution was "knowledge of documented effectiveness" and the key to the documentation was science. However, by this time, science for Fischer and for much of the field, had come to respect single systems designs— uncontrolled methods—as an equivalent of RPCT. "The literature on this topic (single subject designs) increased at an explosive rate in the 1970's," Fischer being its chief popularizer in social work (201). Yet, while single system designs have a place in preliminary research they fail as critical demonstrations, lacking controls, randomized sampling procedures, and large samples. Their essence after all is a sample of one, the smallest possible, and their hospitality to the clinician in the role of researcher is an open invitation to expectancy biases.

In due course, the social work literature enthusiastically supported Fischer's effusions with "scientific" testimonials to its effectiveness. Unfortunately, these studies are still not methodologically sound. There is in fact no evidence of its effectiveness while there are considerable grounds for the conclusion that its defining interventions typically fail.

The Feldman et al. Experiment

Feldman et al. (1983, Feldman and Caplinger 1977) has been frequently cited as an example both of high-quality research in social work and of the field's more recent positive effects. However, it actually provides a prominent example of the characteristic weaknesses of the *best* research in the field and its strained reach for supportive evidence.

Feldman and his colleagues conducted a field experiment in St. Louis between 1970 and 1974 to test the value of group work (one of social work's principal methods) in treating antisocial behavior and, by the authors' clear implication, juvenile delinquency. The experiment was funded by the federal government's National Institute of Mental Health. Feldman et al. randomly assigned 263 antisocial youths between eight and sixteen years of age to a variety of experimental and control conditions: groups run by experienced and inexperienced leaders, groups in which only one or two antisocial youths were mixed among prosocial youths, and groups composed entirely of antisocial youth; and three types of treatment: traditional social group work, group work that employed a behavioral treatment method, and a minimal treatment condition that constituted a placebo control. Treatment consisted of up to twenty-four weekly group meetings of approximately two to three hours throughout the school year.

The experiment was set in a Jewish community center whose "clientele were from the middle and upper-middle socioeconomic strata," 90 percent of whom were Jewish. In contrast 90 percent of the experimental youths were Christian; 34 percent were black; most were drawn from the lower and lower-middle classes. Their mean age was 11.2 years, the majority being 9, 10, or 11 years of age (17 percent, 22 percent and 17 percent, respectively). As a condition of the experiment all the antisocial youths were apparently living with their parents.

The antisocial youths were referred to the experiment through a broad variety of local agencies. The referring agency filled out a questionnaire that counted the referred youths' antisocial acts for one week: hitting, biting, shoving, pinching, slapping, throwing an object, pulling someone's hair, hitting someone with an object, taking something that was not his, saying bad things such as "I'll kill you," not carrying out reasonable requests, and other similar forms of misbehavior. The experiment established a minimal antisocial eligibility score of twenty-one antisocial acts per week. However children who committed serious offenses, such as stealing, assault, arson, and so forth, were specifically excluded from the experiment. The outcomes of the experiment—the degree to which antisocial acts were modified by the interventions—

were scored on standardized reports by parents, the youths themselves, group leaders, and other supposedly neutral observers.

The authors found that the experiment was immensely successful in answering "fundamental" questions in the treatment of antisocial youth.

> Experienced group workers were highly capable change agents. Members of their groups exhibited significant increases in prosocial behavior and significant decreases in antisocial behavior. . . . Youths who were treated by the behavioral method made significant gains in prosocial behavior and corresponding losses in antisocial behavior. In contrast, youths who were treated by traditional group work showed substantial increments in antisocial behavior. . . . The observational data highlighted the importance of the treatment relationships that are forged between youths and their group workers. . . . Simply put *the leader modifies the group and it in turn alters the behavior of individual members* . . . (and therefore) may provide a boost in morale for today's beleaguered schools of social work. In particular, it suggests that social work educators should reemphasize curriculum design, clinical instruction, and field research regarding group work practice. (Emphasis in original)

> As a human service enterprise, the St. Louis Experiment is likely to generate renewed interest in integrative treatment programs for antisocial youths. Indeed, it should encourage traditional community service agencies to reexamine their program priorities. Transportation excluded, the yearly cost for a program such as the St. Louis Experiment would be unlikely to exceed $150 per youth in 1983 dollars. This assumes that professional leaders are employed and that the expenses are distributed equally among groups with an average size of only eight members. By any standard, such an investment would appear to be a worthwhile one not only for a humane society but for a cost-conscious one. . . . The research points convincingly to the effectiveness of integrated treatment programs for young offenders. (Chapter 18 passim)

Unfortunately, the research itself sustains none of these conclusions. Its methods were porous and its relevance to contemporary social problems was doubtful. Many of their findings were small, contradictory, and anomalous. The referred antisocial youths actually reported *fewer* antisocial acts during the eight-week baseline period before treatment than the supposedly normal, nonreferred youths.

The finding that "prior professional experience is, in fact, a key determinant of positive treatment outcomes" is confounded by consistent differences among therapists in addition to prior professional experience. The more experienced leaders were graduate students in social work while the inexperienced therapists were undergraduates who were obviously younger in age, and probably less mature and less experienced in *life*.

The very small reported differences were acknowledged by the authors intermittently throughout the study but certainly not in their conclusions. Their critical findings were that antisocial boys in mixed groups did better than those in groups composed entirely of antisocial boys and that "the antisocial behavior of youths treated by any method or any type of group leader was usually perceived to have declined" as measured by "two very important constituencies, namely the referred boys' parents and their referral agents."

Yet this latter finding would seem to contradict the morale boost to professional social work since the minimal or placebo treatment provided results equivalent to the other treatments. Secondly, the authors unravel the conundrum of antisocial behavior among youths in terms of the positive influence exerted by prosocial peers on antisocial youths. But only twenty-six youths were initially assigned to these groups (and fewer completed treatment) while the findings were based upon observers and observations that were neither independent of the research situation nor blind to the participants' status.

"Group leaders were never told which, if any, of their members had been referred to the agency(66)." Yet this does not mean that the group leaders were blind throughout the study. It defies the most malleable credulity to hold that lower-class Christian youths were not discernible by their comments, assumptions, and references within a middle and upper-middle-class group of Jewish youths. If by no other evidence, their status as referred would become apparent at holiday time, if not the High Holy days, then certainly around Hanukkah. The experiment obviously did not take appropriate steps to guard against the expectancy biases of raters.

The methodology of the study, in spite of the use of randomized assignment, is too leaky to sustain its conclusions and raises the issue of why money was wasted on an experiment that was from the outset incapable of providing credible information. Reliability of measures was low; contrary to the authors' claims an interrater reliability of .51 is terrible. Attrition and censoring were immense problems that on their own vitiate the findings; approximately 60 percent of the participants dropped out before the termination of treatment. Approximately the same percentage of information was lost. Attrition and censoring were even greater in the follow-up periods, with only about 20 percent of the antisocial youth (an attrition of 80 percent) being available for interviews one year after the project. Feldman et al. limply offer the observation that in this sort of experiment such attrition is usual. But this only underscores the generally poor state of research in social services.[2]

The most important finding of the study is not a product of its design but the result of an ex post facto analysis of their data. "We documented assiduously how the *behavior of peers* in a treatment group—regardless of whether the label of 'antisocial' or 'prosocial' might once have been ascribed to them—is the most important factor in group work treatment" (emphasis in original, Feldman and Wodarski 1984). But they did not vary nor control peer behavior as an independent condition in their experiment. In order to establish this finding, which in any event seems to be a common understanding of how young boys behave in recreational settings and could well have been a biased result of their recording procedures, they would need to construct a controlled experiment to test this surmise prospectively.

The initial conceptualization of the experiment was also problematic. The youths that they treated were not serious offenders. They were living in seemingly intact families concerned enough about their sons to seek out care for them and provide time for interviews. The antisocial youths were also very young—actually preadolescents—and because more serious youthful offenders were screened out of the research sample, the findings are of dubious relevance to any social problem.[3]

The experiment after all did not randomly select a sample from a predetermined problem population nor did it explore potential biases in the referral pattern. Indeed the fact that the "youth's self-ratings consistently contradicted the observations of the trained nonparticipants as well as their own group leaders," taken together with the strong possibility of biased reports by the experiment's judges, raises questions about all of the experiment's reported outcomes. Did the children reach the experiment as the result of neurotically overprotective parents and solicitous referral agents? Should the parents, not the children, have been in group work?

Finally, and of greatest moment, the positive outcomes, if they occurred at all, could be attributed to the lavish recreational and social opportunities afforded by this wealthy community center and not by the insights of trained counselors. All the referred children had free run of the center. Therefore, accounting for the putative gains of the experiment simply in terms of inexpensive group leadership ignores the far more substantial, indeed immense, cost of providing community recreation and supervision on a level capable of thwarting antisocial behavior. Rather than a few hours of what the authors admit was frequently uncertain group work, the social milieu of the middle class and their splendid cultural opportunities for social and group interaction are the likely causes of any beneficial outcomes. But this exceeds by many, many thousands of dollars per head the $150 per year that the experiment claimed as the cost of its prosocial outcomes.

The *St. Louis Conundrum* epitomizes the havoc visited on social work research by service to social efficiency. Yet the subsequent reviews of the literature customarily placed Feldman et al. among the field's best research. It randomized between controls and experimental conditions; it took multiple outcome measures; it was conducted by social workers; it tested practice; its initial report (Feldman and Caplinger 1977) appeared as the lead article in the inaugural issue of one of social work's leading refereed journals. Yet the experiment's minimal methodological accommodations to science are patently inadequate to assure credibility even at the most rudimentary levels of information.

The poor quality of the research is itself a conundrum of the popularity of the *St. Louis Experiment* within social work. The community of social service scholars seems to tolerate its conceptual inadequacies, methodological pitfalls, trivial findings, and misleading conclusions as the price for endorsing the professional aspirations of the field.

The Reid and Hanrahan Review

Reid and Hanrahan (1982) reviewed the next generation of social work's studies after Wood. From 1973 to 1979 they were able to identify twenty-two studies, including Feldman and Caplinger (1977), that met their basic inclusion criteria: random assignment of subjects between control and experimental conditions, and interventions by social workers with the goal of improving their client's social functioning. Their happy findings stood in stark contrast with the pessimism of previous reviews. Reid and Hanrahan felt that social work's interventions were well organized and "usually carried out step by step and designed to achieve relatively specific goals." Many employed behavior modification techniques, psychodynamic approaches, and group methods. Their target groups spanned the traditional service populations of social work: "children with behavior problems, predelinquent and troubled youths, parents with children in foster care, families receiving public assistance, couples with marital difficulties, adults with emotional and interpersonal problems, mental patients in aftercare, and elderly people in institutions and in the community."

In addition to a far greater rate of methodologically sophisticated studies (twenty-two in six years compared with Woods' twenty-two in almost twenty years), Reid and Hanrahan underscored the greatly improved outcomes in their group of studies:

> All but two or three of the twenty-two studies yielded findings that could on balance be regarded as positive . . . less than a third of the (Wood) studies produced findings that could on the whole be regarded as positive. . . . Also in marked contrast to the earlier experiments, no recent study that involved a comparison between treated and untreated groups failed to yield at least some evidence of the positive effects of social work intervention. The findings of the recent experiments are grounds for optimism, but they are no cause for complacence. (331)

They pointed to a number of methodological problems that qualified their enthusiasms: some findings were statistically significant but trivial and a few studies reported occasional client deterioration. Nevertheless for Reid and Hanrahan these twenty-two studies proved that: "intervention carried out by social workers could be effective," there was evidence of "promising developments," the field was producing an empirical basis of evidence for effectiveness, and the quality of the field's research had improved.

Yet a close reading of Reid and Hanrahan's twenty-two studies vitiates all of their grounds for optimism. Fully fifteen of their twenty-two studies employed very small samples, twenty-five or less; four of these studies reported samples under ten. A sixteenth study had a sample of only forty-three. The sample sizes in these studies were of particular concern because of their many other flaws that invited researcher expectancy biases: reactive, unstandardized, and subjective measures, and lack of blinding.

The Berger and Rose (1977) study of Interpersonal Skills Training is typical of this group. Their own discussion of their mixed and largely negative findings—measured in "a behavioral role play test"—is far less positive than Reid and Hanrahan's view of the research. Berger and Rose caution that their findings "provide only limited evidence for the efficacy of Interpersonal Skills Training with elderly patients" because successful training when it took place did not generalize to other situations and at follow-up, only eight weeks after training, three of four outcome measures were negative (Berger and Rose, 352).

Reid's own test of his "task-centered approach" to social treatment was also reported as a success (Reid 1978). However, it is deeply flawed while only reporting marginal effectiveness. His demonstration employed forty-four graduate social work students who were enrolled in task-centered training where Reid taught. Each student therapist was assigned two cases: one to be treated with the task-centered approach and the other with a control therapy (supportive attention). Two so-called independent raters assessed segments of audiotaped sessions and rated client outcomes. The principal findings, relating to the subjects' main problems and their overall problem situation, were small but positive and sometimes statistically significant, favoring the task-centered client group by 7 percent to 9 percent.

However, the student therapists, with an obviously large stake in the task-centered approach, were also not blind to the situation of their clients. They may well have induced changes simply by their different attitudes toward the two different sets of clients. The information that was used to evaluate the clients' outcomes was solicited in interviews from the clients themselves, opening wider the possibility of shaded reports (to please their therapists). Moreover, frequent cues were probably present in the recordings that allowed raters to identify a subject's form of treatment while the agreement among different judgments was sometimes unacceptably low (under .50). The research situation was clearly not a test of live practice in the field and seemed likely to have suffered from a host of demonstration effects. The small findings, the question of interrater reliability, the imperfect test situation, the possibility of reactive measures, and the small sample sizes imply that the report of positive findings was both premature and distorted. This was a very compromised study.

Piliavin and Gross (1977) and the Stein project (1976; see also Stein and Gambrill 1977 and Stein 1978) were two of Reid and Hanrahan's six large sample studies that also reported positive findings. However, approximately 50 percent of the samples in Stein and Gambrill were not randomly drawn nor randomly assigned while attrition rates at the two year follow-up point were very large: 40 percent in the experimental group and 25 percent in the control. The research tested the possibility of increasing permanent placements of foster children and reducing

long-term institutional placement through a process of behavioral contracting (based upon behavior modification theory) and intensive services. The control situation provided customary county services. The
project reported positive results: the degree of long-term placement was
considerably less for experimental children, who were returned to their
natural parents about 25 percent more often than children in the control
condition.

However, a number of serious problems compromised the Stein
project. The two groups were not comparable to begin with. Children
with a greater likelihood of return to their parents may have been placed
with greater frequency in the experimental group while those with more
difficult natural families may have ended up disproportionately in the
control group. Indeed more than 50 percent of the foster children were
selected for the different groups by the caseworkers themselves. Stein
worried over the differences between the two groups but he could offer
no assurances that these differences were immaterial.

Furthermore, the staff of the experimental condition was intentionally
oriented to different outcomes than the staff of the control condition. The
control staff was obviously attempting to improve foster care; the experimental staff was trying to remove the children from foster care and
reunite them with their natural parents. But the study takes the point of
view that the return to natural parents is superior. While it may be less of
a draw on the public pocketbook, this is by no means a proven truth. The
children were removed from their parents in the first place because of
gross neglect.

In the end, the Stein project does not meet the randomization criteria
for inclusion by Reid and Hanrahan. It demonstrates little more than the
fact that the orientation of the caseworker can influence the outcomes of
foster care, but does not demonstrate that those outcomes are desirable.
Moreover, Stein and his colleagues were unable to attribute their outcomes to the treatment itself; they were judicious and cautious in interpreting their meaning. In contrast, Reid and Hanrahan reported the
superiority of behavioral contracting over routine service. To repeat, the
value of the outcomes for the children was not measured.

Piliavin and Gross (1977) tested the wisdom of separating social
services from cash payments for recipients of public welfare, a controver-
sial administrative change in the management of public welfare. The
researchers reported that the separation of services from cash assistance

resulted in a decline of requests for services, thereby arguing for the recombination. However, the research did not credibly substantiate its findings. The differences between groups while significant were very small: eighteen monthly requests from the group of seventy compared with eleven requests from the group of seventy-five. Moreover, there was no assessment of whether the requests were reasonable and needed or whether they were simply an artifact of the worker's orientation.

Taken together, Reid and Hanrahan's group of twenty-two studies were neither credible, meaningful, nor well conducted. They represented a weak and misleading pool of research that was not apparently superior to prior cohorts of studies, although positive reports seemed to have been more frequent. A few of the studies, none of them true tests, may indeed have been able to substantiate their positive findings. But such a small number—four or five out of the many thousands that appeared in the literature during the six years of the review period—certainly did not testify to research quality in the social work literature. Such a small number might easily be accounted for by sampling error.

The Rubin Review

In a manner similar to previous reviews, Rubin (1985) screened the batch of social work studies that appeared in journals between 1978 and 1983 to discover whether the literature continued to support Reid and Hanrahan's optimism. Rubin could only identify twelve research projects, reported in thirteen papers, from among more than 6,500 articles, that were able to pass an inclusion criteria similar to previous reviews. Yet contrary to his claims to have found more grounds for social work's effectiveness in these studies, only one of them, an experimental gem conducted by Stein and Test (1980) in Wisconsin, withstands a less flattering methodological critique. All of the other studies that provided evidence of social work's effectiveness, employed grievously flawed methodologies or, in fact, did not support a conclusion of effectiveness. Certainly none, not even Stein and Test, were critical demonstrations of social work's interventive power.[4]

Ironically, the Stein and Test research showed that adequate community care of psychotics was more expensive than institutional care even while their research understated the cost of such care. Although roundly cited in support of the deinstitutionalization policies of the recent years, their investigation of white, family-attached, and young psychotics in a relatively receptive, ethnically homogeneous, and rural community could also be offered as evidence against the wholesale removal of the chronically mentally ill from hospitals.

Stein and Test did seem to demonstrate that the techniques of community care can be successfully implemented, at least in the hands of a highly motivated professional staff. However, they did not prove that deinstitutionalization is desirable for many patients, that their techniques are replicable outside of the their demonstration fishbowl, that their rural success is applicable to urban centers, or that an adequate level of funding could be maintained for patients released to the community. Indeed, most evaluations of the deinstitutionalization experiences of the chronically mentally ill have given substance to these doubts.

But most importantly, Stein and Test is an unusual instance in either the social work or the human service literature generally, of an experiment whose findings may portray actual test conditions and not merely the stakes of researchers or service workers. None of the other studies cited by Rubin either reported findings as positive as those he attributed to them or was conducted credibly in a manner comparable to Stein and Test.

In addition to Stein and Test, Rubin lists six other research reports (five studies) that contained positive outcomes and employed sound methods. Yet one of these six (Tableman et al. 1980) did not really meet Rubin's inclusion criteria for random assignment. Two of the others (Hogarty et al. 1974 and 1979, and Linn et al. 1979) did not report truly positive findings. Their findings were anomalous and equivocal.

The credibility of all of these studies is further limited by other methodological difficulties. Only Linn et al. counted more than fifty in their experimental and control groups. One study (Matson and Senatore 1981) reported samples under fifteen. Attrition was a debilitating factor in Velasquez and McCubbin (1980). Therapists in all of the studies were aware of being in a demonstration project and were conscious of close scrutiny.

In addition, blinding procedures were not adopted; judges, frequently able to identify experimental patients, may not have been truly independent assessors of patient behaviors; patient self-reports were frequently employed. The authors themselves were more skeptical critics of their own methods than Rubin, one confessing that "data are admittedly limited in methodological rigor" (Matson and Senatore, 380).

Furthermore, many of the positive outcomes did not seem to be theoretically valuable. Experimental conditions did not typify actual practice conditions. Even Stein and Test, the most uncrippled of these studies, was only a pilot demonstration and not a definitive test with broad applicability.

The situations of the research also tended to focus on the chronically mentally ill. Therefore, the positive findings, such as they were, may have resulted from lower-level surrogate environments—"highly structured forms of practice"—more than from the socially efficient "therapies" of social work interventions.

Notwithstanding their many methodological problems, these seven reports taken together may have stated only the obvious: even very disabled people (schizophrenics) respond well to non-abusive environments. These environments were not usually constructed by highly trained workers.

To tally it up, of the seven papers that Rubin held up as sound demonstrations of positive social work outcomes: one did not meet his own inclusion criteria; two others did not really show positive outcomes; one other did not have comparable control and experimental groups due to high and differential attrition; none, except Stein and Test and Linn et al. (and even these are questionable), established credibly independent outcome judges; and all but two used very small samples. Positive outcomes, when they occurred, were not technically credible.

Of Rubin's other six research projects, five were grievously flawed, trivial works whose credibility and positive findings Rubin grossly overstates (Reid et al. 1980, Boone et al. 1981, Toseland et al. 1981, Roskin 1982, Berlin 1980). The sixth by Akabas et al. (1982) clearly acknowledged its unfortunate methodological problems and should not have been included.

Rubin unwittingly provided grounds for greater pessimism about both social work and social work research. In the years covered by his review hardly any credible research was performed in the field. Yet the fact that Rubin chose to present a very different picture calls attention to the field's imposing demands for conformity with its false advertisement of itself, the notion that its superficial interventions are making headway against serious social problems.

Other Summaries and Recent Research

Thomlison (1984) and Sheldon (1986) compiled summaries of the literature in social work and allied fields that testified to the growing prowess of its techniques and its research skills. Both relied heavily on the Bergin summaries (Bergin 1971, Bergin and Lambert 1978, Lambert et al. 1986), Smith et al.'s meta-analysis, and textbook treatments of behavior therapy. Sheldon relied upon many of the individual studies of previous reviews (notably Feldman and Caplinger 1977, Berger and Rose 1977, and Reid's work). He also discovered a few more English studies that he considered to be methodologically sound testimonials to social work's effectiveness. Neither Sheldon nor Thomlison scrutinized the base of their evidence; they simply passed along the previous conclusions of Fischer, Reid, and Hanrahan and Rubin. However, their sources and research evidence could only support a skeptical view of the field, not their calm assurance of its therapeutic progress.

Thomlison, like Fischer, took great comfort in behavior therapy:

> The outcome data reporting on programs to produce individual change, such as those for anxiety disorders, sexual problems, psychosis, obesity, alcohol and drug problems, all attest to positive results obtained with behavioral therapy. . . . For example, in 1972, this author explored the application of a behavioral approach to alleviating marital problems. (52)

Thomlison was referring to his own unpublished doctoral dissertation. His other citations to the "outcome data" referred exclusively to summary evaluations of behavior therapy. The chain of reporting—from the actual experience of therapy reported in primary research to summaries of primary research that then led to reviews of the reviews such as Thomlison's— magnified the appearance of efficacy. The base of studies themselves grossly exaggerated the impact of their findings. The summaries expressed some qualifications but relied upon their convergence to report a general trend of positive results. The third order repetitions (e.g., Thomlison) took heart from the fact that previous reviewers had reported a growing body of evidence, a codified scientific literature, weighing in for the curative powers of social work and behavior therapy. But neither the summaries nor Thomlison himself could point to a single definitive test of behavior therapy.

Thomlison's optimism obviously shot past his cited support. Krasnegor (1980) had concluded that "in the drug abuse literature, there is a paucity of design altogether. The vast majority are case reports" (Krasnegor 49). Both of them, however, still exaggerated the capacity of any alcohol or drug program to rehabilitate abusers.

Gelder (1979) in reviewing the impact of behavior therapy on neurotic disorders only touted its efficacy against phobias. But this literature is at best ambiguous and is more accurately summarized as weak, unreliable, and misleading. Kovacs (1979) actually questioned the *clinical* relevance of behavior therapy since relapse was high and many of its benefits were "so easily reversible." Phillips and Ray (1980) presented a deep critique of behavior therapy research that seemed to be inconsistent with their own belief in its efficacy and to conflict with Thomlison's report of their research.

Stunkard and Mahoney (1976) carefully presented the behavioral evidence for the treatment of eating disorders. But this evidence weighed against any conclusion of consistent efficacy or credibility: small sample studies, absence of controls, self-selected patients, small gains (if any gains occurred at all), high relapse rates. Moreover, behavioral treatment was frequently as effective as other interventions. The skeptical alternative remains very strong in these studies (as well as in the remainder of the literature) that the gains, however short-term and small, could not be attributed to the behavioral interventions themselves but only to artifacts of the research situation (pleasing the therapist) and artifacts of patient motivation (after all, the samples only included the highly motivated who had sought out treatment).

In short, the summaries do not support Thomlison's effusions while the primary base of research does not support the positive findings of the summaries, only their doubts.

Sheldon's studies actually deepen the critique of the field. In particular, Rose and Marshall (1974), an elaborate experiment in school social work but failing to employ randomized controls or other standard safeguards against bias, would not have been included in any of the American reviews.

Rose and Marshall claim that their interventions—averaging only about four hours of social casework per youth over a two-year period—lowered juvenile delinquency in experimental schools compared to untreated youth in nonrandomized "control" schools. But in experimental schools delinquent youth were referred to social workers while in the control schools they were referred to the police. Delinquency was measured not in terms of the youths' behavior but in terms of police reports. Obviously, those referred to the police probably generated a greater number of police reports than those referred to social workers. But the behaviors of both groups of youths may have been precisely the same (marginally delinquent youth may even have had a more therapeutic experience with a policeman than with a social worker).

Thomlison, Sheldon, their sources, and the more recent literature testify to the continuing compliance of social work with the myths of social efficiency. Through the convenience of porous research, the field's weak, inexpensive, and socially compatible interventions are recast into the heroic mold of effective techniques against social problems. The field has created a litany of proof—the Bergin reviews, Smith et al., and by now, Reid and Hanrahan and Rubin—and a battery of weak research methods—vulgarized randomization, bogus objectivity—to arrive at reaffirmations of its preventive, rehabilitative, and curative prowess.

Following the recent fashion in summary reviews, Videka-Sherman's (1988) two meta-analyses (reported in a single paper) attempted to identify the factors that led to successful social work outpatient treatment of chronic mental illness and of less severe mental illness. Contrary to her own conclusions for modest effectiveness, her analyses actually undercut both the value of treatment and the community of researchers who conducted the studies.

Her first meta-analysis covered thirty-eight methodologically acceptable studies, that is, studies that utilized control groups, social work practitioners, and less severely ill patients. She reported that "the average experimental client had a better outcome than 69 percent of control group clients" (328). However, she neglected to add that these were group comparisons in which the controls started at 50 percent. In other words the improvement was 19 percent if it existed at all and it may not have. As she reported, only four of the thirty-eight studies were randomly sampled from the problem population. Fourteen of the studies did not randomize patients to the experimental and control conditions. Only fifteen of the studies enjoyed "high internal validity (random assignment, low mortality rates, and no other discernible threats to validity)" (327). Nevertheless, psychological functioning was the principal outcome criteria, which almost invariably was measured by patient self-reports or practitioner reports and therefore "tended to be reactive" (327). In addition:

Control groups that received no intervention were a small proportion of the comparison groups studied as were defined interventions, placebo conditions, treatment dropouts, control groups on waiting lists, and intact nonintervention groups (such as a similar client population in a nearby unserved community). (327)

Finally, the base of studies for both meta-analyses contained a confusing and inconsistent array of interventions. "Standard treatment" usually remained undefined; thus it was conceivable that the standard treatment in one study was the experimental treatment in another" (327). The cumulative benefits of experimental conditions may have added up to little more than the ability of expectancy biases to induce the appearance of improvement under favored conditions.

The second meta-analysis—social work outpatient interventions with the chronically mentally ill—involved twenty-three "quasiexperimental or experimental studies," a weaker base than Videka-Sherman's first meta-analysis. She computed an effect size that implied only a 12 percent gain for the group of social work interventions. In addition, the base of studies were marred in the same way as the previous studies that measured effectiveness with the less mentally ill.

On the strength of her two meta-analyses, funded by the National Association of Social Workers, Videka-Sherman drew lessons for social work practice while also identifying factors that led to successful treatment. Yet the quality of the research leads to very different conclusions. In the first instance, the small gains need to be discounted by the absence of placebo controls and the use of reactive measures. These two problems by themselves invalidate any reported gain. But in the context of the other methodological flaws, particularly the large number of samples that were not drawn randomly from the problem populations, these meta-analyses raise the possibility that social work treatment may actually be harmful or, more likely, unrelated to outcomes.

Nonetheless Videka-Sherman's two meta-analyses, in spite of their limitations, are still the most systematic and objective summary reviews in social work since Fischer's "revolution." A cautionary note about weak methods seems to have become obligatory in any discussion of the social work literature (see also Polster 1986 and Frankel 1988). But neither the cautions nor the actual conditions of the studies themselves seem capable of softening the field's militant optimism toward its own effectiveness.

A skeptical reading of the literature repeatedly suggests the possibility of actual harm or at least the prolongation of the problem situation by the use of ineffective techniques. The body of behavioral treatment experiments characteristically employ seemingly weak, marginally relevant, and short-term reinforcements. In the absence of therapy, some of their clients would be exposed to the far harsher penalties of life, perhaps more successfully smoothing out their personality abrasions. To the extent that this may be so, the problems of these patients are prolonged for the interests of their therapists and as a result of the field's inadequate research. The persistence of consistently self-serving and useless research begs for an estimate of the impact that deferring more effective, humane, or appropriate treatments may have on the patient populations.

The more recent outcome studies that incorporated randomized designs—not yet anthologized in meta-analyses and critical summaries—repeated the field's common fallacies. Their common methodological failings and their trivial research questions may even signify a decline in the quality and relevance of social work's literature. Short-term behavioral techniques were the most prominent interventions among social work's recent batch of promising leads.

Edelson and Syers (1990) randomly assigned 283 men who battered their mates to one of three forms of therapy based upon either educational techniques, self-help, or a combination of both. They reported small benefits for the self-help treatment at follow-up. However, they employed neither a nontreatment nor a placebo control; their outcome measures relied upon self-reports; and their sample sizes were small. More damaging to their claims, 46 percent of their subjects did not complete treatment while only 33 percent were available for their follow-up interviews.

Hall and Rose (1987) employed groups of only eight subjects in each. Their findings were inconsistent although they claimed that therapy reduced parent-adolescent conflicts. Hepler and Rose (1988) claimed that eight weekly forty-five minute sessions improved the social skills of their experimental class of school children. However, their contrast class was not randomized. Outcomes were measured by role-play and subjective, questionably reliable indicators.

Toseland et al. (1989) tested the effectiveness of two kinds of support groups for people who were caring for elderly relatives. One group was run by the care givers themselves, one by professionals, and one group, providing only respite from care giving, was employed as a control. The interventions were applied in eight weekly two-hour sessions. The findings were mixed but tended to favor the peer counseling group, contradicting the value of professional social work. Both interventions were slightly superior to the control condition. However, measures may have been reactive, as the authors pointed out, and the initial report of gains may have simply expressed the subjects' pleasure in being assigned to an experimental group and disappointment in being assigned to the control group. Toseland (1990) reported in a one-year follow-up study that these benefits had largely washed out since the *controls* reported improvements during the follow-up period while the experimental groups either maintained their gains or reported slight losses.

Kirkham and Schilling (1989) compared the effectiveness of life skills training and traditional parenting training for 230 mothers of children with developmental disabilities. The two-hour sessions were run twice per week for nine weeks. They found no differences between the two techniques. Their analysis provided virtually no justification for the superiority of skills training. Yet they concluded that their interventions were valuable.

Tolman and Rose (1989) ran an experiment in stress reduction. They compared a "multiple methods" condition with relaxation therapy and a wait-list control. Treatment involved eight weekly two-hour sessions. All measures were based upon client self-reports. None of their groups contained more than fourteen subjects. They found that stress in the *wait-list group* declined at statistically significant levels. "Although change scores were in the predicted direction on every measure, comparisons (between the experimental) treatments and with the wait-list conditions were not statistically significant" (62). Yet they refused to accept their negative results, insisting that tension reductions were "demonstrably clinically significant" (62). In disregard of their own research logic, they ignored their proof that time itself seemed to have accounted for stress reduction. Moreover, their subjects may not have been severely or chronically stressed to begin with. Whitney and Rose (1989) repeated the same errors and exaggerations in their similar demonstration.

The most recent randomized outcome studies in social work refused to acknowledge the obvious failures of their weak interventions, their trivial research questions, and their inadequate research methodologies. They consistently strained for effectiveness, attempting in conclusions and after-the-fact analyses to resuscitate obviously inconclusive findings that affirmed the value of professional practice and the "clinical significance" of their inexpensive techniques. Yet their conclusions frequently contradicted their own evidence while their methodologies were too compromised to sustain any credible finding. Randomization was not adequate protection against true belief.

Social work's flat-earthers dominate the field. The critical tradition is a minor voice in the chorus of social work and the social services. Ginzberg et al. (1988), a rare exception, documented the futility of weak interventions to prevent four problems among adolescents: drunk driving, drug abuse, pregnancy, and dropping out of school.

> There is no easy way, really no way, of identifying prospectively the high-risk drivers.
> . . . Society can only deal with drunk driving by exploring new approaches to reducing automobile fatalities. (70)

> Despite the fact that drug programs of various types have been in operation for more than twenty years, there is little objective evidence about the effectiveness of these programs. To date, only anticigarette smoking programs have had any success. . . . (103)

> The excessive level of school dropouts among inner-city minority youth, their disturbingly high unemployment rate, and their subsequent marginal attachment to the regular work force are interrelated and should be seen as a single problem of severe social maladjustment. (120)

> In the case of teenage pregnancy leading to unwed motherhood, the outlook for primary prevention is bleak. . . . (126)

Their conclusions are equally applicable across the board to long-standing social problems in the United States. While the authors were not social workers (Ginzberg is an economist), their observations exemplify the tone of the critical tradition in social work and the social services. Those observations are the essential components of the dilemma of America's social welfare:

> (T)he ineffective performance of adolescents and young adults is a consequence of dysfunctional components of the developmental cycle starting from conception and birth to their eighteenth or twenty-first year. The absence of a father in the household; living in poverty, often on welfare; growing up in a disorganized ghetto area; suffering the indignities of racism; attending malfunctioning schools; bereft of models of successful relatives, friends, and neighbors; exposed from early age to violence and crime; unable to meet most employer's hiring requirements—and the many additional societal pathogens that militate against normal growth and development in the ghetto—all coalesce to produce ineffective performance. The amazing fact is not that so many young people growing up in such adverse conditions fall off the track . . .

but that such a large number manage, despite their cumulative hardships, to find a place for themselves in a society that has failed to provide them with anything like the range of opportunities available to young people growing up in middle-class families. . . .

. . . this observation about the much larger number of young people who are at risk relative to the numbers who fail helps to explain why the preventive approach is so severely limited. There is no way that even a benevolent society, which wanted to reduce human wastage by adopting strong intervention devices early in the life of a child growing up under severely disadvantaged circumstances, would be able to identify those most likely to fail so that it could start on a corrective program. And no society, even one as affluent as the United States, has shown the desire, much less the will, to tax away such a large part of the earnings of the rich and the middle class in order to correct the inequality of opportunity for minority youth. (129)

Conclusions

Ginzberg's arguments are largely ignored in the scriptures of social work's effectiveness. Its pseudoscientific literature has reinforced a psychotherapeutic role, given perhaps its most prominent recent expression by Wakefield (1988a and 1988b). In fulfilling the ambitions of the field for professional status, Wakefield argued that social work's central mission is to distribute positive self-images, a new "psychological good" justified on the basis of "psychological justice." Yet there is no credible evidence that either psychotherapy or social work is successful in this feat of self-worth nor that a positive self-image is instrumental in resolving social problems. To the contrary, Lasch and others provide considerable grounds on which to argue that professional missions such as Wakefield's testify to the field's narcissism more than to its commitment to resolve social problems. Social work seems to have slipped its mooring from client problems, tying itself increasingly to the ambitions of its practitioners.

The scientific eccentricities of social work are indulged by a society that takes comfort in the lap of its fables. Successful social work does not imply helping people solve their problems. To the contrary, it means successfully promoting the symbols of cheap cure at the expense of those people. The severe economic and budgetary pinches on the poor of the last decade or so have not awakened the field's researchers out of their psychotherapeutic reveries. The poor and other lower-status groups have had to compete for social work's attention against those who are being refitted with more positive self images.

The behavior modification outcome studies—the most ballistic of social work's recent enthusiasms—mock Skinner's work. They fail to isolate the conditioning process (as in a "Skinner box"). They fail to establish either the relevance or the power of their reinforcers. The inadequacies of their research methodologies permit the expectancy biases of the researchers to determine outcomes, confirming the field's hope that its superficial, inexpensive, short-term, and nondisruptive "reinforcements" can modify dysfunctional behaviors.

In contrast with the community of skeptical scientists that tested Skinnerian principles on animals, the poor research in social work suggests a cultish betrayal of the spirit of science. Social work's outcome research has been about the same poor product for decades. The self-deception of Fischer's improvised scientific revolution cosseted the field's pool of consistently distorted and inconclusive primary studies.

Neither social rehabilitation nor psychic comfort seem ever to have been reliable outcomes of social service. They have obviously failed to provide alternative institutions for those deprived of families, training, community, jobs, and so forth. Indeed, efficient solutions may not exist, while effective solutions, perhaps the result of social services that create greater social and economic equality, may be costly, socially disruptive, and therefore politically impractical.

In a futile effort to resolve this dilemma, social work and the other human service professions may be exhausting their special mandate to provide human services. They may even be weakening their standing as sources of programmatic expertise.

By laying claims to scientific professionalism, social work is asserting the ability of objective knowledge to alter social conditions. Yet the critique of an objective social science, posed by diverse scholars such as Marx, Foucault, and Ravetz and carried through by many others, has pointed to the many instances when the convenience of the powerful dictates social truth.

Reported outcomes seem to have improved over a period of time in which funding for services was severely reduced. However, the analysis of those studies suggests that the field's improved effectiveness is more mendacious than real. The literature seems out of touch with populations of service. Its distortions in portraying the failures of superficial interventions sidestep a politically awkward advocacy for those in need—the public welfare caseload, including foster children and children in trouble as well as dependent families, the homeless, the working poor, and the near poor. In denying science, the field denies benevolence.

It is worth speculating on the effect of adjusting each period of social work research for the influence of the culture's dominant ethos. Rosenthal's estimate of expectancy biases might well wash out the differences between the negative studies of the skeptical 1960s and the positive research findings of the narcissistic 1980s. Indeed the collective direction of the field's research during each fashion of social thought may be little more than one measure of the culture's power over its separate institutions.

Although the cadence of critical thought in social work may be slower than in many areas of the social sciences, the results are about the same throughout. Social scientists, more often than social workers, have evaluated social services, especially those programs more clearly tied to income supports and the labor force. Economists in particular have raised their banner over the social service territory that has direct ties to broader public policy. But economists have failed as profoundly as their less sophisticated peers to provide credible statements of outcomes even while their work appears to be methodologically more sophisticated. Indeed, in their identification with the interests of dominant social organizations and their easy ability to convince themselves that they serve the public good, economists may be more malleable pawns in the play of power than social workers, the visceral evangels of social services.

Notes

1. Unique in the sense of maintaining class boundaries and prerogatives even while instituting reforms in the name of a classless society. Richard Titmuss pointed out that middle class doctors will always find a way to serve a middle-class clientele; his sample was unfortunately restricted to England.

2. The project's few other critics, Spergel (1984a, 1984b) in particular, also pointed to "ecological" problems that obscure important differences by substituting group means for individual behavior and a host of statistically questionable practices and outcomes. Braukman (1984), contradicting Spergel, claims that Feldman et al. fail to control for either maturation or selection biases.

   The Feldman and Wodarski (1984) exchange with Spergel (1984a and 1984b) begins to reveal the spitefulness of the field toward dissenting views, and Spergel is hardly a heretic. The emotional appeal to a political audience in their last paragraph hints at the unreasoning self-protectiveness of social service research:

What course would Spergel propose for social work when it seeks to deal with antisocial youths? As suggested in his review, would he wait until youths have been arrested five or six times, become impervious to treatment, and produce incalculable personal and financial costs for society? . . . Ironically, during the course of his review, Spergel applauded our intervention strategy. Yet, he did not seem to realize that there is no truly credible basis for doing so except for the data that appear in the *St. Louis Experiment*.

3. Spergel raised this point with them (1984a). Their response: "Spergel attempted to fault us for inadequately measuring a phenomena that we never sought to study, namely juvenile delinquency" (Feldman and Wodarski, 1984). Yet the first sentence in their book reads: "This book reports the findings of a unique and highly successful treatment program for antisocial and delinquent youths" (Feldman et al., ix).
4. Occasional portions of this analysis of Rubin's study originally appeared in my essay "Rational Claims to Effectiveness in Social Work's Critical Literature."

4

Economics, Social Policy Analysis, and Welfare Reform

Aid to Families with Dependent Children (AFDC) is a very small welfare program but a fierce battleground for domestic policy. The total federal, state, and local benefit payments for AFDC in 1987 amounted to only $17.1 billion (1988 dollars). The federal share, something over 50 percent of the total, amounted to only 3.6 percent of total federal social welfare spending and 1.7 percent of the federal budget. Total federal spending on the poor for that year, which includes the Foodstamp program, Medicaid, Supplemental Security Income, and other means-tested programs, only amounted to 11.8 percent of total federal spending and only 3.6 percent of the gross national product (Marmor et. al., chap.4, passim). Nevertheless, the relationship between the poor and the labor force and consequently their claims on public welfare preoccupies much of domestic policy.

Distinct from the physically and mentally disabled, recipients of AFDC and other means-tested programs are presumably capable of working, that is, they are "able-bodied." The debate over whether to support them focuses on whether their need is primarily a result of market conditions, that is, structural factors such as the absence of jobs and skills, or whether their unemployment results from their own moral shortcomings such as laziness. If the conditions of the poor are due to their own immorality, then the logic of social discourse in the United States denies them any relief of their misery. In contrast, welfare assistance is sanctioned for the poor when structural factors are seen to be the causes of unemployment.

This dispute over the nature of dependency loses any sort of neutral innocence in the face of powerful economic and social interests, present in most nations, that benefit directly from large pools of low-skilled, underemployed workers and large numbers of culturally marginal people. Yet there is a deep dispute over whether the *long-term* effects of such conditions actually benefit the culture by disciplining the labor force through the lessons of a stern necessity or whether they shred the tranquil possibilities for a humane and productive society. Indeed, the differences over this single issue are among the clearest distinctions between the polar visions of man and society that animate the conservative and liberal philosophies even while both points of view seek to maintain a strong tie between the provisions of welfare and work.

Two sets of elaborate social experiments conducted by the policy professions, notably economics, set out to test whether specific suggestions for reforming the welfare system would also maintain recipients' relationship to the work force. In the first instance the Negative Income Tax experiments of the late 1960s and early 1970s tested the degree to which a guaranteed welfare payment would interfere with the volition of recipients to work. In the second instance, the Evaluation of State Work/Welfare Initiatives examined whether minimally funded programs for the AFDC population would be able to coax them into unsubsidized jobs, saving taxpayers money. Definitive research outcomes would have had far-reaching influence on social policy.

In both cases the researchers insisted that their studies would settle policy debates over whether to accept or to reject specific reform proposals. The researchers' claims were rooted in the methodological rigor of their studies, particularly the use of randomized controls as supplements to the customary techniques of objective, coherent, unbiased research. This application of randomized controls to large field experiments represented the only definitive method by which the research outcomes could have been unequivocally attributed to the experimental interventions, that is, the specific reform proposals. In this way their advice to public forums would carry a legitimate scientific cachet. Only the promise of definitive advice could have justified the enormous costs of the research.

Yet any research "with policy implications is part of an adversary process [in which] the adversaries are contending for power, not truth" (Aaron in Hausman and Wise, 275). Policy studies provide partisan ammunition. The pursuit of power and the factional nature of the policy process itself, often acting through the stakes of professionals, researchers, and experts, may distort the outcomes of even the most sophisticated experiments.

The costs of producing information are usually very large. Few tests can be afforded. Often only one experiment or research opportunity may be possible. In these situations the research findings exert a unique influence that is disproportionate to the scientific value of the study itself. Because replication—the customary process of validating findings in mature scientific disciplines—is usually impossible, the adversarial dispute tends to center on the credibility of a study's findings and conclusions—the degree to which its information was produced through rigorous, objective methods.

The credibility of policy research also touches on the skill and probity of the researchers in protecting the research process from biases. By extension the stakes of the researchers reflect the stakes of their home disciplines that provide both the theoretical justification and the specific methodologies and instruments for the research.

Many personal and institutional stakes ride upon the outcomes of a test of a program's effectiveness. The demonstration situation itself frequently creates special conditions —unique motivations, unusual staff efforts, atypical participant behaviors, and special bureaucratic climates— that will not carry over into the program's institutionalized form. A temporary enthusiasm to create positive outcomes may grip the experimental staffs, motivated by their jobs and by possible promotions if the demonstrations are more broadly adopted.

Policy researchers usually have great stakes in positive findings in addition to the scientific merits of the study itself. Researchers are deeply committed to their insights, not simply because they may be correct but because being correct confers more material advantages. Positive findings testify to the insight of program designers and researchers in developing and implementing successful program innovations. Positive findings, not just credible findings, enhance their ability to compete for new research grants and testify to their value as trustees, board members, consultants, teachers, managers, authors, lecturers, and savants.

Wisdom has many extrinsic benefits. Power is also frequently served by the appearance of wisdom, the classic Faustian temptation. In this sense, a critical analysis of an important study is not simply a narrow assessment of its methodology; it also reflects upon the legitimacy, skill, prestige, and utility of a community of scholars and their academic discipline—whether their research and their vision were true insights or merely convenient social myth.

The Negative Income Tax Experiments

By the later 1960s the national debate over poverty and welfare had reached the point at which many claimed that reform rested upon a negative income tax (NIT). In turn, the political feasibility of an NIT seemed to hinge on the issue of cost, the amount of money above current expenditures that an NIT would entail. "The heart of the [cost] controversy was the question of work disincentives; that is, whether a guaranteed income would cause low-income able-bodied individuals to work less" (Brasilevsky and Hum, 1984, 1).

Proponents of an NIT argued that it would "rationalize the existing patchwork of welfare programs" in terms of adequacy, fairness, and administrative efficiency (Brasilevsky and Hum, 6–7). At the time, state payments varied greatly. An AFDC recipient in Mississippi was far less fortunate than a recipient with similar needs who lived in New York, even considering the difference in cost of living. Yet benefits for a recipient in New York were also inadequate while the system itself discouraged work efforts to raise income. Except for a minimal amount (a small "disregard"), earnings while on AFDC at that time were applied dollar for dollar against the welfare grant. In 1979 the average monthly payment to families with dependent children was $87.48 in Mississippi, $371.62 in New York, $278.39 in Pennsylvania, $205.75 in Virginia, and $272.38 nationally (Danziger and Plotnick, 1981, 140–41).

In addition, its proponents claimed that the NIT would help to eradicate the stigma of welfare programs, while also reducing the racism and blunt tactics of labor control employed by many state departments of welfare. The administrative structure of the NIT was designed to deliver benefits impersonally, in the manner of paying taxes and receiving refund checks in the mail. Moreover, by reducing the large amount of personnel required to calculate benefits and provide surveillance of claims, the new "tax" system for welfare was estimated to be very cost effective.

On the other side opponents argued that an NIT was going to be more expensive, impractical, poorly targeted, damaging to the work ethic of the United States, bureaucratically demanding, and would lead to social disintegration. Alternative plans ran from a system of demograts

(Schorr's plan for universal child allowances) to simple suggestions for reforming the current system.

Unfortunately, no agreement existed on how much work disincentive, cost, disruption, and inefficiency was serious or how little was tolerable. These policy experiments were conducted without standards of what would constitute success and failure.

The complexity of choosing specific program dimensions of an NIT resulted from the competitive values implied by different levels of guarantee, by different marginal tax rates, and by the implications of the resulting break-even points; decisions on two of these variables determined the third. In this way, the selection of a level of adequacy (guarantee) and a level to either stimulate or retard the work effort (marginal tax rate) of recipients, fixed the program on a level of equity— the break-even point below which people would be subsidized and above which people would pay taxes. A generous guarantee and a high stimulus to work (low marginal tax rate) would create a break-even point that entailed subsidizing a large number, even a majority, of Americans. In contrast a low level of guarantee and a high marginal tax rate, while costing less (and thereby producing a low break-even point), would tend to provide inadequate levels of support—a necessary concern of any welfare program—and to discourage work, a result anathema to Americans. Moreover, any attempt to segregate groups of people eligible for an NIT from those who would be covered through more customary procedures, reinstituted the centuries-old problem of distinguishing the worthy from the unworthy poor and thus restored the need for a large bureaucracy, necessarily discretionary and abusive, to investigate claims.

It is clear that the more generous the program, as measured by high support levels and low taxation rates, the larger will be the total program costs of a guaranteed annual income (GAI). This results because non-workers would receive larger amounts, low-income workers would keep a larger proportion of their earnings, and a larger proportion of the population would be recipients since high guarantees and low tax rates have the effect of raising the income level (called the breakeven point) below which NIT payments are made by the government. Consequently, attempting to eliminate poverty by providing income payments to the poor through a GAI can be very costly, depending on the support level and tax rate chosen. At the same time attitudes toward income support in general, and toward the poor in particular, are strongly conditioned by the work ethic and the institutional fact of labor markets. A guaranteed income could lessen work incentives, perhaps to the point of net social detriment. Just how much less people would work in response to a guaranteed income no one can confidently say. And it is not clear that nonexperimental data can provide answers to this very important question. (Brasilevsky and Hum)

The march to experimentation in order "to get the facts" followed the simplifying assumption that the elimination of poverty was an income maintenance problem alone—poverty as economic insufficiency. In this sense, the argument over an NIT largely rested with its costs in relation to work effort, how much disincentive to work was created by the different marginal tax rates. The economic definition of poverty inherent in a broad NIT denied the concept of poverty as a cultural residue of personal and societal failures that needed to be handled through either changes in the individual's behaviors or changes in the culture or both. To the extent that poverty resulted from long-standing and noxious social attitudes toward race and class and not simply from the unfortunate imperfections of the economic system, an NIT would face difficult legislative barriers erected by those attitudes. In this way, the legislative progress of an NIT was a test of its technical merits as well as its implicit assumptions about American poverty and American social attitudes.

Together with the other contemporary social experiments, the NIT demonstrations represented and probably still represent the pinnacle of sophistication and the largest classical field experiments ever conducted by the policy sciences in the human services. The NIT experiments were designed both to discover the effects of different program "treatments" and to select the one that best fit with contemporary values to minimize costs. In only the most superficial ways did the NIT experiments attempt to measure social and political impacts. In no way was the NIT tested against alternative approaches such as demogrants, work training and public employment programs, and deep reforms of then current welfare (e.g., nationalizing its administration).

The researchers were program advocates, usually politically liberal economists and other social scientists who decided on the major questions to be addressed by the experiments, the conditions of the tests, the content and form of the analyses, and the conditions for publishing and disseminating the results. While they were impelled by the noblest motives to do well on behalf of their fellow citizens, they were also motivated in more immediate ways by the imperatives of their profession. In particular, they made a tacit, although probably conscious, assumption that income poverty could be politically and logically separated from concerns with other, usually social, causes of poverty.

Partially on the strength of these experiments, economics was looking at the possibility of becoming a truly experimental science by applying its rational technical sophistication to large classical field tests of theory and policy options. The NIT experiments were designed to test specific program options, but they also provided a convenient stage for modern economics to demonstrate its unique soundness as the policy science of choice.

This seems to have already occurred. But if these studies are any measure of the field's capacity for objective advice, precision in estimating outcomes, and unbiased research—and indeed they should be—then the role of economics should be reconsidered in light of its live performance, not potential technical sophistication. In the event, "the pressures of the moment propelled an experiment into the field before many (design issues) could be adequately thought through and resolved" (Haveman 588).

There were four American NIT experiments (and one independent Canadian experiment, the Manitoba Basic Annual Income Experiment: see Brasilevsky and Hum). The first experiment, the New Jersey Graduated Work Incentive Experiment, began to enroll families in 1968. It was designed to test the work response of the working poor. In order to be eligible for the experiment, families had to contain a male between eighteen and fifty-eight who was currently receiving a customary income under 150 percent of the poverty line. The experiment enrolled 1,357 families who were then assigned to a control group or to one of several treatments (marginal tax rates of 30 percent, 50 percent, and 70 percent and guarantees of 50 percent, 75 percent, 100 percent, and 125 percent of the poverty line). The resulting sample was not representative of the low-income population of the United States, containing a higher proportion of nonwhites, large families, and young family heads.

The Rural Income Maintenance Experiment enrolled low income rural families in North Carolina and Iowa. It was designed to last for three years and had treatment conditions similar to the New Jersey experiment. It also included female headed families and families headed by an aged person. Eight hundred and nine families were enrolled.

The Gary Income Maintenance Program was designed for a three-year period to focus on the work behavior of black female headed families in a ghetto setting. The sample contained 1,800 families of whom 60 percent were headed by females. In addition to the outcomes measured by the other experiments, the Gary program also estimated their demand for social services and education. A referral worker was made available and different levels of day care subsidies (35 percent, 60 percent, 80 percent, and 100 percent) were provided.

The Seattle-Denver Income Maintenance Experiment was the largest and most elaborate of the experiments. In addition to the standard outcomes of labor force participation, it also measured family stability and the effects of inexpensive manpower programs and training subsidies on the work behavior of enrolled families. These samples were stratified by customary income as well as by race and number of family heads. The experiment utilized declining tax rates in addition to the fixed rates of the other experiments. Annual support levels were guaranteed at $3,800, $4,800, and $5,600 per year. In all there were eleven different treatment packages. Moreover, the 4,800 families in the research sample—some of whom earned more than 150 percent of the poverty line, the cutoff point of the other experiments—were enrolled for three, five, and twenty-year durations.

The Results

The adoption of an NIT seemed to depend politically upon the degree to which enrolled families withdrew from the labor market. Initial findings from the New Jersey experiment were encouraging, at least from the perspective of NIT advocates. The hours worked for whites and Hispanics declined modestly, 6 percent and 1 percent respectively. The work behavior of the black husbands increased slightly, "defying plausible explanation." The work behavior of wives declined enormously, in some cases by more than 30 percent. However, few of the differences were statistically significant, possibly in view of the small subsamples. Relatively few of the sampled families contained working wives. In short, the New Jersey experiment found small and insignificant labor supply effects. Total family earnings were only slightly affected, implying that an NIT would entail no dramatic increase in costs over existing welfare programs. However, the New Jersey experiment could not "detect consistently significant effects in response to variations in either the support level or the tax rate, (it) failed to find significant results or explanations for the 'unusual behavior' of black families, and (it) remains 'puzzled' by the perplexities of ethnic differences" (Brasilevsky and Hum).

The rural experiments tended to confirm the small effects of the New Jersey NIT experiment on the work reductions of male heads of families. Few of the differences were statistically significant. However, "for families in which wages constituted the major source of income, the relative experimental differential measured by total income was minus 13 percent for the eight state aggregate" (Brasilevsky and Hum). As in New Jersey, there was a large negative response of wives and dependents, but again their contribution to total family income was small.

The Gary experiments, concentrating on black, female headed families, further corroborated the previous findings: modest declines in work behavior of 2.9 percent to 6.5 percent. However, very high reductions, 26 percent to 30 percent, were reported for the female headed homes.

The fourth set of experiments, Seattle-Denver, corrected some of the methodological flaws of the other experiments. However, its findings contradicted their results, reporting consistently high work disincentives: work effort declined 5.4 percent for husbands, 22.0 percent for wives, and 11.2 percent for female headed families. Higher guarantee levels and higher tax rates caused even greater work reductions.

Few of the social effects seemed to conform to prevalent social preferences for stable families or work effort. The rates of marital dissolution were much higher in the experimental groups than in the controls. The NIT frequently increased divorce rates by more than 40 percent and in some cases by more than 60 percent, probably because they allowed women to become economically independent of their husbands (Keeley 1987). In addition, these experiments found that enrollees used the education and training vouchers "to pay for schooling they would have obtained in the absence of the program; . . . there was little payoff for the incremental investment" (Haveman, 591).

The Controversy

The findings, irregularly published, caused considerable debate. The initial New Jersey experiment probably underestimated the withdrawal of labor, perhaps as a result of the unwitting defects of the initial design: self-selection (attrition), censorship, truncation, and small samples (Brasilevsky and Hum). The criticisms of the rural experiments were also deep; "our general conclusion is that the analysis . . . can provide no scientific evidence, one way or another, on labor supply of farm operators under a guaranteed annual income" (Brasilevsky and Hum, 152).

Initial reports from the Seattle-Denver experiments described large and significant differences but they were not analyzed in the same way as the other experiments and did not specify what the actual differences were. Later analyses put the group differences in the 10 percent range, suggesting that the costs of an NIT would be considerable.

The criticism of the experiments, on methodological, administrative, and conceptual grounds, has been profound, raising fundamental questions about the value of these kinds of policy tools and the role of the policy professions, particularly economics, in satisfying the public's requirements for accurate policy data.

Many of the criticisms stem from one particular problem. The reliability of the reported earnings greatly affected the value of the research findings, its ability to anticipate the true behaviors of participants in an implemented NIT. Earnings data were largely self-reported by participants. Subsequent analyses have shown that the Gary data were grossly underreported, by more than 30 percent (Greenberg et al.) and that the Seattle-Denver data were also seriously flawed (Greenberg and Halsey). These analyses suggested considerable cheating, a central concern in current programs and one of even larger concern in any reform. The problem of underreporting inflated the differences between experimental and control groups.

The extensive problem of cheating itself argues against an NIT on grounds of civic orderliness and equality. It suggests perhaps that other kinds of programs—children's demogrants, public jobs, and job training programs—might be better targeted on the poor than an NIT. But the research did not really test the social desirability of an NIT, only its labor participation effects, which were tested poorly. The problems of data validation were recognized and then largely ignored by the researchers (Robins). In the end this *single* problem, a rudimentary issue in even the simplest research, undermines the reliability of the experiments.

Also, because of resource constraints and the decision to test many different benefit packages, the samples were small. However, small samples require large outcomes in order to achieve statistical significance. This design decision endorsed the preferences of the researchers, who as advocates of an NIT hoped to minimize the differences

between experimental subjects and controls and thus minimize the inter-
polated costs of an NIT.

Hausman and Wise have argued strongly and with seeming success
that a simpler design should have been adopted: large untruncated
samples, fewer treatment conditions, and a less biased sampling procedure. These may not be the sorts of criticisms that can be simply
discounted as the wisdom of hindsight. Many of these theoretical concerns had been worked out in the academic literature prior to the experiments.

It is also questionable whether the study conditions adequately anticipated live conditions under an established NIT. The limited time
frame of the experiments—typically a three-year enrollment—probably
discouraged many enrollees from leaving stable employment. Experimental group participants may not have fully understood the conditions of the programs (Ferber and Hirsch). Attrition was considerable.
Those just above the break-even point—an essential and large group that
would presumably be affected by any NIT—were not studied.

The more accurate and humbling conclusion that should have been
reached is that little was learned. Differences were neither statistically
significant nor scientifically credible; the studies were poorly administered.

Moreover, the experiments were neither conceptualized nor designed
in a manner that could settle policy disputes. Their narrow interpretation
of the problem of welfare reform for purposes of research and experimentation in the context of then current American society prevented direct
comparison with alternative programs that may have been more in tune
with contemporary values and the needs of the poor themselves. The
experiments began with the assumption that "an NIT to assist the poor
and the near poor was arguably less problematic (in terms of work
disincentives) than many had predicted" (Berk et al.). Yet even if the
experiments had produced findings to endorse an NIT (that is, little
difference between the experimental groups and the controls), there
would still have remained large, unaddressed obstacles to its adoption
based on the social characteristics of the United States: the nation's stake
in the availability of low income workers, the effect of an NIT on those
not studied (i.e., above the break-even points), the effect of an NIT on
deep American values such as personal responsibility for economic

success, and the sizable issue of who was going to pay for the substantial benefits (Neubeck and Roach).

By not addressing alternative programs, the experiments ignored the powerful possibility that an NIT was not a shortcut to resolve the problem of dependency and poverty in the United States. The economists imposed the limitations of their field—a preference to measure labor force participation—on a social problem that in the end engulfed the analysis. Many of the flaws in the research—in particular the validation of data, social effects, sample size, and the complexity of the issue—could and should have been anticipated.

The formal social experiments of the 1960s and 1970s were very expensive. Haveman estimated that the total costs of the ten "major social experiments" approximated $1.1 billion (in 1983 dollars). The Seattle-Denver experiment, the largest of the NIT studies, spent $97.8 million for research and administration ($132.7 in total costs). The four NIT experiments spent over $450 million. Did the experiments justify their costs?

Many economists are enthusiastic defenders of their value. "There is . . . some consensus that the gain in knowledge was worth the money, and we are part of this consensus" (Brasilevsky and Hum, 212). Even those who have been most critical of their technical and design flaws, Haveman and Stafford as examples, felt that "the estimates from the experiments are, in general, more reliable than those available from non-experimental studies. This assessment, of course, does not say that the contribution to knowledge provided by the experiments is worth the cost" (Haveman).

But in the end, best estimates may not be good enough, especially where they cannot settle the policy dispute that provided the rationale for the studies in the first place. No side in the debate over an NIT was served by the experiments. Liberals could not say with confidence that an implemented NIT would largely maintain the labor force participation rates of enrollees and conservatives could not say with confidence that it would be disrupted. The experiments may have dispelled fears of outliers, that is, enormous changes in labor force participation rates. However, they may not have done even this much, especially in light of the temporary nature of the experiments and the possibility of widespread cheating in an implemented NIT. In short, no credible finding stands out against the background static of the NIT experiments' methodological problems.

Moreover, the NIT experiments were not well-situated within a theory of poverty and welfare that would have permitted labor force participation to be assessed against the extended social effects of implementing this novel welfare program. Particularly for this reason, the longer range and more important considerations of social cohesion, mobility, and stratification were all assumed, fallaciously from the beginning, to relate simply to the labor force participation of the poor. A recent critic of the experiments has even argued that

> contrary to many early claims, it is no longer clear that a low tax rate on earnings will act as a spur toward greater work effort. Even if this prediction were correct for people who are already collecting benefits (which is debatable), a lower tax rate would make more people eligible for transfer benefits and would probably reduce their work effort. Paradoxically, an extremely high tax rate in transfer programs might be optimal from the point of view of minimizing aggregate work disincentives. It now also appears doubtful that a universal transfer system would be less disruptive to family life than the current system of categorical aid. (Burtless, 75)

Did the analytic professions learn a lesson from their technical failures on the NIT? The Manpower Development Research Corporation (MDRC) was a principal legatee of the NIT studies and the other social experiments of the 1960s and 1970s. Although more modest in scope and cost than the NIT experiments, MDRC's studies of work initiatives for welfare recipients embodied many of the same flaws of the earlier social experiments. The failure of both sets of studies also suggests that the flaws of the research were more than innocent imperfections in research designs, representing the institutional accommodations of the social sciences to the preferences of the dominant culture. Far from Aaron's simple claim that policy research is a conservative drag on implementation, these studies boldly implemented the culture's demand for symbols of efficient solutions to social problems.

MDRC's Demonstrations of Work Initiatives
for Welfare Recipients

During the 1980s, the Manpower Development Research Corporation (MDRC) evaluated state employment programs for recipients of AFDC and in some cases for recipients of AFDC-U, an even smaller categorical program designed for families in which both parents were unemployed.

These two programs, unlike Unemployment Insurance, only covered indigent families and children.

The MDRC studies entered the welfare debate promising to define the "critical relationship between work and dependency" from a presumably neutral position, seeking only to define the proportion of welfare recipients that could be put back to work and the costs for doing so (Gueron 1986a). As with the NIT studies, the institutional interests that gave rise to the research also created incentives that corrupted MDRC's ability to fulfill its research tasks.

The MDRC studies evaluated eleven state responses to a portion of the Omnibus Budget Reconciliation Act of 1981 (OBRA). They were designed to measure the effectiveness of the existing work programs for welfare recipients (the Work Incentive Program (WIN) and in some cases even WIN's replacement, the WIN Demo Program) against the new state experiments. OBRA encouraged "workfare"—the placement of welfare recipients in unsubsidized jobs. The states were allowed to require recipients, as a condition of receiving welfare, to take specific jobs, to search for work, and to participate in training and other experiences intended to equip them with the skills or attitudes necessary to find work.

The workfare provisions together with many other provisions of OBRA were assaults on the principles of American social welfare that had given rise to the Social Security Act in the 1930s and to liberalizations of its procedures and benefits in the decades afterwards. These principals were antagonistic to workfare and to the notion of coercing work out of the poor. They tended to assume that the poor were largely victims of economic imperfections that created unemployment and of social imperfections that produced unequal opportunities.

OBRA's assumptions were very different. It contained the early legislative initiatives of President Reagan's newly elected conservative administration. OBRA reduced federal subsidies for the poor who were characterized as lazy and promiscuous. The OBRA policy amendments also theorized that the welfare reductions would prod the poor to find jobs. Moreover, the welfare expenditures were seen as diversions from economic investment and therefore as threats to the long-term prosperity of the nation. The poor would be better served by a growing economy that offered them employment than by an economy whose growth was imprudently sacrificed for the welfare of the unproductive and the immoral.

However, liberals and conservatives both accepted the dictum of practical politics. They were looking for programs that would reduce the welfare rolls. The cost of government and its growing deficit were transcending the narrow ideological debate over the causes of dependency. Moreover, following the failure of the NIT experiments to provide a convincing alternative to the welfare system, the findings of the MDRC studies naturally provided new guidance for reform. Indeed, they eventually supported the rationale for Senator Moynihan's politically popular reform proposals, the Family Security Act of 1988.

The MDRC studies were designed to answer three questions that were immediately relevant to the practical policy debate. Is it feasible to impose work obligations as a condition of receiving welfare? What do workfare programs look like in practice and how do recipients view the mandatory work requirements? What are their impacts on dependency and cost? The evaluations were not simply neutral program assessments, but also, by their unique claims to scientific rigor, tests of the underlying political philosophies that inspired the OBRA amendments. Successful demonstrations that noncoercive, well-run, relatively inexpensive programs could use to reduce the welfare rolls and save money in the long run would be historic advances in social welfare. An ability to credibly prove the impacts of the demonstrations would also be historic advances in social science. In this sense, the MDRC experiments tested the rare skills and special insights of the human service professions themselves. Therefore, the possibility of proving successful program impacts on the welfare population created enormous incentives for the researchers, demonstration workers, and their institutionalized bases in universities, social service agencies, and legislatures.

The work programs, initially designed by the states, embodied OBRA's assumptions that the poor perpetuated their own problems. These culture-of-poverty assumptions about dependency produced programs to equip recipients with marketable skills and to modify their attitudes and behaviors in order to encourage them to look for a job and then hold onto it.

It is not possible within the design and data of the MDRC studies to assess whether the service staffs themselves struck a moralizing posture, judging the AFDC recipients to be responsible for their own conditions, or simply viewed their unfavorable market position through lenses of failed schools, families, and communities. However, all of the experimental interventions, whether neutral or moralistic, were relatively inexpensive, short-term programs that fit into the current pattern of social services. Parsimony was their chief theme, relatively inexpensive and nondisruptive social service programs whose purpose was to coax recipients off of the welfare roles. The programs shared many similarities with the casework approaches of social rehabilitation programs.

The MDRC studies were funded in large part by the Ford Foundation and also by the state bureaus that designed the experimental programs and, in some cases, by additional philanthropic sources. MDRC obviously depended for support upon the agencies that it evaluated as well as organizations, the Ford Foundation in particular, that had subsidized their views on the issues of American welfare.

The Ford Foundation had been the patrician source of moneys for the Grey Area projects and the Mobilization for Youth experiments in "opportunity theory" during the 1950s and early 1960s. These programs drafted the blueprint for the Office of Economic Opportunity and the other programs of the War on Poverty.

More recently, the Ford Foundation continued to set the fashion in American philanthropy with its awards program for "Innovations in State and Local Government" administered through the John F. Kennedy School of Government at Harvard University. In 1991 these two liberal pillars provided ten awards, among them:

> The K-Six Early Intervention Program of Fresno County, California, helps children beat the odds of school failure through early diagnosis of problems and massive intervention. Unexcused absences have dropped by 40 percent and referrals for misbehavior are down by 70 percent.

> Maryland's Friends of the Family transforms high-risk families with young children from passive consumers of public services into active partners in developing services tailored to their needs.

> The Philadelphia Anti-Graffitti Network replaces urban scrawl with urban art. Former vandals have cleaned 40,000 city walls and have painted 1,000 murals under the guidance of professional artists. (Steinbach 1991)

Although MDRC had been established with the high-minded intent to avoid the ethical pitfalls of contract research, their studies were staged before a very attentive audience of partisans, some of whom were providing funds for the research. The Ford Foundation, Harvard University, the states, the MDRC board and its staff seemed to share a symmetrical optimism that a sizable portion of welfare dependency could be corrected efficiently through modest social welfare interventions. Even a small success—signs of hope, new grounds for optimism, promising leads—would endorse a cushioned reality in which the human service professions handle contemporary need within the limitations of social and political preferences.

Failure of the MDRC experiments would have been unsettling. It would imply that huge numbers of Americans could not work because jobs did not exist and because their skills were at such a rudimentary level that even if jobs did exist they could not perform them. This condition of vast deprivation and inequality would not be amenable to inexpensive solution. If the problem of welfare was to be solved, then massive funds would be required and the society itself would have to stretch its tolerances and hopes to make room for more, compensated workers. The implications of such a finding would have challenged the underpinnings of both the conservative administration in Washington *and* the more liberal view that assumed that efficient responses to social problems were possible.

MDRC's senior staff members were drawn from the quantitative Ivy League streams of the social sciences, usually economics. The board of MDRC itself as well as the consultants for the work initiative studies reflected the rationalistic intellectual influences of the 1960s and 1970s, in some cases including economists who had worked on or supported the NIT studies. The state sites were not randomly chosen. Rather, states that wished to experiment with work for welfare recipients were invited to hire MDRC to evaluate their programs.

MDRC, in a manner similar to the NIT studies, sought to assure the credibility of their findings by employing a prospective, randomized design in addition to the customary procedures of objective, coherent social science. "It is very rare to be able to conduct an evaluation with this degree of reliability. . . . The study for the first time provides rigorous answers" to the question of these programs' effectiveness (Gueron 1987, 20 and 17). In this way the MDRC studies embodied the ambitions of the policy disciplines for standing as true experimental sciences.

Six Principal MDRC Studies

Maryland. The main purpose of this study was to evaluate the Options Program (OP) in Baltimore that was designed to replace the customary

WIN program. The WIN program was mandated for "all single parents of children older than five years who apply for or receive AFDC" and AFDC-U (Friedlander et al. 1985a). The WIN program attempted to place its enrollees directly into the labor force although with very little preparation or training. It tended to reach only a small portion of eligible enrollees and its placement record was very poor. Moreover, far fewer remained successfully in their jobs than were placed.

In contrast, OP sought long-term positive effects by recognizing that many welfare recipients and enrollees lacked the necessary skills and perhaps even the appropriate attitudes to find and hold a job. Therefore, OP made a wide variety of "employability services" available to enrollees in addition to direct placement services, (i.e., group and individual job search). The "employability services" included unpaid work experience, basic literacy training, preparation for the general equivalency diploma, some personal counseling, and on-the-job training. The "employability services" were purchased from supposedly "innovative agencies." OP offered these structured services to 50 percent of its caseload. In contrast WIN typically reached only about 3 percent of its caseload with similar services. OP cost an average of $950 more per enrollee than the WIN control.

This $950 additional per capita investment in OP enrollees represented the operationalized, specified conditions of a socially efficient work program for welfare recipients— presumably the increment above customary and failed services sufficient to fill the employment deficits of welfare recipients. As such, it is a measure of inequality and the degree to which that equality is amenable to correction. Written in the large, that is, as representative of similar budgets and strategies for addressing need, the disparity between failed program efforts and the amount of money required to correct those disparities (the OP budget) were profound statements about the nature of American society—the magnitude of its deprivations and the costs for filling them.

OP assumed that simple skill preparation would be sufficient to allow welfare recipients to find and keep remunerative jobs and that the consequent costs to the taxpayer for welfare would decline. OP fit conveniently into the then current welfare model. The hope was that for its small additional costs, $950 per subject, an important success could be purchased that netted out to the benefit of society, if not solely to the taxpayer.

In contrast, failure would imply that the assumptions behind the program—particularly its estimates of client need and the nature of employability—were wrong. OP's failure would resurrect the necessity of far greater funds to close the disparity between the status of clients and the requirements of the labor market. By implication, this would both indict the skills of program designers—the "social workers" and advocates of the program, as well as the researchers—and the culture that tolerated such persistent disparities among its members.

The experimental sample contained more than three thousand applicants for welfare and recipients of welfare who were randomly assigned to the experimental OP or to a WIN control. The experiment lasted for three years. Evaluations were conducted after fifteen months and after three years. Data was collected from a variety of state agencies, the enrollees and the staff.

In the end, the evaluators reported that OP was modestly successful. OP was able to target its services on enrollees' needs. Its components were heavily utilized. Enrollees (who found work) and their supervisors claimed that their activities were not make-work. Those placed reported that their jobs, usually clerical or service positions paying at or near the minimum wage, were satisfying.

Measured over the one-year period following initial services, OP seemed to have greater impact than the WIN control. The three-year follow-up evaluation reported that most gains for the OP enrollees occurred in the second and third year. They earned an average of $7,638 over the three-year period in contrast to the WIN control average of $6,595, a difference of $1,043. Impacts were "all stronger for sample members who lacked recent work experience. On the basis of these findings, the researchers claimed a modest victory . . . " (Friedlander et al. 1985a).

Yet, the differences between groups are actually tiny and frequently not even statistically significant. The difference in average earnings translates into less than $10 per week for the three-year period and about $3 per week for the first year. The savings in welfare are less than thirty cents per week. Indeed, the impacts of OP are so minimal that even small lapses in the research's rigor would destroy credibility in their reality.

But the methodological problems of the MDRC research in Baltimore, particularly uncontrolled demonstration effects and the reliability of data, were actually very large. Moreover, in this case, the contract agencies, facing renegotiations on the basis of their performance with the OP clients, were in an even more vulnerable position than agencies within the civil service. In addition, these OP contract agencies possibly employed superior workers and offered better services than the WIN staff. It is not clear then whether the services themselves, the conditions of service, or the personnel providing the services accounted for the differences between the groups. Therefore, the findings may exaggerate the effectiveness of a standard OP program, that is, after the enthusiasm of a demonstration period has worn down to customary levels of staff motivation.

The experimental samples, in comparison with the welfare caseload, contained a much higher proportion of applicants than recipients and presumably a less debilitated, more motivated group of people. Therefore, the findings, such as they are, probably overstate the impact of OP services on the existing welfare caseload.

There is also a serious unanswered question about biases and inaccuracies in reported earnings. The largest and most important differences between groups are in their total earnings. Yet these are the least reliable differences. Presumably welfare payments were accurately reported; OP clients may have accurately reported their earnings sensing that they were under scrutiny. But the controls may have underreported their income to a greater extent, perhaps to the customary extent of AFDC clients. Indeed, the same problems of reliable income reports that beset the NIT studies also hampered this one. The researchers did not conduct thorough reliability checks. This problem alone may be sufficient to eat up all of the differences between groups.

The survey data covering client satisfaction and the nature of paid and unpaid work experiences is highly suspect, coming from participants with a stake in a particular report. Under more usual conditions of program operation, respondents might feel far freer to report greater dissatisfaction.

The study's cost/benefit analysis suggests that while OP may cost the taxpayer a small amount, in the long run society benefits. However, this analysis neglects many of the extended consequences of favoring one particular group of people for jobs in a tight job market. OP found existing jobs for welfare clients. They did not create new jobs. Someone who was not a welfare client did not receive the job. That unemployed person would have to spend down his or her resources in order to qualify for welfare. The amount of those savings that are spent down in becoming eligible for welfare can be viewed as an unintended subsidy (or transfer) to the current welfare client who received the job. This transfer effect perversely forces some of the poorest people in society to support each other.

In addition, increasing the number of candidates for low paying jobs may suppress wages generally for low-paid employees. This again tends to pit poorer people against each other with possibly unfortunate effects on the social fabric of American society. Moreover, while the research itself is couched in terms of the satisfaction and personal benefits of economic self-sufficiency, these concepts do not necessarily carry over into the returns of marginal jobs to either the workers or to the society itself.

A very subtle attitude distinguishes the encouraging staff from the punitive staff. While sanctioning of participants for infractions was rare during the demonstration, a routinized program might turn far more frequently to the kinds of historically prominent punishments associated with a coercive labor force policy.

An accurate benefit/cost analysis implies estimates of the extended social and economic consequences of OP and not just the narrow budgetary implications that are simple to measure. In the end, the small incremental investments in OP did not seem to produce much nor did the study evaluate its impact credibly. The potential biases and reliability problems vitiate any finding. The more judicious conclusion is that no conclusion is possible. The lessons of Baltimore remain indeterminate.

San Diego. In San Diego, two experimental interventions were compared with a low service control. The study lasted for three years. It collected information from state records, a survey of applicants, and interviews with a small sample of clients and staff. It randomized study participants and led the authors to conclude that "because of the rigor of the design, any statistically significant difference between groups could be safely attributed to the program's treatments" (Goldman et al.).

The first experimental condition, the Employment Preparation Program (EPP), "provides job search workshops designed to teach welfare recipients how to find unsubsidized jobs" (Goldman et al., ix). The second experimental condition added a work experience requirement, the Experimental Work Experience Program (EWEP), that offered job search followed by a mandatory period, for those who did not find work, "in which welfare recipients work[ed] in public or private non-profit agencies in exchange for their benefits" (Goldman et al., ix). The controls received "very minimal WIN services."

EPP cost approximately $400 per capita, a minimal amount, to which the EWEP component added about $80. The San Diego study enrolled a very large number, 3,408 AFDC-U applicants along with 3,596 AFDC applicants. These two groups, presumably representing different levels of preparation for work, were analyzed separately.

The authors claimed that both EPP and EWEP made "substantial" and similar impacts on the percent of AFDC enrollees employed at any time during the thirty-nine week follow-up period. Both experimental groups employed approximately 10 percent more than the control group. The total differential in pay for the thirty-nine weeks averaged $391 for EWEP participants and $506 for EPP participants. This works out to $10 per week and $13 per week respectively—statistically significant but seemingly unimportant. None of the other differences were clearly significant except that the EWEP group of AFDC-U participants seemed to require less welfare support than the controls. Almost two-thirds of all AFDC-U groups were employed at some point during the study. Neither job search nor work experience seemed to make any impact on the experimental groups.

In spite of very ambiguous findings (the controls did *better* than the experimental group along one measure), the authors concluded that the interventions yielded a net social benefit. "Not only does society as a whole benefit . . . but . . . welfare applicants and taxpayers . . . benefit as well" (Goldman et al., 168). Yet the methodological problems here were the same as in Baltimore. In spite of randomization, San Diego's porous methodology—demonstration effects, unreliable data, and inadequate benefit/cost considerations—vitiates any conclusion. Nevertheless, the researchers insisted that the experiment produced "substantial increases in employment and earnings" (Goldman et al.).

The researchers rejected the apparent meaning of their own data that weak, superficial interventions had hardly any impact at all on serious employment problems. Taken at its own face value, the evidence argues for terminating these sorts of interventions.

Arkansas. The Arkansas experiment compared its WORK Program that "gives a new emphasis to participation in employment services" to a customary WIN-type program in which clients "received virtually no services beyond assessment" (Friedlander et al. 1985a, 148). The experimental WORK program offered a fixed sequence of required activities: two weeks of group job search followed by sixty days of individual job search and finally mandatory unpaid work experiences of twenty to thirty hours for each of two weeks for those who did not find jobs. The local Winthrop Rockefeller Foundation chipped in with Ford Foundation and the state to fund the study.

The Arkansas sample contained a large number of mothers who had children younger than the WIN mandatory group. Fifty percent of the 1,153 AFDC mothers in the sample had children between three and six years of age. Eighty-six percent of them were black.

The findings showed that only 38 percent "ever participated" (for at least one day) in the experimental program. Only 20 percent participated in the WIN control. Moreover, rates of participation in the work experience were low (about 3 percent), while the program was poorly implemented at one of the two experimental sites. Nevertheless, those who did work and those who supervised the workers claimed that the tasks were real and the experience was valuable.

WORK staff members were given guidelines to spend more time with highly employable participants. This also seems to be the pattern in the other experiments: low participation and a tendency to favor the more employable. The reasons for nonparticipation, actually attrition in many cases, were not measured, although here as in other sites it seemed to stem from a combination of factors: leaving welfare for a job or marriage, the choices of staff in refusing to penalize nonparticipation (creating a largely voluntary program), and true attrition.

The possibility of large real attrition may raise the specter more eloquently than any poorly conceived and possibly reactive survey of client attitudes that the workfare programs may have been unpleasant, abusive, and stigmatizing. The enrollees' nonparticipation—a tacit strike—supports the speculation that the programs may have caused some harm. In any event, the research did not check into this possibility.

In spite of these problems the study concluded that "against the backdrop of low pre-program employment, the WORK Program was effective in helping its enrollees achieve modest improvements" (Friedlander et al. 1985a, xvii). "Clear reductions in welfare receipt were found for WORK Program enrollees" (Friedlander et al. 1985a, xviii). This "clear" reduction—only 6.9 percent and only in the third quarter of the follow-up period—was associated with a welfare payment reduction of $43 or about $3 per week.

The plausibility of the these tiny, marginally significant findings is sabotaged by the study's many design problems. These tiny differences push the limits of modesty. They may result from a few motivated clients in the experimental group being given a chance for unsubsidized work. This sort of selectivity bias, "creaming," does not testify to the slight but palpable value of the experimental intervention but rather to a more reasonable conclusion that its weak interventions produced inadequate results, if any at all.

Particularly at this site and probably at the others, the researchers stretched positive findings, presenting their data in a manner that exaggerates the success of the experimental intervention. "Over the nine month follow-up period welfare savings per recipient were nearly six times higher than the savings per applicant" (Friedlander et al. 1985a, xxii). But the actual savings were only $176 vs. $29, that is only $4.60 per week vs. $0.75 per week. Moreover, the difference is significant merely at the .05 level.

The authors tend to ignore their five quarter follow-up report on applicants that reported the controls doing better than the experimentals. For the follow-up year, controls averaged $813 in total earnings while experimentals only earned $633. Again the weekly average difference is tiny as are all of the others. None of these differences are statistically significant. Yet statistical significance did not bar the authors from reporting trends in the other, shorter-term data that tended to support their views of the WORK program's effectiveness.

The gains in employment and earnings were not sufficient to offset losses to recipients in Medicaid and AFDC. In other words, by removing people from assistance, the program obviously acted more on behalf of taxpayers than on those in need. It is noteworthy that this occurred amid the wretched poverty and low-payment levels of high unemployment Arkansas. The researchers seemed proud of their program's success.

The true conclusion, here as in the other sites, is that no conclusion should be drawn about the effectiveness of the experimental interventions except to raise the conjecture that it did not appear to be very beneficial. The experience particularly in Arkansas might have also raised the question of whether its goals were reasonable or even laudable. In whose interest is it to force unremunerative jobs, indeed jobs that provide benefits below subsistence, on impoverished people? In exercising their interpretive discretion, who do the researchers represent, and in crafting their myths of program efficacy, whose position are they advocating? Clearly in Arkansas, the researchers used weak, contradictory, and implausible findings to write the decisive metaphors of the myth of work. Apparently, too, the consultants to the project and the MDRC board were well enough satisfied with the study and its interpretation by the researchers to allow it to be published.

West Virginia. The West Virginia experiment tested the feasibility of classic "workfare," that is, requiring work in payment for welfare. The experimental condition, the Community Work Experience Program (CWEP), was applied to both the AFDC and the AFDC-U recipients. Only the AFDC group was randomly assigned—1,853 to CWEP and 1,841 to a low-service WIN-type control. The AFDC-U experiment was intended to test the maximum feasibility of maximum participation in a workfare program, not its impact. Participation, initially defined as mandatory, ended up to be voluntary because of staff decisions. Data were collected from sources similar to the other studies.

The authors stated that "overall the findings of this study indicate that the state succeeded in its principal objective: providing a substantial number of welfare recipients with productive, long-term work experience—with the aim to maintain skills and morale—in a labor market suffering one of the highest unemployment rates in the nation" (Friedlander et al. 1986, vii). However, "CWEP had no short-term impacts on the employment or earnings of AFDC women" although "small reductions in welfare receipt for the women were evident at the end of the 21-month period" (Friedlander et al. 1986, xvi). Indeed after their seven quarter follow-up there was virtually no difference between experimentals and controls. Still,

> lengthy work assignments—combined with productivity levels equal to or surpassing those of regular employees—led to substantial value of CWEP output for AFDCs. *Supervisors interviewed in the CWEP jobs judged the women to be, on average, slightly more productive than regular* employees. For experimental registrants, the value of output per CWEP participant averaged $3,400 over the five-year projection period. . . . (Friedlander et al. 1986, xix, emphasis added)

> [Nevertheless], CWEP did not lead to any financial gains for the welfare recipients. . . . As anticipated by state officials, CWEP cost rather than saved money for government budgets. However, when the value of goods and services produced by

CWEP workers is factored in, the public at large clearly gained. (Friedlander et al. 1986)

Yet again, the study's benefit/cost analysis did not include estimates of the impact of providing employment to welfare recipients as opposed to offering them real tasks for competitive employment, nor of the suppressive effect that a full blown forced work program would have on public salaries. The authors limply excuse their experiment in coercive labor by concluding that "as implemented in West Virginia, workfare was not the punitive instrument that it is often feared to be. CWEP also did not invent the work ethic for welfare recipients in West Virginia; rather, it built on the work ethic it found" (xxviii).

Nevertheless, the long-term effects of an *institutionalized* program of workfare cannot be easily extrapolated from the short-term effects of a largely voluntary demonstration. A dangerous long-term resentment may accumulate when participants are forced to work at low wages. The belief that the welfare recipients were apparently working above the customary level of other workers should have raised questions about the possibility of intimidation, fear of losing their welfare payments. Recipients may have been allowed to strain themselves in the forlorn hope that their workfare jobs would somehow protect their futures.

The West Virginia experiment suffers from the methodological flaws of the other studies. It also falls into the trap of projecting weak demonstration data onto the future without a credible longitudinal experience. Indeed, the study lacks a credible basis for claiming an experimental gain. It does however seem pleased to be taking a third world dividend from poor, unemployed workers in a recessionary environment.

The problems of data reliability are acute in this experiment. The authors concede that the state's employment records did not include some sources of income, especially those for domestics. Moreover, many research areas bordered other states and the researchers did not access those state records. "Potential underestimation was a particularly difficult research issue in West Virginia" (66). "Data quality checks . . . revealed that as many as 40 percent of the jobs held by the women either prior to random assignment or after random assignment might not have been reported in West Virginia's data base" (67). The underestimation problem may have been more severe for controls than for experimentals, many of whom were tied up in workfare jobs and many of whom may have felt themselves to be under tight scrutiny. As a possible result, the controls may have been financially much better off than the experimentals, CWEP serving in the end as a policeman and a low-wage taskmaster.

These observations do not condone cheating on welfare. Yet it may be imprudent to force recipients to choose between hunger and unreported side income by providing benefits that are below subsistence. Both choices may breed contempt for society.

In the end, the advertisement of a well-conceived and accurately reported experiment needs to be examined in light of its important social effects, many of which the study ignored. The symbols of program success that the authors created served a parsimonious social welfare policy. But those symbols were not the legitimate summations of credible data.

Maine. The Maine experiment set out to train and to place hard-to-employ welfare mothers in private sector jobs. The experimental condition, Training Opportunities in the Private Sector (TOPS), was distinguished from its control by a sequence of activities: prevocational training, unpaid work experience, and on-the-job training (OJT), which was subsidized by diverting a portion of the AFDC benefit to the employers. A customary low-service WIN Demo program, WEET, was the control. The number of AFDC mothers who volunteered for the experiment was 444; 297 were randomly assigned to TOPS and 147 to WEET.

The net cost of TOPS relative to WEET was $2,244 per participant, an amount that recalls the "intensive" casework approach to dependency:

> The intent behind TOPS' carefully sequenced set of activities—designed to address problems arising from AFDC recipients' low self-esteem as well as their lack of work experience—was to help the women obtain jobs that paid more than the minimum wage and offered opportunities for advancement. Ultimately, these jobs were expected to enable enrollees to move off of welfare entirely. This was a particular concern in Maine where, historically, a relatively large proportion of the caseload worked full time and still received AFDC benefits. (x)

The similarity of the experimental group—its representativeness—to the national pool of long-term dependents was critical if the Maine experience was to speak to the national problem of long-term dependency. In the context of the national problem, a successful TOPS program would have been a historic demonstration of the effectiveness of rational programming and proof that efficient solutions are possible for even recalcitrant social problems. It would have been a tribute to its designers and advocates, testimony to their ability to define the particular conditions of dependency (low self-esteem and motivation, and lack of opportunity) and the strategic interventions (job search and counseling) that would lower the number of long-term unemployed welfare recipients inexpensively ($2,627, but the most spent in any of the MDRC demonstration) and with little fuss (by largely utilizing existing organizations and opportunities—in this case, private sector employment).

The three phases of the TOPS sequence worked as follows:

1. Pre-vocational training lasted two to five weeks and stressed personal growth as well as job-seeking and job-holding skills.

2. Work experience consisted of 20-hour per week, unpaid positions in the public or non-profit sector for up to 12 weeks. The intent was to teach good work habits and provide participants with an employer reference. It was offered to participants who completed Phase 1 but were judged not to be ready for an OJT placement.

3. On-the-job training consisted of placement into subsidized training positions, primarily in the private sector. The training period was a maximum of six months, and the employer subsidy was set at $50 of the new employee's wages. Participants who demonstrated their motivation and acquisition of basic work skills became candidates for OJT. (Auspos, ix)

In order to realize its intent to test the TOPS approach on the hard-to-employ, the experiment was "targeted to single heads of household who had been on welfare for at least six months, were not employed at enrollment (in the experiment) and applied to participate" (Auspos, ix). Although 63 percent of the resulting study group, the 444 volunteers, had been receiving welfare for more than two years, these criteria produced a sample that was decidedly not representative of either the state AFDC caseload or the national caseload. They were almost all white. Half had children under six. More than half were divorced or widowed and 75 percent had a high school diploma or its equivalent (GED)—a relatively high level of education. Furthermore, welfare clients were allowed to volunteer for the experiment while the staff "exercised considerable discretion in deciding whether a particular client was 'appropriate'," meaning that the successful participant had arranged for child care, was in good health, and was literate. The authors acknowledged that

although these women would be characterized as harder-to-employ in terms of their welfare histories and limited recent employment experience, there are indications that the program concentrated on a segment within this group with somewhat more favorable employment prospects. In addition, a number of factors—the high percentage of sample members who were divorced or widowed, the presence of pre-school children, the relatively high level of educational attainment and the absence of employment history—suggest that the women in the TOPS sample may represent a displaced homemaker population, that is, women who discontinued or postponed working for marriage and family and then experienced hard times. (xiii)

This process "creamed" atypical welfare recipients out of the much larger number of long-term welfare recipients. They may even represent an upper limit on the percentage of prime work candidates in the welfare pool since all the available slots for the experiment were not filled. The voluntary nature of participation and the discretionary screening process together with Maine's tight, recessionary labor market produced a group of prime candidates for employment, but not the hard-to-employ candidates that gave meaning to the experiment. These relatively few "displaced homemakers" with appropriate skills and child care arrangements emerged from the large pool of 3,157 WEET registrants (those on AFDC with children over six years of age) and the much larger pool of 16,556 AFDC heads of household in Maine. Since the resulting sample could not test the effectiveness of TOPS intentions, why didn't the researchers select a more representative sample or alternatively why wasn't the study aborted?

In the event, only sixty-nine TOPS enrollees reached the OJT stage; sixty-three of the sixty-nine continued their jobs after training. Seventy percent of these OJT positions entailed service or clerical jobs paying an average of about $4 per hour. One-third paid more; two-thirds paid less.

The authors acknowledge that the OJT subsidy provided a bonus for employers. In comparison with the employers' customary trainees, these AFDC mothers did not require greater training time or attention and their productivity was no lower. Yet the trainees' productivity was not directly observed; their performance was evaluated through interviews with their employers. It seems quite plausible that the highly selective process for screening TOPS participants produced trainees who were more motivated, mature, experienced, and therefore productive employees than the more usual minimum-wage pool of clerical and service workers. Not only did the employers benefit from direct cash subsidies but TOPS also reduced their search costs (interviews, advertisements, agency fees) while delivering to them an unusually productive group of new hires.

Although the authors report a net social benefit for TOPS, the impact of the program itself was insignificant; there was little difference between the experimental TOPS group and the WEET control. "Three quarters of the overall earnings impact in the post program period was due to increased wage rates or hours worked for those who were employed, *rather than to a higher proportion of experimentals who were ever employed*" (Auspos, emphasis added).

Equally high proportions of both groups (TOPS = 81.8 percent and WEET = 80.2 percent) worked at some point during the two and one half year follow-up period during which the average TOPS participant earned $1,745 more that the average WEET participant. But this difference works out to less that $13 per week. The $2,300 difference between the groups that is reported for the full five-year follow-up works out to an even smaller average weekly differential, $10 per TOPS participant.

Ninety-eight percent of both groups relied upon AFDC at some point during the initial 2.5 years, although TOPS participants averaged slightly higher payments. This finding is not statistically significant but it is nonetheless anomalous by being concentrated later in the experiment after the training and counseling periods had ended. This is another instance of the tendency throughout the different studies to report non-significant trends that support the effectiveness of the experimental interventions and ignore incongruent and anomalous data.

The Maine experiment was impaired by the same methodological problems that characterized MDRC's other sites: demonstration effects, nonrepresentative samples, and unreliable data. But here the biases of the authors, probably also reflecting the biases of their auspices, worked into the selection process for study participants and determined the conclusions of the research. Largely based upon the earnings differentials and soft responses to interviews about the value of the work to the participants and their employers, the authors concluded that TOPS was modestly successful in producing a net social gain.

A more reasonable summary of the Maine data, especially in light of the study's flaws, would conclude that TOPS made no difference for its participants. Its costs were not justified in terms of employment gains. OJT subsidies were not needed. Moreover, the study had questionable theoretical importance since the experimental subjects were atypical of either the state caseload or the national problem of dependency.

However, the experiment did suggest that a jobs program, not a counseling program or a superficial training program, might have an impact on dependency and unemployment. The AFDC participants in both groups apparently took full advantage of work opportunities. TOPS had no edge on WEET. A program that provided jobs or access to jobs would probably be attractive to many welfare recipients and presumably to an even larger number of unemployed people not yet impoverished to the point of AFDC eligibility. But a jobs program, especially if it were open to anyone who was unemployed and not just the relatively small number of people on AFDC, would cost far more in terms of public transfers than a relatively underfunded TOPS program reserved for a few qualified AFDC mothers.

The benefit/cost analysis in Maine, as in the other MDRC sites, failed to measure either the social and economic impacts or the capricious redistributive effects of favoring AFDC recipients over other poor but ineligible workers. In recessionary Maine, a fully implemented TOPS program might well tend to depress subsistence wages even further. Finally, the benefit/cost analysis did not include either the social desirability of substituting work for the time that sole remaining parents were spending with their preschool children.

Chicago. The experiment in Chicago was allocated only $130 to $160 per registrant in the test condition, among the smallest amounts of the MDRC sites. Two experimental groups were established in addition to a control group that only received an orientation. One group went through an orientation and then Independent Job Search (IJS). The second experimental group added the requirement of unpaid work in the Illinois Work Experience Program for those who had still not found a job after orientation and IJS. Noncomplying clients were frequently and heavily sanctioned for noncompliance (their welfare checks were reduced). No other MDRC site sanctioned clients as heavily as Chicago.

The authors report "small welfare savings but no statistically significant employment and earnings gains" (Friedlander et al. 1987, ix). The program appears to have saved taxpayers money especially since losses in AFDC and Medicaid exceeded benefits for the IJS groups. There were no statistically significant differences between the two experimental groups or between either of them and the control groups. Approximately one-third of all three groups found some work during the study period while all three groups earned an average of about $1,900 during the 1.25 years of follow-up. Virtually 100 percent of all groups relied upon welfare at some point during the study. Out of a maximum of eighteen months on welfare, all groups averaged between fourteen and fifteen months on welfare during the study period.

The Chicago experiment, repeating all of the methodological flaws of the other experiments, is the case of punitive welfare. Little investment was made and little gain was found.

The *absolute* findings in Chicago (the differences between controls and experimentals) as in the other sites are very small, even in terms of the investments in the experimental programs. The few thousand dollars of difference in work program investments between Chicago and Maine, for example, may simply be too small to make any difference in labor market success. The size of client deprivation may be much greater than the happy assumption that productive employment can be purchased for socially debilitated people with a meager few thousand dollars. In any event, the studies were too flawed to distinguish the outcomes in one site from those in another site. The differences between sites if they existed at all were probably due more to fortuitous situational characteristics of the experimental subjects (e.g., the high educational levels of the "displaced homemakers" in Maine, the relatively buoyant labor market in San Diego) than to the interventive power of the experimental conditions.

But the authors obviously disapproved of the Chicago program suggesting that the cause of the reported failure here in distinction to Maine as one example may lie more in the researchers' attitudes than in actual differences between sites. The researchers may have been offended by a symbolic offering in Chicago that was too thin and too coercive to satisfy their sense of what social efficiency required.

The MDRC Conclusions

The burden for assuring credibility rests squarely on the shoulders of the research. The true scientific test accepts an obligation for instituting protections against possible threats to its validity. MDRC did not accept this burden. Their use of randomized controls was not adequate by itself to prevent their research from falling into the many pitfalls that greatly circumscribe its value. By itself, the plausibility of demonstration effects would be enough to severely curtail the credibility of *large* outcomes. But the MDRC outcomes were very small and rarely reached even low thresholds of statistical significance.

In addition to possibly large distortions created by the experimental nature of the study and the researchers' stakes in positive outcomes, the income data were probably not reliable (as acknowledged in West Virginia), and possibly more understated for controls. This subverts confidence in one of the principal research findings—that experimental participants earned more than controls. Moreover, the survey responses upon which MDRC assessed the quality of the jobs and the clients' satisfaction with their placements may have been reactive to the stakes of researchers and staff and to the fears of participants.

The MDRC analyses are also imperfect. They choose conveniently low thresholds of statistical significance, 0.10, but without addressing the reciprocal problem (beta error) that increased the probability of random significance. Indeed the number of significant findings relative to the number of the study's multiple comparisons is not much greater than could be expected by chance variation.

Furthermore, the experimental samples were not representative either of the state caseloads or of the national caseloads. Those with the likelihood of success were consistently "creamed" from large AFDC caseloads for participation in the experiment. Self-selection (the process by which volunteers were frequently accepted as study participants) probably produced participants who were exceptionally motivated to seek employment. Other restrictive selection criteria (e.g., the presence of child care arrangements, education, and so forth) also created unrepresentative pools of experimental subjects whose experience cannot be easily generalized to populations of greater concern. Moreover, the voluntary participation in many of the MDRC studies may have contributed to demonstration effects. It is unlikely that the states selected for the research are representative of the nation. In short, the sampling procedures adopted by the studies prevented MDRC from addressing the problems that justified the experiments in the first place. Their "lessons" are not broadly applicable.

The benefit/cost comparisons neglected important considerations, particularly the capricious distributive effects that result from giving priority for scarce jobs to welfare recipients over other near-poor workers and the effects on general wages of increasing the labor pool without increasing the number of jobs. The social and political effects of the demonstrations, for example on the attitudes of the public toward welfare, were also ignored in the benefit/cost tabulations.

Variations in sampling procedures, in the intensity of services, in local situations, in characteristics of the welfare groups, and so forth prevent comparisons among the sites and again limit the possibility for drawing general lessons.

The conclusions of the study are not faithful to its data, even ignoring for the moment the many methodological flaws. Significance is marginal. Anomalous findings (the occasions in which control groups did better than experimental groups) were ignored. Moreover, the practical importance of very small weekly gains, a few dollars in many cases, is neither apparent nor addressed by the researchers themselves.

A more judicious interpretation of the MDRC experience concluded that "most workfare jobs (the MDRC placements) do not provide opportunities for the kinds of skill development that is likely to lead to long term employability" (Weidman et al., 113). Strategies that lead to long-term employability need to remove the real obstructions that prevent the welfare caseload from finding and keeping jobs: low grade-point averages, limited work experience, age and sex (biases of employers), absence of telephones, cars and driver's licenses, poor interview skills, failure on job tests, naïveté about job search, unwillingness to relocate and restrictions on what constitutes an acceptable job, loss of welfare benefits, and so on. The MDRC interventions handled only the smallest of these obstacles. They did not address the more intractable problems of people on welfare, particularly their lack of marketable skills. These problems are very costly to overcome.

The small outcomes, particularly in light of plausible demonstration effects, data problems, analytic shortcomings and biases, raise the possibility that control groups may actually have done better than experimental groups, perhaps *because* of the greater amount of time that experimental staffs spent with experimental participants. The staffs of welfare departments have accumulated a long history of abuse toward applicants and recipients of welfare. Customary, low-service WIN programs seem to ignore clients. Did experimental staffs display condescending or disparaging attitudes toward participants? Did they stigmatize them or in other ways discourage them from seeking work? The studies provide few fine-grained and credible descriptions of the program processes. Why assume that the intentions of demonstration staffs worked themselves out in nurturing or otherwise acceptable ways?

The methodological shortcomings of the studies do not inhibit Judith Gueron, the president of MDRC and the principal research investigator, from drawing important findings, powerful conclusions, and lessons to guide welfare reform: "The striking feature of the programs studied by MDRC is their consistently positive outcomes" (Gueron 1990).

> Typically within six to nine months of registering with the new program, about half of the AFDC group had taken part in some activity; and substantial additional numbers had left the welfare rolls and the program. . . . The programs also led to some welfare savings. . . . The programs were often most helpful for certain segments of the welfare caseload (AFDC mothers vs. AFDC-U fathers). . . . When benefits were compared with costs results were generally positive. . . . In San Diego an average dollar spent on the program for AFDC women led to estimated budget savings over a five year period of over two dollars . . . results dispel the notion that employment and training interventions do not work. . . . (Gueron 1987)

> The programs produced "a notable substitution of earnings for welfare and proved cost effective, suggesting that the success can be repeated on a larger scale . . . " (Gueron 1990, 94).

Only fleeting attention is given to necessary cautions in interpreting the studies. Even this is phrased as a tribute to the research, "the magnitude of the changes was relatively modest . . . thus they will not move substantial numbers of people out of poverty" (Gueron 1987). Nevertheless, the MDRC

> findings have provided important lessons as Congress attempts to decide whether welfare programs should continue to be broad entitlements or instead should become 'reciprocal obligations,' whereby work—or participation in an activity leading to work—is required in return for public aid . . . 1) it is feasible under certain conditions . . . to tie the receipt of welfare to participation obligations . . . ; 2) a number of quite different ways of structuring and targeting these programs will yield effective results. . . ; 3)in cases in which states chose to operate mandatory workfare, the interim results do not support the strongest claims of critics or of advocates . . . ; 4) the programs led to relatively modest increases in employment, which in some cases translated into even smaller welfare savings. (Gueron 1990)

But the research itself sustains none of these lessons or conclusions. In fact the conclusions are misleading, conforming more to the theater of American social myth—slow but steady progress, two steps forward one step back—than to the reality of the nation's needs.

MDRC lacked scholarly caution. Its self-serving advocacy of weak interventions that may have actually been harmful does not fulfill the requirements for accurate policy information. It also provides no benefit to welfare clients who may need more intense social services if they are to become productive Americans. The findings do, however, reinforce the social myths of their auspices. The MDRC study staff could have taken courage from the example set by Eli Ginzberg, one of their own distinguished board members, to report the apparent failure of cheap social services to correct grievous social problems.

The War between Science and Politics

The NIT experiments tested structural reform and the MDRC studies tested social services. Both were designed to respond to questions about poverty and welfare in order to settle important policy debates. These experiments are on the most sophisticated levels that policy research has reached in the human services outside of medicine. Indeed, the NIT experiments may be the most elaborate large-scale social experiments ever attempted. They are among the most expensive.

The credibility of the findings of each set of experiments was seriously compromised by methodological flaws and by the researchers' biases. In both cases the researchers were program advocates. In both cases the reported findings and conclusions exaggerated the attractiveness of the experimental interventions. The practice of science was the casualty in the war between convenience and reality.

The methodological flaws that have invalidated the NIT and the MDRC studies testify to the difficulty of creating credible policy information through the policy sciences. These experiences are characteristic of social policy research. The MDRC and the NIT studies and perhaps the whole genre of policy research, in their subtle accommodations to the preferences of authors, auspices, and powerful institutionalized interests, may be a new expressive art that uses the forms of science as a sculptor uses clay. They did not describe an independent reality that settled important policy issues. They negotiated that reality in the material terms of science within the factional environment of public policy. This was not their avowed function. This was their chosen role.

Both series of experimental interventions embody the assumptions of social efficiency: that inexpensive interventions would be effective in achieving their goals and, by implication, that they would not disrupt established societal relationships. But these assumptions were not sustained. The effectiveness of the interventions was not demonstrated. Their social impacts were not adequately considered. Important lessons were not credibly taught. At best the findings are indeterminate. At worst, they are measures of researcher bias—the extent to which the stakes of the researchers percolated through porous methods to determine the outcomes of the experiments.

Parsimonious solutions for poverty and welfare dependency have not been demonstrated. Income guarantees will probably disrupt American culture greatly. A little bit of job search and counseling confers little benefit. On the one hand, American society is too deeply bound by its own values, work in this case. On the other hand, the MDRC failures begin to hint at the immense deprivations that exist in the rigidities of the culture. Both failures mark points below the minimum required to make impacts on social problems; if solutions are to be found more needs to be spent.

The misleading research disguises the depth of social need in the United States, depriving the large number of people toward the bottom of the social rewards ladder—the poor, the near poor, and the working poor—of a voice on their behalf. The studies falsely suggest that important and telling differences among social groups—differences that probably lie at the root of much misery and many social problems—can be reduced by relatively inexpensive and nondisruptive social welfare programs. These convenient myths impede the possibility of resolving the nation's social problems.

5

Juvenile Delinquency and Drug Addiction

Juvenile delinquency and drug abuse are compelling social problems in the United States. They often coincide. Nearly half of serious juvenile offenders are also abusers of multiple illicit drugs (Hawkins et al. 1988).

Data from the 1988 National Household Survey on Drug Abuse indicate that perhaps as many as 500,000 Americans under the age of twenty-six had taken illicit drugs intravenously in the preceding year; probably more than 800,000 youths used hallucinogens such as LSD; more than 300,000 youths used crack cocaine; more than 1.5 million youths used cocaine; more than 6 million youths used marijuana. Drug abuse by adolescents, that is, by those under twenty-one, may account for approximately half of these estimates.

While the levels of adolescent and youth drug use are alarming, in the few years prior to 1990, and generally since the early 1970s, there was a slight but steady decrease among adolescents in the abuse of the most threatening of the illicit drugs: heroin, crack and other forms of cocaine, marijuana, pills, and so forth. However, subtle reporting problems may have reduced the reliability of data drawn from surveys, such as the National Household Survey on Drug Use, that have described these trends (Sidney 1990). Increased social disapproval may have suppressed the report of illicit drug use, particularly among adolescents, without actually changing their behaviors. While the apparent although slight recent decline is politically comforting, it is not credible, especially since the surveys do not appear to be making efforts to repair their accuracy.

In 1988, 2.1 million arrests were made for serious crimes; 600,000 involved juveniles. In the United States, the juvenile years produce the highest rates of criminal activity; arrest rates for property crime peak at the age of sixteen (falling 50 percent by the age of twenty) and for violent crime peak at the age of sixteen. The effects of crime—victimization rates—are startling. The lifetime probability is 83 percent that a twelve-year-old in 1987 will suffer one or more violent crimes at some point in life; the probability is 25 percent for three or more violent crimes. There is a 40 percent chance that the twelve-year-old will suffer a robbery or assault resulting in injury and an 87 percent probability of experiencing three or more personal thefts (Siegel and Senna 1991, passim).

Reports of crimes, as opposed to arrests and other data drawn from the Uniform Crime Reports, draw a gloomier portrait of crime in the United States. According to the National Crime Survey, 35.8 million crimes occurred in 1988: "6 million crimes of violence, 14 million personal thefts and 15.8 million household crimes, such as burglary" (Siegel and Senna 1991). Many victims do not report crimes. "About 50 percent of the crimes of violence, 72 percent of the personal crimes of theft, and 60 percent of the household crimes are not reported" to police (Siegel and Senna 1991, 35).

Self-reported delinquent acts by the high school class of 1988 indicated widespread criminal misbehavior: 23 percent were in trouble with police; 1.7 percent committed arson; 9 percent stole more than $50; 27 percent admitted to breaking and entering; 30 percent shoplifted; 3 percent used a weapon to steal. These were probably low estimates of the actual extent of youth crime since self-report surveys typically exclude the incarcerated and thereby the most delinquent youths (all data from Siegel and Senna 1991).

There are many thousands of treatment programs for delinquent youth and drug abusers. They cost billions and employ hundreds of thousands of doctors, psychiatrists, psychologists, social workers, corrections officers, police, paraprofessionals, nurses, and support personnel. The indirect costs to society in terms of crime, fear, social disruption, and economic losses are many multiples more than the direct costs to handle the problems.

Although still a minor theme, the spread of AIDS rings a note of terror into the problem of delinquency and drug abuse. AIDS most frequently enters the heterosexual population through intravenous drug use, usually heroin. To the extent that AIDS is also transmitted by heterosexual intercourse, addict behavior becomes an insidious threat. Many prostitutes are intravenous heroin addicts. Many of them are also very young.

The impact of AIDS on intravenous drug abusers is only beginning to be assessed. According to the surveillance system of the Centers for Disease Control, over 25 percent of all reported adult and adolescent cases of AIDS in the United States are attributable to intravenous drug abuse, and the percentage is growing. However, the effect of AIDS on intravenous drug abusers has been even greater than indicated by AIDS case data. . . . According to reports from the National Institute on Drug abuse, there are an estimated 1.1 to 1.3 million intravenous drug abusers in the United States. . . . Between 70 percent and nearly 100 percent of intravenous drug abusers share the use of injection equipment. . . . About 70 percent of those born in the United States and reported to the CDC as having AIDS attribute their infection to heterosexual contact with an intravenous drug abuser. (Leukefeld 1990)

The nation is seeking advice to reduce juvenile crime and drug abuse in a way that is consistent with national values. This implies that, in order to be feasible, a solution must also be inexpensive, both economically and socially. Particularly now, in light of unprecedented peacetime federal budget deficits and debt obligations, any social initiative, especially for poor and blue-collar beneficiaries, seems constrained by these characteristic demands for social efficiency.

It may well be that the cycle of attention to domestic problems is beginning again and, in a manner similar to the 1950s, youth delinquency and addiction may be one of the first items on the broader social agenda of contemporary American life. Have the human service professions—criminology, sociology, psychology, psychiatry, and social work—developed sound ways to treat and to prevent juvenile delinquency and drug addiction? Have they learned lessons from past successes and failures to guide future social policy? Is their advice based upon credible fact?

Social Rehabilitation and Programs to Prevent and Treat Juvenile Delinquency

Social rehabilitation and prevention have been the typical promise of juvenile delinquency programs, even those run with the principal goal of "incapacitation," that is, prisons of one sort or another. Yet the possibility that undesirable behaviors, frequently associated with long-standing material, social, or psychological deprivation, can be quickly corrected through a relatively small and inexpensive amount of professional attention belies the more common observation that human behavior is resistant to change.

The epistemic fix of the social services—finding what works—is illuminated in the administration and evaluation of California's Community Treatment Program (CTP) (Palmer 1974). CTP has been one of the better described instances of the many "promising leads" to reduce juvenile crime. Its failures as both social research and social remedy have not been improved upon in more recent projects. Indeed, most programs go unevaluated. CTP was an influential, highly elaborated experiment in social rehabilitation—"one of the most wide-ranging and ambitious therapeutic studies." Nonetheless, CTP may be remembered more for the failure of its research staff to modify their preconceptions—their expectancies—in a larger commitment to scientific objectivity than for its advocacy of intensive community treatment.

The Community Treatment Program

Backed by federal research funds, the CTP experiment was conducted between 1961 and 1974 to answer two basic questions. First, between 1961 and 1969, the experiment tested the ability of intensive community treatment to reduce recidivism among juvenile delinquents. The second stage of the experiment, beginning in 1969, attempted to test whether CTP's more troublesome youths would benefit from a short period of restrictive care in a residential facility before being released to the intensive community program.

In each of its two phases, juvenile offenders were randomly assigned to groups that received the experimental care or to control groups that received the customary services of the California Youth Authority. Eight hundred two boys and 212 girls participated in the first part of the experiment. As described by the CTP itself, community-based treatment was designed as standard but intensive social casework provided by a parole agent who could also make referrals to a variety of backup services. The parole agent, working with the same individuals over a period of years, was assigned a small and stable caseload of between eight and twelve. Placement planning decisions were made carefully and were closely monitored. The parole agent also acted as an advocate for the youths, linking them to agencies that provided employment and education. He was readily accessible in the event of emergencies and met with his wards in their own environment in addition to more formal office visits, while also providing extensive surveillance of the youths in the community: nights and weekends, wherever they socialized, worked, or went to school.

The parole agent acted as the referral source to the following services: individual and group counseling; group, foster, or other kinds of out-of-home placements; an accredited school program within the CTP community center building; recreational, cultural, and social programs. CTP embodied a sophisticated differential approach to service; youthful offenders were psychologically typed, matched with an individualized treatment plan, and monitored. As reported by the researchers, CTP provided optimal social casework.

Some of the CTP findings were reported in accessible scholarly journals, usually by Ted Palmer, CTP's research director. Yet the largest amount of both program material and outcomes were available only through unpublished agency documents of the California Youth Authority. Despite a large attentive audience for the results of correctional programs and a great many books by the researchers themselves on corrections and rehabilitation, no complete or even modestly satisfying description of CTP appeared through customary channels of publication. Indeed, the most complete and coherent description of CTP was made by Paul Lerman, the project's major critic (Lerman 1984).

In 1974, CTP announced great success in the first stage of the experiment, especially with the largest group of youthful offenders, "the Neurotics," who accounted for as many as 75 percent of the Youth Authority's caseload. During the course of the experiment, the control group of "Neurotics"—those who did not receive intensive community services—were arrested 2.7 times more often than the experimental group of "Neurotics," those who received intensive services. "In practical terms," wrote Palmer, "this would mean 1,400 fewer arrests per career, for every 1,000 'neurotic' youths in the CTP program as compared with an equal number of these youths within the traditional program." While the youths were in the program itself, recidivism rates were 66 percent for controls and 45 percent for experimental youths. Within forty-eight months after participation in the experiment, controls averaged 1.88 convictions while the figure for experimentals was only 1.58 (Palmer 1974).

The outcomes for the other psychological types, the "Power-Oriented" and the "Passive Conformist" youths, suggested that intensive supervision failed to reduce their criminal behaviors. "Power-Oriented" controls, those who went through the customary Youth Authority services, had lower recidivism rates than the experimental subjects who received intensive services. Still, the force of the study lay in its success with the "Neurotics," by far the largest portion of the caseload.

The second stage of the experiment focused on youthful offenders who did not benefit from the earlier experiment, that is, the more recalcitrant within each psychological group. The researchers found conclusive evidence that "delinquent behavior of the Youth Authority's more troubled, troublesome and/or restive wards may be substantially reduced"—provided that they are first worked with in "residential settings before being released to community care" (Palmer 1974).

CTP Considered. This would be wonderful news if it were true. However, all of CTP's findings are vitiated by imperfections in the research design, the principal one being a lack of objective measurement, "blind" impartiality. Rather, evaluations were made by research staff and parole agents who had stakes in the experiment's success. Decisions to revoke probation, a measure of the program's failure, depended upon the discretion of the parole officers themselves. Paul Lerman's most penetrating criticism of CTP held that the reported recidivism data— probation revocations, crimes, arrests, convictions, and so forth—were sensitive to the stakes of the project and in the end underestimated the true criminal behavior of the youths.

Moreover, the actual receipt of services was not measured. The researchers did not look at the degree to which control subjects absorbed many of the same kinds of social services that the experimentals received, albeit not from the same sources or through the same channels. Many of the rehabilitation services that were available to experimentals through the community-based program were also available to controls through the referrals of their probation officers.

The experimental youths actually received less than the reported community care and more of a variety of unlabeled substitutes for detention. In order to keep reported recidivism rates low for experimentals, various forms of home detention were employed in lieu of actually revoking probation. Moreover, much of the intensive supervision seems to have been devoted to administrative staff tasks and not to care itself. In the end, service differences between experimentals and controls, the essential condition of the experiment, may have been small or nonexistent and therefore the reported outcomes may have measured research distortion more than recidivism.

It is also notable that CTP's published research reports differed greatly from Lerman's descriptions of the program's operation. Judging from his reanalysis of the mimeographed project information, CTP functioned far more as a detention program than as a treatment program, tacitly acknowledging the difficulty of handling delinquent youths. Apparently treatment changed the ways in which the youths were handled, but it did not change their delinquent behavior.

In the end, CTP resolved the epistemic fix of social service—the tension between political convenience and objective reality—through a common strategy: the creation of false evidence of effectiveness. Far from being the most egregious example of a bad study, CTP has emerged as the typical case of juvenile delinquency treatment research.

The Martinson Debate

In 1974, Robert Martinson published an essay based upon a study of the contemporary professional knowledge in corrections that he and his colleagues had conducted for the state of New York. After considerable difficulty, *The Effectiveness of Correctional Treatment* was finally published in 1975 (Lipton et al.). It is a rare expression of the critical tradition in the human services. The authors had searched the literature of corrections between 1945 and 1967 for credible evaluations of corrections programs. They identified 231 studies, representing less than 25 percent of the available outcome literature, that met their inclusion criteria: a specific evaluation of a treatment procedure, the use of independent measures of outcome, and the comparison of outcomes with a control group.

Martinson's essay has become another citation classic. Few outcome evaluations of corrections programs have been published after 1974 without some reference to the epigrammatic summary of Martinson's position—nothing works: "*With few and isolated exceptions, the rehabilitative efforts that have been reported so far have had no appreciable effect on recidivism. Studies that have been done since our summary was completed (i.e., after 1967) do not present any major grounds for altering that original conclusion*" (emphasis in original, Martinson 1974).

Martinson extended his gloomy summary of program outcomes to cover the very poor quality of the research itself, particularly the frequent problem of experimenter bias, that is, the expectancy effects created by "enthusiasts." The Warren studies of intensive supervision that he criticized were the linear ancestors and the inspiration for Palmer's CTP experiments. Martinson's discussion of experimenter bias on the basis of Johnson's later experiment goes to the heart of the problem:

> Johnson, like Warren, assigned experimental subjects to small caseloads and his experiment had the virtue of being performed with two separate populations and at two different times. But in contrast with the Warren case, the Johnson experiment did not engage in a large continuing attempt to choose the experimental counselors specially, to train them specially, and to keep them informed about the progress and importance of the experiment. The first time the experiment was performed, the experimental youths had a slightly lower revocation rate than the controls at six months. But the second time, the experimentals did *not* do better than their controls; indeed, they did slightly worse. And with the experimentals from the first group— those who *had* shown an improvement after six months—this effect wore off at 18 months. In the Johnson study, my colleagues and I found, 'intensive' supervision did *not* increase the experimental youths' risk of detention. Instead, what was happening with the Johnson experiment was that the first time it had been performed—just as in the Warren study— the experimentals were simply revoked less often per number of offenses committed, and they were revoked for offenses more serious than those which prompted revocation among the controls. The second time around, this 'policy' discrepancy disappeared; and when it did, the 'improved' performance of the experimentals disappeared as well. The enthusiasm guiding the project had simply worn off in the absence of reinforcement. . . . One must conclude that the 'benefits' of intensive supervision for youthful offenders may stem not so much from a 'treatment' effect as from a 'policy' effect—that such supervision, so far as we now know, results not in rehabilitation but in a decision to look the other way when an offense is committed. (Emphasis in original, Martinson 1974, 45-46)

In addition to expectancy effects, Martinson and his colleagues found other methodological faults with the 231 studies that they reviewed. There was a pattern in which studies "found effects without making any truly rigorous attempts to exclude competing hypotheses," utilized poor measures of outcomes, incorporated short follow-up periods, and failed to account for "system" effects that may have produced their positive findings. Studies were rarely replicated. "It is just possible that some of our treatment programs *are* working to some extent, but that our research is so bad that it is incapable of telling."

Lundman, McFarlane, and Scarpitti (1976) tended to support Martinson's skepticism, "it appears unlikely that any of these [corrections] projects prevented delinquent behavior." However, their explanation of the failures characteristically ignored the weakness of the interventions themselves. Their position that the wrong problem was being addressed maintained the underlying belief that professionally focused cures were possible and that the causal entity was a specific and treatable social disease. But this common faith in efficient cures had certainly not been encouraged by Martinson's research.

Yet Martinson did provide a ray of hope. Although community programs failed to rehabilitate criminal offenders, they did no worse than prisons while they cost considerably less. Yet decarceration exacts at least a social price, since the general crime rate would probably increase. As Martinson pointed out in a later essay, rehabilitation programs and corrections in general need to be focused on the problem of the general crime rate, not individual offenders (Martinson 1976). While prison did not rehabilitate, it did take likely offenders off of the streets. Still, prison is a very expensive crime prevention program.

Nevertheless, the alternatives to prison are so few and so poorly supported by credible research that it is difficult to find any evidence, let alone any systematic and consecutive body of evidence, that refutes the position that "nothing works." This is not surprising in consideration of the superficial interventions that the rehabilitation literature offers to handle delinquent behaviors—usually little more than a few hours of conversation and a series of light penalties for infractions. It is fanciful to expect either committed criminals or the severely disturbed and deprived to "reform" without the provision of genuine opportunities to lead nondeviant lives. The 231 attempts at corrections did not provide these alternatives, customarily offering punishment or temporary, shallow, and incomplete "treatments" that lacked the resources to substitute for failed families, school systems, job markets, and communities.

In support of this criticism, a later review of the corrections literature by the National Academy of Sciences (NAS) pointed out that

> a more penetrating inquiry into the nature of the problem of rehabilitation and programs and methods that have been tried leads to the conclusion that there is even less in the research than meets the eye. The techniques that have been tested seem rarely to have been devised to be strong enough to offer realistic hope that they would rehabilitate offenders, especially imprisoned felons. (Sechrest et al. 1979, 3)

Yet the provision of powerful interventions, especially to populations at risk of delinquency, would be very costly because of the large numbers who would be eligible for service by virtue either of their actual delinquency or of their high potential for delinquency. Apart from not knowing what works, the problem of cost impedes the search for effective corrections programs.

The NAS review came to a less qualified summary conclusion than Martinson and his colleagues about both the effectiveness of corrections and the quality of the corrections literature. NAS pointed to the large number of "fugitive" research findings in the corrections literature that appeared to influence public policy. These "technical reports, unpublished papers, [and] articles published in out-of-the-way places" (recalling Palmer's mimeographed reports on CTP) pose a problem of quality since they do not go through even the minimal peer review procedures of the field's journals. NAS also felt that the Martinson group had been too inclusive and inattentive to the many debilitating methodological flaws contained in their 231 studies. Eight percent contained no comparison group; 29 percent were not prospective experiments; and fully 35 percent did not use random procedures to assign subjects to experimental and control groups.

Martinson had argued that some few programs *appeared* to be promising—the "soft" nothing works position. In contrast, the National Academy of Science's committee stated the "hard" position bluntly:

> the entire body of research appears to justify only the conclusion that we do not know of any program or method of rehabilitation that could be guaranteed to reduce the criminal activity of released offenders. Although a generous reviewer of the literature might discern some glimmers of hope, those glimmers are so few, so scattered, and so inconsistent that they do not serve as a basis for any recommendation other than continued research. (3)

In 1984, Rutter and Giller published an exhaustive review of the juvenile delinquency literature. They attempted to be good diplomats, staying true to the failures of the research while still staying loyal to the field:

> Our review of research into prevention and intervention has emphasized the many actions which have not yet been subjected to evaluation, and the extensive conceptual and methodological problems in the research which has been undertaken. It is obvious that the empirical findings do not yet justify any firm recommendations on 'what works' in preventing delinquency or reducing recidivism. Nevertheless, it would be wrong to underestimate how much has been achieved and how much we know. Already the research findings provide some important lessons in planning future policies. (317)

However, their subsequent discussion fails to identify the research that supports their hopefulness. To the contrary they eloquently point to the many shortcomings of behavioral approaches (the uncertainty of any lasting effects), counseling and psychotherapy ("are of no value"), "therapeutic and correctional regimes in institutions" (no consistent effects), and so forth. On its own merits, their thorough review of the program literature provides support for the NAS report. Yet for all the attempts at prevention and rehabilitation that they reviewed, not one of them provided a customary cultural environment; none attempted to compensate for previous abuses and deprivations. Most attempts at rehabilitation were professional interventions that applied the rare skills and insights of various theories of corrections at relatively low levels of cost.

The very few isolated and unreplicated instances of successful outcomes could easily be accounted for by a variety of alternative explanations. Their samples may simply have been fortunate, containing by chance a large number of youths in the experimental group who would reform in any event or a large number of youths in the control who would deteriorate under any circumstances or both. The researchers may have distorted measures and procedures. In the many cases in which no control was employed, the positive effects may have simply been the result of maturation which carried along the intervention on its coattails. Particularly in the instance of fugitive publication, the positive outcomes may simply have been bogus. Without replication, these so-called successes provide no lessons at all.

The more appropriate conclusion to have been reached on the massive evidence of Rutter and Giller is that something was faulty with the scholarly enterprise of delinquency research itself. Yet even after an immense number of failed reports, program designers were still claiming that weak, theoretically improbable solutions to delinquency should be attempted.

The Gottfredson Review

Gottfredson (1987) reevaluated a class of treatment and prevention programs that employed Guided Group Interaction (GGI), a sometimes highly confrontational technique.

GGI is an intervention that aims to develop a group using free discussion and an open atmosphere and that assumes delinquents must learn to conform to conventional social rules by gaining more social rewards through conformity than through nonconformity. GGI is expected to encourage participants to recognize problems with their behavior, attitudes, and values. An adult leader is active in guiding the development of a group by asking questions, creating norms of reassurance, repeating ideas expressed in the group, and summarizing important ideas. Descriptions—but not evaluations—or these methods with suggestions for their use are numerous. (Gottfredson 673)

In the Highfields Project (reported in 1957 and 1958), delinquent boys sixteen and seventeen years of age were assigned by juvenile courts to probation at the Highfields Residential Facility or to incarceration in a state reformatory. Youths stayed at Highfields for four months where they worked for a token amount of pay ($0.50 per day) and attended GGI sessions five days per week. Youths at the reformatory stayed for one year.

The authors reported that recidivism was lower for Highfields boys than those who went through the reformatory: "Highfields rehabilitates [a] high proportion of boys in a four-month period, whereas most other facilities keep boys at least three times as long. Not only is this fact important in itself, but it is important because Highfields is relatively much less expensive per boy treated than is the conventional facility" (Gottfredson, 675). However, Gottfredson noted important differences between the two groups that predicted lower recidivism for the Highlands group. Moreover, his reanalysis of the original data provided no support for a treatment effect on white youth and inconclusive evidence for a treatment effect on black youth.

The Essexfields demonstrations (reported in 1967) were similar to Highfields, even beginning their groups with some of the Highfields boys. Again, their comparison groups were not equivalent even while there was no demonstration of treatment group superiority.

In turn the Collegefields community treatment demonstration (reported in 1967) began with Essexfields boys. The study design called for boys to be randomly assigned to the community treatment condition or to one of two standard probation controls. The experimental condition consisted of daily GGI and academic coursework. GGI was a harsh and punitive intervention in Collegefields.

The experimenters claimed that "'in all major aspects . . . [Collegefields was] a successful program for the rehabilitation of 14 and 15 year old delinquents.'" However, these judgments were largely based upon staff reports; the recidivism rates of experimentals was the same as controls on standard probation. The dropout rate in the experimental condition was also high, perhaps a result of the unpleasantness, and perhaps even the cruelty, of GGI in this demonstration. Once again, randomization was breached with the result that controls could have been expected to show higher recidivism rates. Therefore, in Collegefields, as in other experiments, the failure of treated subjects to show lower recidivism raised the possibility that GGI may have actually been harmful.

The Silverlake experiment (reported in 1971) tested community-based services against the standard residential treatment. Delinquents working and residing in the community received GGI five days per week in 1.5 hour sessions. Although recidivism for both groups during the follow-up year was the same, the evaluators noted that the seriousness of offenses declined for both groups equally. Gottfredson felt that these decreases may have been due to "selection-regression or measurement artifacts" (686). Nonetheless, the evaluators claimed that the experiment was a success since the community program cost $303 per month while the residential program cost $363 per month (implying even greater disparities in total costs since the community program was much shorter) in producing similar results.

The Provo experiment (reported in 1974) was designed as a community treatment program that was even less expensive than the Highlands project. Youths worked and lived in the community and participated in GGI part of each day. The experiment called itself a success: recidivism was higher for standard probation than for those in experimental treatment (an average of 1.3 arrests and .85 arrests respectively). However, Gottfredson notes that after treatment, which involved considerable surveillance, recidivism was the same for both groups.

The Marshall Program employed highly confrontative GGI techniques but failed to implement a true experimental design. As a result the experimental group was at a lower risk of recidivism. Nonetheless no differences in recidivism were reported between experimental and control groups. A later reanalysis in 1970 found a higher failure rate for the treated group, reprising the theme of harm.

A variety of school-based interventions attempted to prevent delinquent behaviors among high-risk youth. In a characteristic understatement, Gottfredson noted that they have been "subjected to evaluations of varying quality." The Omaha Public Schools Program reported improvements in suspension rates for the treated group of students. However, these results were based upon a "grossly non equivalent comparison group design." Gottfredson's reanalysis shows that treated students had a much higher suspension rate than comparison group students.

Gross methodological problems invalidate other positive reports from "experiments" in Rock Island, Berrien County, and Chicago. In Chicago, the evaluations were conducted by an incompetent and possibly unscrupulous proprietary firm, M & E Associates. M & E Associates reported a randomization design that they in fact never implemented.

Gottfredson stops short of indicting the community of researchers that produced the studies he criticizes so severely. Yet in addition to his criticisms, largely based upon imperfect comparison groups and faulty statistical analyses, the studies also tolerated reactive measures, short follow-up periods, and questionably reliable instruments. They also failed to employ neutral judges or, even more importantly, to check on the accuracy of the recidivism data. In spite of obviously self-serving evaluations of programs that could reasonably be considered cruel in some instances, Gottfredson concluded that some experiments were promising (e.g., Essexfields).

A conclusion less ambiguous than Gottfredson's seems warranted, one more in keeping with the CTP experience. GGI seems to have been a coldly militant series of attempts to decrease and prevent youth crime at very low costs. In either its institutional forms or its less expensive community forms, GGI interventions were incapable of correcting delinquent behaviors; they may even have encouraged them. The GGI experience also raises ethical questions; unlegislated and unadjudicated penalties were imposed upon unwitting subjects, albeit in the name of science and the social good.

Box Scores and Meta-analyses

Following the recent fashion, a number of box scores and meta-analyses have summarized the separate empirical studies of juvenile delinquency treatment. Their breadth of inclusion has been uniformly compromised by their failures at depth, especially their gullibility in endorsing the credibility of their base of studies. In spite of their frequent attempts to identify promising leads and hopeful signs, Martinson's conclusion is still reasonable: nothing seems to have worked.

Garrett (1985) conducted a meta-analysis of all treatment studies of adjudicated delinquents in residential settings that appeared in the professional literature between 1960 and 1983 and that made any comparisons, (e.g., controls or a pre/post test design). Garrett's conclusions, based upon 111 studies, would seem to contradict Martinson's bleak summary: "The major finding of this quantitative integration of primary research results is that, yes, treatment of adjudicated delinquents in residential settings does work" (303–4).

However, of her 111 studies, only 37 percent employed a randomized design while more than 25 percent employed no comparison group of any kind. The mean effect size for the uncontrolled studies was 1.15 (implying that treated groups were 37 percent better off after treatment) and for the controlled studies only .25 (treated groups being 10 percent better off than controls). Moreover, Garrett averaged significant findings along with those that were not significant, which makes the conclusions impossible to analyze except in pointing out that the size of her reported findings may have been inflated by effects that could have been due to chance.

The importance of her findings are further suspect since most of them relate not to more objective behavioral measures, such as recidivism, but to measures of institutional adjustment. Many of these softer measures were made by residential staff and researchers with a stake in positive outcomes. Garrett seems to acknowledge this problem, although reluctantly: "One can argue, however, that adjusting to and meeting demands and expectations in the institutional environment may help to prepare the youth to meet the demands and expectations of the noninstitutional world if the treatment program is designed to facilitate that transfer" (305). Yet the absence of credible evidence that this transfer occurred suggests that institutional adjustment may have little impact on juvenile delinquency. This point of skepticism is given force by the barren conditions of many of these institutions.

Garrett identifies an average effect size for all treatments of only .37, which translates into an improvement of only 14 percent. The weak, frequently uncontrolled, and biased base of her studies does not refute the single alternative possibility that any positive effects that take place are due simply to the maturation of the delinquents themselves and not to any element of residential care. But there are many more alternatives made plausible by the weakness of her base of studies: expectancy

effects, noncomparable groups, nonsignificant findings, biased reporting. In the end Garrett has not refuted Martinson or identified a single
study that credibly testifies to the successful treatment of adjudicated
juvenile delinquents.

Lab and Whitehead (1988) conducted a box-score analysis of the
impact of delinquency intervention programs on recidivism during the
ten years between 1975 and 1984: diversion programs, community
interventions (probation and parole), institutional and residential
programs, and other programs (Outward Bound and Scared Straight).
Somewhat more rigorous than Garrett, they only included studies that
contained comparison groups. They identified fifty-five studies that
made eighty-five numerical comparisons.

> The results are far from encouraging for rehabilitation proponents. Disregarding tests
> of statistical significance, 45 of the comparisons showed no impact or negative impact
> for the various interventions with juvenile offenders while 40 interventions showed
> positive impact. Where authors reported tests of significance, only 15 comparisons
> were in favor of the experimental group, whereas 33 showed no impact or a negative
> impact. Based on these statistics, it is hard to reaffirm rehabilitation. (77)

Even greater pessimism seems warranted. Lab and Whitehead failed
to explore the quality of the studies themselves. Of the fifty-five studies
only twenty-one studies employed randomized designs while only
twelve of these twenty-one contained samples larger than fifty. Of these
twelve studies with the larger samples, three reported positive findings,
two reported mixed findings, and seven reported negative findings or
failed to find differences between their experimental and control groups.

Moreover, the Lab and Whitehead analysis is insensitive to the lessons
of CTP. These studies exhibited the range of other methodological pitfalls
that circumscribe their value: nonrepresentative samples, noncomparable groups, biases in reporting, and lack of treatment integrity.
Furthermore, the basic reliability of the recidivism data seemed to be a
problem. Kirigin et al. (1982), included in this meta-analysis, only
obtained accuracy rates of approximately 80 percent for their coders in
transferring data from police records. Most other studies do not report
reliability checks on the recidivism data; presumably they are not routinely carried out.

Whitehead and Lab (1989) conducted a meta-analysis on a similar
base of studies that appeared in the professional journals between 1975
and 1984 inclusive. This meta-analysis confirmed their box-score

analysis while it also failed to go beyond a superficial critique of the base of studies. Of the fifty studies that met their inclusion criteria, only eighteen studies employed randomized controls. The issue of ineffectiveness and even harm keeps reemerging:

> The analysis of correctional intervention in this article could be considered to be overly lenient in its interpretation of [positive outcomes]. We have opted to consider any phi value exceeding .20 to be an indication of program effectiveness. . . . This choice is very generous and could be criticized for being too low. A more rigorous selection phi around .40 to .50 would lead to a more conclusive finding that juvenile correctional treatment is highly ineffective. The current use of .20 was chosen to err on the side of finding positive results. Interestingly, even this low figure fails to support claims of efficacy by most interventions. (291)

In their impatience for correcting delinquency, societies have at times tolerated extremely harsh and punitive interventions—maiming, isolation, barbaric detention, whipping, deprivation of rights, food, exercise, and so forth. Some of the expressions of GGI—"Boot Camps" and "Scared Straight"—begin to suggest abuse. Many of the conditions of juvenile corrections institutions are still barbaric. Very few of the studied rehabilitation programs provided extensive, long-term treatment conditions that approximated customary cultural conditions. The best of the program settings for juvenile delinquents may provide an adequate but temporary congregate situation for a small number of extremely disturbed children. But these programs are representative neither of treatment settings nor of delinquents. They are also extremely expensive.

Perhaps the undertone of deterioration in treatment signals primitive and inhumane conditions within some juvenile corrections programs. Perhaps too, deterioration implies a profound and *appropriate* rejection of the failed interventions among the delinquents themselves and a confirmation of a delinquent pattern of life. The cruelty of some so-called professional interventions seem quite capable of causing anger, even rage and hatred, among disturbed juveniles.

Replies to Lab and Whitehead and the Notion of Consistent Ineffectiveness

Some loyalists like CTP's Palmer (1991) rejected the Lab and Whitehead analyses in a manner similar to their argument with Martinson some years before. Palmer simply ignored the logic of Lab and Whitehead's two summary evaluations, choosing to misrepresent and distort their findings. As one example: "Using fairly *stringent* success criteria, (Whitehead and Lab) found that 24 percent to 32 percent of the studies evidenced what they called 'program effectiveness' [success]" (emphasis added, Palmer 1991, 335). Whitehead and Lab argued that their criteria were actually too low and called for much higher criteria of success.

Other critics of Whitehead and Lab reanalyzed their base of studies, pressing for conclusions more favorable to juvenile corrections programs. Izzo and Ross (1990) found that corrections programs that contained a cognitive component were "more than twice as effective as programs that did not" (138). Unfortunately, the cognitive component accounted for an improvement of only 6 percent.

In perhaps the most sophisticated attack on Whitehead and Lab, Andrews et al.(1990b) carried much of the psychotherapeutic outcome literature into corrections. They claimed to have developed a selective appraisal of that literature, leading to recommendations for "appropriate" treatments. Quite consciously (dedicating the essay to CTP's Palmer), they intended their review to support traditional rehabilitation for offenders on the grounds of effectiveness.

However, the poor quality of their base of studies again undercuts the authority of their claims to program success. Andrews et al. reviewed two sets of outcome studies. The first group of studies included forty-five of Whitehead and Lab's original fifty; five were excluded because they appeared to overlap with others in the group. The second group

> included 35 studies in [the Andrews et al.] research files as of February 1989 that were not included in the Whitehead and Lab set but had employed binary measures of recidivism. [These studies] date from the 1950's through 1989, but they are not purported to be a representative sample of any particular time period. . . . [They provide] a convenient means of exploring, albeit tentatively, how well conclusions based on the Whitehead and Lab sample may generalize to adult samples. (377)

On the basis of their analysis, they reached a variety of happy conclusions, in particular that "appropriate treatment— treatment that is delivered to higher risk cases, that targets crimogenic need, and that is matched with the learning styles of offenders—will reduce recidivism" (377).

But even if their analysis was technically acceptable, and this is disputed in Lab and Whitehead's response (1990), their conclusions cannot be sustained by the outcomes reported through those studies, by their own poor methodology, or by the process by which they augmented their initial group of forty-five studies.

Andrews et al.'s (1990a) correlation between the type of treatment and recidivism is small and has little theoretical importance in predicting effective interventions. Andrews et al. interpreted this correlation between treatment and recidivism to indicate a causative relationship—that community corrections produced positive outcomes. This is unwarranted by the methodologies of the underlying studies. The correlation could be explained by the biases of those studies, by factors in the selection of subjects for service, by the maturation of the subjects and by other pitfalls of the research. Also troubling because of the poorly controlled base of studies is the possibility that program success may have been explained by "creaming"; those who received treatment and went on to productive lives and to being counted as program successes may not have needed the treatments in the first place.

Moreover, the augmented group of studies prevents either generalization or, more importantly, any sort of definitive conclusion based upon their inherent quality. Not one of them is a credible test of an intervention. All of them are marred by serious methodological and theoretical flaws that forestall even tentative conclusions about hopeful leads, let alone an exquisite confirmation of differential diagnosis and treatment in juvenile corrections.

The landscape of the base of the Andrews et al. studies prior to 1984 was covered adequately by Martinson, Sechrest, and Rutter and Giller. None of the post 1983 studies included by Andrews et al. (1990a) relieve its bleakness. Schneider and Schneider (1984) compared two types of restitution programs for juvenile offenders. In one, the juveniles' restitutions were carefully supervised; in the other, an "ad hoc" approach, they were not. The researchers found that those who completed restitution payments were less likely to commit crimes in the future and that a greater proportion of those who were carefully supervised fulfilled their restitution obligations. The authors repeatedly suggested that fulfillment of restitution prevents recidivism: "successful completion makes a difference in terms of the likelihood of reoffending . . . [restitution programs] provide an opportunity to have a positive effect on recidivism rates." Those who completed restitution were less deviant than those who did not even while the delinquencies themselves were relatively minor property offenses.

Yet these results would seem to be a very natural effect of supervision while their small apparent impact on recidivism is very speculative. Supervision, not restitution, may have accounted for the outcomes. In any event the follow-up period was too short to make an informed judgment. Furthermore, the study was conducted in Dane County, Wisconsin suggesting that, whatever its findings, they were probably not relevant to the common urban setting of juvenile delinquency. This trivial, illogical, poorly designed study fails to demonstrate the value of restitution programs in combating the recidivism of juvenile delinquents.

Barton et al. (1985) was one of the pillars of Andrews et al.'s reliance upon psychotherapy for delinquents. However, nothing in Barton et al. distinguishes it from the previous critique of psychotherapy and family therapy outcome research. Barton et al. reported on three extensions of Functional Family Therapy (FFT): to new populations, in utilizing less formally trained therapists, and in new treatment contexts. FFT is a technique to improve communication within families.

In their extension of FFT to paraprofessional therapists, eight undergraduate students received sixteen two-hour training sessions. They found a 26 percent recidivism rate for experimental subjects during the thirteen month follow-up period. In declaring success, the authors compare this 26 percent recidivism with "the 51 percent base-rate annual recidivism rate for this juvenile court district as a whole" (19). This comparison is made without demonstrating that their study sample is in any way comparable to underlying population of juvenile delinquents. Presumably the court referrals to this project were not random and some selection factor probably screened out higher-risk offenders. The authors make no comment on the severity of their subjects' offenses. Moreover, the study utilized no control group of any kind with the result that the findings have little meaning. They certainly do not provide credible evidence for success.

The second extension, to foster placement, was in essence an extemporaneous study conducted by two FFT trainees who "unbeknownst to the (other) trainers and their supervisors . . . decided to implement FFT into their casework and to perform an evaluation of the effectiveness of the procedure for their own professional decision making and caseload management" (20). Randomization procedures were not utilized. Reliability checks were not made. Expectancy biases were not controlled. The similarity of comparison groups was not established. Data were reconstructed from logs. In the end, this is an ad hoc, intuitive study. It provides no credible outcome information.

The third extension of FFT, to "hard core delinquents," reported that the frequency of offenses decreased by more than 50 percent among the group of delinquents who received FFT. However, neither randomization nor a nontreatment control were utilized. The treatment integrity of the comparison groups was suspect while the groups were not comparable. Moreover, the "offenses" and the way that they were tabulated looked suspiciously like CTP's with the result that the recidivism rate may well have been reactive to the researchers' ambitions. This is particularly important in light of the small size of the experimental sample—thirty.

In short, FFT does not provide even a reasonable level of preliminary support for its effectiveness. Indeed the three studies suggest that the researchers, in pressing for positive findings, ignored a prudent skepticism, failing to apply standard methodological safeguards. The report is cultish in its fervor for FFT and falls below even the common levels of contemporary research in juvenile corrections.

In spite of his apparent intent, Shorts (1986) actually provided evidence of ineffectiveness. The research showed that association with delinquents in a community program did not have the effect of increasing recidivism. But the research also suggested that the community program—a series of very minimal services—was not more effective than unserved controls in reducing recidivism.

Andrews et al. cite their own previous research (1986) to test a central tenet of "appropriate treatment," the risk principle: "intensive controls and services are best reserved for higher risk cases" (377). However, their study sample is restricted to property crimes among a pool of delinquents in Ottawa, Canada while they did not conduct any follow-up after the period of treatment (probation, in this case). As a result, their findings—a reduction of recidivism by approximately 50 percent—can be attributed to the temporary surveillance of intensive supervision and not to their experimental conditions. Their finding also seems to be trivial: higher-risk groups need greater surveillance. Moreover, the intensive supervision was based upon highly motivated volunteers, a research condition that is not easily replicated in practice.

Ross et al. (1988) rather than providing evidence that support Andrews et al., actually provide a basis for questioning all corrections studies that fail to provide placebo controls. Ross et al. compared the value of cognitive treatment for high-risk adult probationers to two randomized controls, one that received regular probation and another (Life Skills training) that was designed as a placebo for their cognitive treatment— the Reasoning and Rehabilitation Project. Their results indicated that 30 percent (seven out of twenty-three) of the regular probation group subsequently received a sentence of imprisonment while there were no recidivists in the experimental cognitive treatment group (twenty-two subjects) and only 11 percent (two out of seventeen) of the placebo control group were recidivists. They considered their experiment to be a success, choosing to compare the experimental group's outcome with regular probation. Andrews et al. repeat this comparison in their review. However, the appropriate comparison is with the placebo control, not the nontreatment control. In this case the difference is not significant; cognitive treatment is not superior to a placebo control.

Ignoring their problems with attrition, small samples, and the possibility that involvement in the experimental group may have itself discouraged sentences of imprisonment or otherwise depressed the report of recidivism, the study hints at an immense potential discrepancy between nontreatment controls and placebo controls. If nontreatment controls were equivalent to placebo controls, then the two untreated groups should have experienced similar outcomes. They clearly were not equivalent with the implication that comparison of experimental outcomes to nontreatment controls that are not placebos for treatment may distort outcomes in favor of effectiveness.

In spite of the convenience of methodologically porous and frequently trivial research, Andrews et al. still reported only a modest average benefit—23 percent improvement—for "appropriate" interventions. Yet their crop of studies transcend issues of effectiveness. Negative or positive, they are simply not credible statements of their programs' outcomes. As a result, the Andrews et al. conclusions are misleading. The value of "appropriate" treatment has neither been put to a true test nor substantiated by the research that they cite.

The Recent Literature

The recent juvenile corrections literature, as well as the augmented group of current studies included in Andrews et al., fails as profoundly as earlier research to provide credible support for the rehabilitative ideal.

Its only positive findings substantiate the obvious: while in prison offenders do not commit crimes in the community.

Rausch (1983) tested the ability of three types of diversion programs to reduce juvenile recidivism in comparison with "normal court processing and disposition." The Deinstitutionalization of Status Offenders (DSO) project provided two types of minimal care alternatives and one kind of "maximum intervention."

In the end Rausch reported no statistically significant or practically important differences between the recidivism rates of the four groups. Between 40 percent and 47 percent of each group fell to recidivism. Neither the minimal care alternative nor the few additional hours of "maximum" care (largely eaten up in assessment services, administration, and referral) made any difference to the youths. "Maximum" takes on an ironic and somewhat misleading meaning in light of the short duration and superficiality of the services that were actually provided: maximum in the sense of what society allocates for its poor and troubled youngsters—the maximum charitable dosage—but not maximum in terms of what may be required to correct the criminal behaviors of adolescents and certainly not maximum relative to the customary care given by most parents to their children.

In light of the large number of minimal intervention failures with juvenile delinquents, it is quixotic to expect that the few additional hours of attention that constituted "maximum" care would have been able to change entrenched behaviors. Indeed, if the maximum treatment group had showed lower recidivism, then the issue would have been raised of whether any intervention at all was necessary to achieve this result or whether some other selection or processing characteristic of this poorly conducted experiment accounted for the result.

Moreover, the author acknowledged that the reported conditions of care may have been inaccurate. In this and in a huge number of other studies, the question of treatment integrity remains open: whether the treated youths actually received the reported services. Few researchers bother to check for treatment integrity in any of their experimental conditions.

Klein (1986) randomly assigned "juvenile offenders of mid-range seriousness" to release, two conditions of community treatment (one that assured the provision of social services and one that relied upon customary referral patterns), and court petition. Klein found that the rearrest rates of the released and treated groups were occasionally lower than the court-petitioned group. This led Klein to conclude that some evidence is provided for labeling theory, that arrests are a result of self-perceptions and social definitions. However, the research ignores the possibility that surveillance itself leads to rearrest, with the group most scrutinized producing the greatest number of arrests. Moreover, the research lacks descriptions of the offenders, community services, and randomization procedures.

Kagan et al. (1987) tested the effectiveness of a home-based counseling program for delinquent and disturbed youths who were at risk of long-term institutionalization. Twenty-nine children, from chronically unstable families, who would have been sent to institutions for long periods were instead diverted to foster homes for a thirty-day assessment program during which their families received counseling. Sixteen of the twenty-nine were returned home after this thirty-day period. During the thirty-day period the children's delinquent behaviors decreased while their school performance improved.

The follow-up evaluation (conducted an average of eleven months after the assessment period) was based on responses by only twenty of the twenty-nine families—an attrition of 31 percent. It revealed that 52 percent of the children were still with their families although 63 percent of those families still reported serious problems with their youngsters. The more aggressive children and those with more problems were less likely to return home than both the nonaggressive children and those with fewer problems. The authors point out that the program was extraordinarily efficient, saving the county $76,000 for the assessment period alone while the savings for the nineteen months of the experiment may have exceeded $1 million.

However, the study was not controlled in any way; improvements over customary outcomes, if they existed at all, might have been attributed to better assessment or greater surveillance of the families and not to the counseling intervention. Moreover, without extensive follow-up and appropriate controls, it was not apparent that the children who were returned to their families were better off than if they had gone to an institution. However, it was apparent that the taxpayers benefitted, at least in the short run.

The authors acknowledged that the foster placements were very difficult to find for these children. It probably took a heroic effort on the part of the staff and the foster families to sustain care throughout the program. As a result, the remission of problems during the foster placement may well have been a demonstration effect that cannot be replicated in the customary field conditions of foster care. Yet the study did not detail the substance of the foster care, and without controls, the effect of the foster placement itself, presumably with very patient and caring people, cannot be separated from the impact of the counseling effect on the children's families as the cause of the children's successful placements.

Decent family environments for children—perhaps the essence of foster care—may have gone further to resolve their problems than any elegance of professional diagnosis and treatment. But the study was not designed to test the effects of relatively permanent and decent placements on delinquent and disturbed youth. The cost for continuing this level of care over the long run would probably not have saved the county money.

Instead, Kagan et al. chose only to test, and poorly at that, the draconian choice between abusive families and abusive institutions. As with many other studies of deinstitutionalized care, the service outcomes in the short-run appear to be equivalent and the taxpayer can save money by choosing the less costly alternative in the righteous belief that quality is preserved. Characteristically, Kagan et al. were silent on the extended costs of community neglect. Far from providing a service to the children, Kagan et al. deprived them of a just compassionate voice by failing to address the value of a decent home environment. They obviously preferred to establish the value of their professional intervention.

Davidson et al. (1987) tested the impact of four types of paraprofessional counseling approaches on the recidivism of juvenile offenses. The four counseling conditions were compared with two controls—a placebo control and the standard treatment.

Davidson et al. reported that the integrity and intensity of the treatments were maintained as per the intentions of the experiment. They found no differences between the outcomes of the different treatments when measured by the youths' self-reports of criminal activities. Moreover, recidivism as measured by court petitions at the two-year follow-up showed no significant differences between the different experimental groups. However, an aggregation of groups treated outside of the court system showed a statistically significant decrease in recidivism compared with an aggregation of the groups treated within the court system (the standard treatment control and the action condition set within the court system). But Davidson et al. did not present tabulations of other measures of recidivism or other aggregations that may not have supported their conclusions. Outcomes measured by incarceration and conviction rates would be particularly relevant. For all the comparisons that Davidson et al. seemed to make, they failed to report the many important ones that probably did not reach statistical significance. Their few positive findings may well have been merely the chance artifacts of multiple comparisons.

In mitigation of their failure to produce important, consistent, or statistically significant findings, they pointed out that their findings were nevertheless in a positive direction that would have been significant if their samples were larger. Yet they are stuck with science. Their research produced marginal, anomalous findings that did not reach levels of statistical significance. As they reluctantly acknowledge, the direction of some of their findings contradicts many previous studies that reported positive outcomes.

In reporting their findings, Davidson et al. caution that "the experimental treatments were implemented under conditions seldom operative in typical service agencies . . . [that] overgeneralization to existing treatments for juvenile offenders is clearly unwarranted" (74). Yet they failed to add that two of their conditions contained extremely small samples of twelve and were collected during only one year of the study while a third condition contained only twenty-four subjects assigned during only two years. But neither their own cautions, nor the fact that the juveniles failed to report any differences in their criminal behavior, nor the fact that many of their principal results failed to achieve statistical significance inhibited Davidson et al. from selecting a few shreds of evidence to reach conclusions of far-reaching theoretical and practical importance:

> The results of this study suggested several possible explanations for the causes of recidivism . . . The results also indicated that conducting interventions outside the influence of the court may beneficially influence recidivism. Such explanations support the notions for labeling theory. . . . In other words, just removing juveniles from the court and pairing them with a volunteer may have positive effects. In addition, examination of the performance of [one of the smallest conditions] indicated the potential importance of supervisor and supervision setting, although this suggestion must be viewed quite tentatively. . . . In conclusion, these results present a replication of earlier findings about the relative impact of diverting juvenile offenders from the legal system and using intensive nonprofessional treatments . . . .

This is the sort of research that begs for replication, and certainly not Andrews et al.'s uncritical acceptance. As of 1991, the field had not yet published a replication of the research.

Shivrattan et al. (1988) tested whether eight sessions of social interaction skills would reduce delinquent behaviors. They tested this in an experiment with forty-five incarcerated males between the ages of fifteen to seventeen who were randomly divided into three groups.

Appraisals of outcomes were based upon different scales: Jesness Behavior Checklists (observer ratings and self-ratings), the Minnesota Multiphasic Personality Inventory (MMPI), and probation reports. At the termination of the training the stress group showed slight improvement on the MMPI while the social skills group showed some improvement on the Jesness scales.

At follow-up, there were no significant differences on the MMPI while there were small gains for both observer and self-reports on the Jesness measures of conformity. Shivrattan et al. concluded that the experiment was a success.

However, the differences at follow-up did not sustain the authors' conclusions. The differences were small and only emerged on the Jesness scales; no differences were found on the more reliable MMPI. Moreover, the Jesness scores resulted from the reports of observers—the training teachers and the staff of the residential school—who had a stake in the success of the experiment.

Sechrest (1989) evaluated a shock intervention program, (i.e., "boot camp"), in Florida.

> Shock incarceration stresses discipline and purports to have the same results as military recruit training with respect to developing positive attitudes toward authority and providing physical conditioning. . . . For most states, system goals include reducing prison crowding and system costs, and ultimately recidivism and its related costs. . . . The primary technique, or 'treatment tool' is teaching discipline through the use of military 'boot camp' techniques. A new 'recruit' . . . is shouted at and referred to as a maggot, scumbag, boy, a fool, or a nobody, and repeatedly threatened with transfer to the main facility where he may be sexually abused, he is told, if he fails the program. In Florida the 'pukes' must pull together or they are all punished as a group, which is standard recruit fare. The [National Institute of Justice] report points out that the Army no longer uses these types of abusive and degrading techniques as part of their training, preferring to use 'voice commands' and other forms of motivation. (16-17)

A randomized design was not incorporated. Comparisons with similar groups of youthful offenders and between graduates and nongraduates of the program in Florida did not indicate program success. Moreover, program participants did not appear to be a group of high-risk or serious offenders: "very few of [them] have been tried on probation and, of those who have been, far fewer have violated community control" (17).

Sechrest suggested that the point of the programs may not lie in their ability to rehabilitate:

> Shock incarceration programs appear to have less appeal to corrections officials than to the public or its representatives. The programs have great media appeal, and are widely publicized as meeting the need to 'do something' about the crime problem. The public appeal is similar to that for the 'scared straight' and 'shock' probation and parole concepts of the early 1980's, none of which have proven effective on close examination. (16)

The programs appeared to be relatively inexpensive. They also appeared to create a number of problems, encouraging the "sadistic tendencies" of correctional officers that "can and has gotten out of control in some instances" (18). The confrontational style may also have caused greater recidivism. Sechrest concluded that shock incarceration techniques were failures whose persistence could be explained only by its public popularity and not by any evidence of their success.

Weisz et al. (1990): A Flawed but Still Useful Standard for Outcome Research in the Human Services

The social services occasionally produce a valuable study even while it may depart from an RPCT design. Weisz et al. (1990) evaluated a court mandated treatment program—the Willie M Program—for juvenile delinquents in North Carolina. The consent decree that established the program by requiring that all delinquents be served precluded a randomized, nontreatment design.

Weisz et al. framed their research against the "appropriate treatment" philosophy of Andrews et al.:

> The core of the program is intensive case management. Each Willie M class member is assigned a trained case manager who works with a clinical/educational treatment team to determine the class member's treatment needs and arrange for an individually tailored array of services targeted to those needs. Officials classify the services into about 20 traditional categories (e.g., outpatient psychotherapy, inpatient treatment, recreation). To be certified as class members, individuals must be judged 'seriously emotionally, neurologically, or mentally handicapped' and must show 'violent or assaultive behavior'. . . . Once certified, youths receive services averaging about

$25,000 per year. During the period studied here, young people 'aged out' of the program 6 months after turning 18, or at the end of the same fiscal year, whichever period was longer. . . . It has been suggested that the program may serve as a model of appropriate interventions with seriously disturbed youngsters . . . and the program does show some of the characteristics of 'appropriateness' described by Andrews et al. . . . However, there has not yet been empirical assessment of program effects. Such assessment has been hampered by a key problem: the lack of a true no-treatment control group to which the treated youth can be compared. Not only are program officials reluctant, on ethical grounds, to assign any class member to a no-treatment control condition, but the consent decree associated with the program prohibits denial of services that are deemed needed and appropriate. (721)

Weisz et al. reported no substantial differences in subsequent arrests between the two groups—those who received minimal services and those who received intensive services. Secondary comparisons, testing the Andrews et al. theory, suggested that "appropriate care," that is, intensive case management and services, did not modify the criminal behaviors of supposedly receptive delinquents.

Although the individualized case management provided through the Willie M Program seems reasonable in theory, its effectiveness would certainly depend on whether the case manager has an array of effective services from which to choose. Neither the present findings nor the evidence reviewed in the introduction provide a clear indication that a rich array of such services exist. (727)

Weisz et al. called for additions to services, "to employ precisely focused model treatment programs based on interventions for which success has been documented in treatment outcome research" (727). Unfortunately those documentations are not credible and are critiqued throughout the previous discussion. If the tests of those programs' effectiveness had been subjected to the rigor and research temper of the Weisz et al. analysis, they would have produced the same gloomy conclusions.

Yet a forceful and perhaps more accurate summary of the Weisz study might point away from their loyalties to psychotherapy and other minimal interventions and toward the problem of embedded social patterns of abuse. Their study offers little hope—particularly because of their uncertainty about whether mandated services were actually received, that is, whether the service system blocked the intentions of the courts —that superficial services can compensate for the violence visited on poor and minority groups, in this case, by Southern culture.

The study has deep meaning for both corrections and social services. Intensive services—at least as delivered under court direction through the Willie M Program—made little difference to the futures of juvenile offenders and seemed unable to reduce criminal recidivism. If important changes are to occur, then much more powerful efforts to change social and personal behaviors are required, in this case for juvenile corrections, but also more broadly for other populations of need: the mentally ill, the poor, near poor, and those on welfare, recipients of social services and social work services, and so forth.

A Summary: Juvenile Delinquency Programs

Weisz et al. is a rare instance of skeptical and thorough social service research. Weisz et al. seemed capable of walling off their results from their own professional preferences—in this case a commitment to psychotherapy. Yet failing to randomize subjects, Weisz et al. did not definitively test the impact of the Willie M Program. Nevertheless, it is excellent preliminary research, screening outcomes through a sophisticated voice of doubt.

Yet the small critical tradition, articulate in corrections, is still not an effective counterfoil to false claims of effectiveness. The rehabilitative ideal persists without credible proofs of effectiveness and blocks out the possibility of experiments that consider more intensive, more humane, and more promising alternatives. Nothing seems to work; reported studies of promising leads are not credible; and the interventions themselves are superficial, inadequate, and sometimes cruel.

Drug Abuse

Much of the drug abuse literature fits a common pattern. Essays, summaries, and research reports begin with the nature of the problem they are investigating, discuss the consistency of past failures, and then make a statement to the effect that although little has worked there are still hopeful leads. The report or study then describes the preferred intervention, coming to the conclusion that it is effective on the basis, invariably, of "empirical" evidence.

Yet in the end, the drug abuse literature contains few studies of outcomes and none of them are credible. Few are even rigorous in a preliminary sense such as Weisz et al.'s evaluation of the Willie M Program. Not one essay can point confidently to a body of reassuring evidence. Rumors of success have been spread in a back-alley sort of a way through fugitive publications, frequently government reports, that sidestep any independent or critical review. The disjuncture between the rhetoric of the literature and the quality of its proofs is wide, profound, and when it comes from government agencies, disturbing. Government misrepresentation, most recently in battlefront reports from its War on Drugs, has apparently been serving electoral needs for good publicity.

The federal government's lead program agency on substance abuse prevention, the Office of Substance Abuse Prevention (OSAP), is pressing eight strategies focused on the individual, the peer group, education through parents, schools, student assistance programs, teachers, the mass media, and law. It can offer no evidence of effectiveness for any of its approaches, attempting to prove its effectiveness through six unevaluated case studies (Amatetti 1989). The National Institute on Drug Abuse (NIDA) and the National Institute of Mental Health (NIMH), the principal federal research agencies that study substance abuse, have also failed to identify effective programs.

The common theme running through all of the failures, which is the practical equivalent of all of the drug abuse prevention and treatment programs, has been unacknowledged: the interventions are weak and inadequate to address the problem. Definitions of the problem itself—the fundamental bridges into treatment theory—remain unmodified by empirical evidence, testifying to the doctrinaire immovability of social attitudes and professional stakes in handling drug abuse. Addiction services are caught up with the rituals of rationality —reported in the outcome studies—and with the political convenience of their superficial interventions that reaffirm faith in professional care.

Yet children who become addicted are rarely the products of caring, stable families, attentive schools, and effective communities. The number of adolescent addicts is an index, and a very powerful one, of the failure of the American culture, the breakdown of its basic institutions of socialization. Among poorer groups, there are few surrogates for these failures. As a result, drug addiction is more frequent and its effects are more profound in poorer communities than in wealthier populations. While many adolescent addicts may be vicious and irredeemable—drug fiends for a previous generation—they have been deprived of customary American rights of protection.

If drug abuse is to be prevented and treated, either the customary institutions of American culture need to be provided to deprived populations at adequate levels, an immensely expensive enterprise, or techniques need to be developed that break the circuit of deprivation and addiction. Effective shortcuts—either in their preventive form or as treatment for addiction—have not been demonstrated.

In this sense, outcome research is more than a managerial technique to improve efficiency; it tests political policy. OSAP's own consultant on prevention program evaluation, while discounting the importance of the research in the field, could not get around the many failures to demonstrate rehabilitation or prevention:

> The majority of evaluation studies of individual programs—not only in prevention research but in all of social science research—have failed to find positive outcomes for psychosocial interventions, thus making the transfer of research findings to the field of psychology, mental health, social services, and of course prevention, particularly problematic. . . . One significant outcome of this situation is a tendency for some critics to forcefully denounce entire programs of professional practice. . . . Instead of examining the various levels at which their evaluation might have failed, the researchers concluded a basic tenet of prevention philosophy should be discarded. (Bernard, 497-98)

OSAP's consultant recommended peer programs to prevent substance abuse on the basis of a meta-analysis by Tobler (1986). The consultant identified 98 studies from among Tobler's 143 that met the consultant's inclusion criteria: quantitative outcome measures, control or comparison groups, subjects in grades six through twelve, and primary prevention as a goal ("i.e. assisting youth to develop mature, positive attitudes, values, behaviors, skills, and life styles") (Bernard, 501). However, more than one-third of these studies were fugitive reports, never emerging in refereed journals. Very few utilized randomization or nontreatment controls. The interventions were invariably weak and the outcomes were frequently ambiguous, small, and dependent upon researcher assessments of outcomes and the self-reports of subjects.

But of particular note, few of Tobler's 98 studies directly measured *drug abuse prevention*. They measured attitudes and behaviors that were assumed to relate, *eventually*, to drug abuse. Few of Tobler's studies directly compared the differential incidence of drug abuse in an experimental group that received the peer program and a control group that did not. In addition, as Bernard points out, the majority of Tobler's studies were not focused on prime populations of risk but on relatively affluent, younger children who even in the absence of the experimental interventions were unlikely to abuse drugs. Another of the OSAP's principal consultants recommended a series of prevention strategies without citing a single instance of a credible demonstration of their effectiveness (Amatetti, appendix H).

Methadone maintenance for heroin addicts and the associated pharmacological treatments (LAMM, naltrexone, and others) have come as close as any to approximating a cure (Nirenberg and Maisto 1987). But this "cure" stretches the common sense of the term. More than 60 percent of those in methadone programs abuse other substances. There are also a number of side effects to the different drugs. In the few instances of successful maintenance on methadone the success rates were associated with the patients' maturity and social stability. The inability of research to separate these factors and others that are unrelated to the methadone maintenance program from the power of the program itself—a confounding of factors—may have the perverse political effect of retarding the emergence of programs that can produce true abstinence for highly motivated addicts. These misleading studies serve to justify a program that only offers an alternative addiction, although one that is less socially disruptive than heroin.

Moreover, some of the so-called abstinent in methadone programs (as in others) are simply reducing their tolerance for heroin, having developed a habit they cannot afford. These false cures will relapse as soon as the addicts' needs are reduced to affordable levels. Methadone is characteristically ineffective with juveniles. It also treats only a very small proportion of the drug abuse problem. Yet even while it fails to address the characteristic problems of addiction or the largest portion of addicts or to offer true cure, methadone maintenance is the most successful of all programs to treat drug abuse.

Two NIDA reports (Beschner and Friedman [1979] and Friedman and Beschner [1985]) provided state-of-the-art assessments of treatments for adolescent drug abuse. Their review touched on the variety of adolescent drug services and programs: individual, group, family, and peer counseling, meditation, supervised work experience, educational services, referral services, vocational training, runaway houses, group homes, free clinics, day-care centers, therapeutic communities, halfway houses, outpatient clinics, school programs, and youth centers.

Even the apparently successful drug programs have not been able to offer proof of their effectiveness, since few youth-serving agencies have the research capacity or resources to conduct adequate program evaluations. As a result, there are limited treatment options for youthful drug abusers, their families, and for the community or court referral systems who must arrange for drug treatment without adequate assurance of its suitability. (1985, 537)

The long list of services have failed to put forward any credible proof of their effectiveness even while "apparent" successes are frequently reported in a fugitive literature of qualitative research, annual reports, program descriptions, and personal testimonials. The youth-serving agencies, customarily dominated by professionals, view evaluation as a threat to their missions. The Door, "an innovative total approach" to adolescent drug abuse, is typical of these sorts of rumored successes. It was reported as a program success in both state-of-the-art reviews.

The Door

The Door in New York City offers troubled and drug abusing adolescents a comprehensive array of free professional, paraprofessional, and volunteer services—"psychiatric counseling, sex counseling, nutrition counseling, an information and contact center, educational/vocational counseling, legal counseling, a rap line/hotline, creative workshops, an in-service training program, and drug education and community outreach programs." The Door's services are predicated upon a variety of assumptions: the effectiveness of professional techniques, most notably counseling and psychotherapy, the need for coordination among professional helpers, and the sufficiency of these services in curing adolescents.

But the Door has not been evaluated nor have any of its funding sources insisted upon rigorous accountability. To the contrary, Friedman and Beschner (1985) accepted the Door's own qualitative self-report for inclusion in the federal government's state-of-the-art review of youth drug treatment programs (Shapiro in Friedman and Beschner 1985, Smith in Beschner and Friedman 1979). Belief in the efficacy of the Door has been the product of its good public relations, its staff's social acuity in fund-raising, and its obedience to the voluntaristic dictates of a conservative Republican administration.

In fact, the Door is so special that it has the pick of New York City's vast client population. The Door has established formal eligibility criteria for admission to their services (and their staff may apply informal criteria) that screen out the highest-risk youths. It is an act of faith to conclude that their services are either effective or that their chosen client group is in need of such intensive care. Moreover, the Door's pattern of seeking out wealthy patrons and the evangelical style of their staff reinforce the private sector orientation of social services, a traditional strategy of service that has been ineffective against social problems.

The Door is a paradigmatic case of the belief that scarce resources should be spent on a client group that can benefit the most from them. Yet this program, and the human services generally, cannot demonstrate their engineered ability to successfully treat even the most susceptible client groups. The possibility will remain strong that any success that emerges from the Door is simply the result of a selection bias in choosing clients. Moreover, by resisting independent evaluation and by straining to control perceptions of its worth, the Door undercuts its own claims for advocacy on behalf of needy adolescents. Is it protecting its clients or is it building an undeserved reputation for its staff?

In the most crucial sense, the Door is not an experiment in social services but a reinforcement of the revelatory style in discovering hopeful leads. If the Door is delivering so-called intensive care at the frontiers of professional knowledge and it is not successful, then other remedies are required. Conversely, if that care is successful, then it is important to establish the causes or at least the conditions of success. The failure to provide an adequate picture of outcomes at the Door, as well as in other programs for youth and in the human services generally, deprives the society of an accurate view of its problems. It also deprives youth of an effective voice on its behalf.

The environment of the Door is exactly wrong for its "experimental learning laboratory" and any other research that its own staff may conduct. Any attempt to test its potential effectiveness is susceptible to the expectancy biases of its organizational assumptions mediated through the dogma of its staff. The initial stumbling block to credible outcome data lies in professional self-interest but the deeper impediment, that tolerates such intransigence, is located in the motives of the culture itself. The myth of professional altruism and the myth of social efficiency are natural allies.

Beschner and Friedman (1979) also included a report of the most comprehensive quantitative study of program effectiveness available at that date. Between 1969 and 1973, the Drug Abuse Reporting Program

(DARP) "collected patient reports on 43,943 clients who were admitted
to treatment for drug abuse at fifty-two agencies located throughout the
United States and Puerto Rico." This massive activity was conducted on
contract between NIDA and the Institute of Behavioral Research at Texas
Christian University. Sells and Simpson report on follow-up interviews
with a subsample of youths. The reports were apparently filed by the
treatment programs themselves, not by independent research staffs. The
near 44,000 reports produced a research file of almost 28,000 reports,
representing an immense loss of data due to patient noncompliance, and
a variety of other "substantive" factors.

The data compared the effectiveness of methadone maintenance,
therapeutic communities, outpatient drug free programs, and detoxification programs. Sells and Simpson report that at the time that treatment
was terminated,

> the gross outcome results . . . showed substantial reductions of drug use and
> criminality during all treatment and smaller but statistically significant improvements
> on other criteria as well (productive activities, employment, beer and wine consump-
> tion). Overall, methadone maintenance showed more effects than other types, par-
> ticularly no opioid use and criminality.

The completion rates for treatment were extremely low: only 14
percent of the youth assigned to methadone maintenance completed
treatment, 15 percent completed therapeutic communities, 27 percent
completed drug free outpatient programs, and 25 percent completed
detoxification programs. On the basis of the follow-up data, Sells and
Simpson report that treatment gains were largely maintained.

However, the follow-up interviews apparently did not include a
urinalysis, relying upon patient self-reports. The follow-up sample was
probably not representative, as the authors acknowledge, of the base of
young patients in DARP, while that base itself was not representative of
those in treatment. Moreover, approximately 45 percent of the data was
lost due to censoring.

In addition, patients were not randomized to the different treatment
modalities while the base of participating drug programs was itself not
randomly selected from the many thousands of programs then operating.
Presumably the programs that participated in DARP were among the
more motivated and therefore may have represented a superior quality.
There were no nontreatment or placebo treatment controls.

Program attrition was immense and the reported outcomes were very mixed. No outcomes were independently validated. But even the few positive outcomes, impaired as they were by a faulty methodology, could not be attributed to treatment since few youths completed their treatment plans and the study did not include any basis (nontreatment or placebo treatment controls) on which to estimate natural remission.

In short, DARP was a very expensive data collection effort, funded by the federal government and conducted by a compatible university, that failed to provide credible or representative information. Its incompetence, even within a field of weak research, is monumental; DARP tromped into almost every possible pitfall of research. Moreover, the presentation of DARP's follow-up with youth in Beschner and Friedman is also frequently incomplete, dense, poorly edited, and undefined, suggesting perhaps a conscious attempt to mislead.

Friedman and Beschner (1985) report on a more current but similar outcome data set, the Treatment Outcome Perspective Study (TOPS), that is also detailed in a more recent and comprehensive report (Hubbard et al. 1989). It studied the "natural history" of 11,750 drug abusers in publicly funded drug programs—fourteen residential treatment programs and eleven outpatient programs. The subjects consisted of all applicants for treatment to these programs in ten different communities from 1979 to 1981. The follow-up sample, interviewed one and two years after treatment, consisted of 375 adolescent patients of whom only 240 (64 percent) were successfully interviewed. Data was collected from questionnaires.

The findings followed predictable patterns: the report of drug-related problems declined during treatment. Follow-up interviews indicated that drug-related and other behaviors were improved compared with similar behaviors before treatment but were not as good as during treatment.

Criminal activity and the use of alcohol seemed to have increased. Hubbard et al. concluded that drug programs for adolescents showed "some positive outcomes." However, even this conclusion, modest at least in comparison with DARP, needs to be discounted. The study relied on interviews without urinalysis; it did not randomize subjects; its interview rate was very low and presumably it missed data from many program failures; it did not employ appropriate control groups and therefore could not attribute any of its findings to treatment; and finally, it had no ability to generalize from its patient sample to the population of drug abusers.

Although far more coherent in its write-up than DARP, and a bit more forthcoming, TOPS deserves a very similar judgment. Because of its many failures, it provides no credible information, even on a preliminary level of research.

It is reasonable to discount NIDA's state-of-the-art publications as government disinformation. The perceptions advertised by Beschner and Friedman have not been corrected or even tested in the nongovernment literature. Indeed, funding for that research customarily comes from the federal government, from the very office that produced the propaganda.

The American public has come to trust the probity of many federal agencies that collect data. The Census Bureau, the Bureau of Labor Statistics, and the National Institutes of Health, as three examples, have earned extraordinary reputations for careful research. The decennial census is one of the social science's few claims to art. Unfortunately the aura of these agencies has shielded others that need far greater scrutiny.

Each federal agency that produces credible information has been able to develop a constituency that allows it to do so. However, a large amount of federal data is produced by agencies that are vulnerable to frank political interference. Indeed, much federal data, especially concerning program outcomes, is produced by consultant firms and so-called think tanks whose profitability depends clearly on the favor of the agencies they are hired to evaluate. The inevitable competition of interests compromises accuracy and integrity.

The partisan contamination of objective data is endemic to government. It exists in one of its severest forms among the agencies charged with the evaluation of programs to treat and prevent drug abuse. Their community of scholars has not established strong traditions of independent research or other fire walls between program evaluation and sectarian stakes in reported effectiveness.

Drug services for adolescents as well as for adults have been ineffective. The research has been misleading even while frequently reporting failed interventions. The problems of DARP and TOPS are not structural impediments inherent in the nature of the programs and problems. They are the result of an inadequate will to evaluate outcomes and an unnecessary level of incompetence that is tolerated by the government—OSAP, NIDA, and NIMH.

Recent administrations setting out to degrade public service have succeeded. Indeed, the situation may be worsening as the public sector retrenches its commitment to social services. Outcome studies subsequent to Beschner and Friedman's two reports have provided little basis upon which to alter the judgments of ineffective programs and of poor quality research.

Recent Studies

Szapocznik et al. (1983) compared two methods of time-limited family therapy—one person and conjoint—for treating drug abuse. Families were randomized to the two treatment conditions. However, a nontreatment control was specifically not employed, the researchers judging that family therapy is an intervention of proven effectiveness: "a large body of literature has evolved that substantiates the effectiveness of family therapy approaches with a number of presenting problems, including adolescents' drug abuse" (896). Sixty-two hispanic families were accepted for the study having met the following criteria: at least one "drug-using" member between twelve and twenty years old who is neither psychotic nor in need of hospitalization nor in need of detoxication, at least two other family members who are willing to come in for therapy sessions. A battery of assessment instruments based upon videotaped sessions and patient self-reports were administered before therapy, after therapy, and at follow-up, which took place six to twelve months after therapy.

The authors concluded that "the two time-limited therapeutic interventions developed as part of this study for use with this population were found to be highly effective at termination and follow-up, thus suggesting that it is possible to make effective interventions with this population without the necessity of long-term therapy" (896). However, only thirty-seven of the sixty-two families in the experiment completed at least four therapy sessions and both the pre- and post-test assessment. This produces an initial attrition of 40 percent. Only twenty-four of these thirty-seven completed the follow-up assessment. Thus the study's analysis is compromised by an attrition of 61 percent. Attrition in drug studies is a basis of presumed failure.

Furthermore, the measures were highly suspect and amenable to the biases of the researchers. Videotaped sessions may not capture typical client behaviors. The so-called neutral raters were not independent of a stake in family therapy generally; they were also aware that all subjects were in therapy and thus inclined to judge improvement over time. The extent of drug abuse was measured by self-report and not independently verified by urinalysis.

Even more injurious to the claims of the researchers for the broad applicability of their findings, the clients were probably not typical of the problem of drug abuse, even within the hispanic community. The study did not establish the severity of the problem among the youngsters. Moreover, the sample of families sought out therapy and presented themselves with their children for sessions. They were obviously highly motivated to correct the problem among their children. This is even truer of the group that survived attrition.

At every point, the research tolerated biased selection processes that culled the sample for success. In the end, the research itself and its acceptance for publication expressed the ambitions of the field more than any possibility that twelve sessions of family therapy is a hopeful lead in curing drug abuse among adolescents.

Dolan et al. (1985) was somewhat more successful in their use of contracting. Contracting is a common and popular therapeutic process by which patients and counselors decide on specific goals for treatment, sanctions for failing to abide by the contract, and rewards for achieving goals.

Eleven of their patients were successful, ten were not. However, only two of the eleven successes were severe abusers prior to contracting while eight of the ten failures were severe abusers. The degree of abuse during the baseline period predicted almost all of the outcomes. No control group was employed by the study and therefore it is not possible to assess the degree to which natural remission of moderate abuse may account for the findings. The follow-up period was only sixty days.

The utility of this questionable success with moderately abusing methadone maintenance patients was circumscribed by a very small and selective patient sample of older addicts and the use of relatively severe sanctions. Without a very powerful incentive, it would not seem to be a promising lead, especially for juveniles. Moreover, the degree of success, especially within the limitations of the study's design, fails to provide a sanction of enduring efficacy for the use of strong aversive motivators in the treatment of drug addicts. This observation is made *a fortiori* for the case of youngsters.

Magura et al. (1987) tested the value of contracting in a methadone maintenance program serving 350 patients in New York City. The authors reported mixed outcomes. "The findings indicate that behavioral contracts were much less successful in curbing drug abuse than in promoting other behavioral changes, perhaps because the rewards offered could not compete with the more powerful attraction of drug use or because these clients were not yet emotionally ready to deal with their drug problem." Drug abuse here meant the use of illicit drugs while in the program and not a reduction in the licit addiction to methadone. Of the eleven contracts for illicit drug use, only two succeeded. Twelve of the sixteen nondrug-related contracts succeeded.

However, even these modest outcomes need to be discounted by the study's many problems. While the drug contract outcomes were presumably tested by urinalysis, the other "behavioral" outcomes were not rated objectively, relying upon patient report and observation. The success of contracts was judged only shortly after treatment. Contrary to the authors' claims, the study did not take place under "typical" conditions. While the clinical setting may have been typical of other clinics, the introduction of research, especially without any blind ratings of "behavioral" outcomes, probably distorted the representativeness of the test itself.

Furthermore, the client population was not representative of the underlying addict population. Their sample was older, average age was thirty-four, and more than most other factors, age tends to predict cure. They were in a methadone maintenance program and therefore they were presumably more motivated than those outside of methadone programs. They were an elite group even within this population, having been selected for contracting because of their appropriateness, that is, their maturity; only twenty-four patients out of a caseload of 350 were selected for contracting. In addition, the research utilized no comparison group of any sort.

The more appropriate conclusion is that even under optimal conditions with motivated clients, no important treatment effect (those related to drug use) was achieved while the "behavioral" changes were poorly substantiated, of indeterminate value, and probably transitory. Nevertheless, the authors insisted upon a number of conclusions that have "implications for practice." In a bit of professional breast beating, the authors pushed forward their conclusion that social workers with master's of social work degrees were apparently more successful than the paraprofessionals and their one colleague with a counseling degree.

Yet the methodology of their study could not test this conclusion. (Perhaps the paraprofessionals, naively expecting a drug program to change addictive behaviors, focused more on the drug contracts.) The shreds of wisdom that the authors pluck out of their research (short-term contracts, older patients, etc.) testify to their refusal to acknowledge the common canons of objective research. The value of contracting in treating addicts was not demonstrated. Based upon Magura et al. contracting is not a hopeful lead for adults and therefore it may even be more futile for adolescents.

Hawkins et al. (1988) found empirical support in the social service literature for a large number of professional and low-cost approaches to identify, prevent, treat, and control juvenile delinquency and drug addiction: early childhood education with parent involvement, life skills training in schools, cognitive interpersonal skills training, proactive classroom management, law-related education, problem solving and behavioral skills training, social influence strategies in schools, enhancement of instruction to broaden academic success, and school-based health clinics. These strategies "have shown promise in reducing identified risk factors for delinquency and drug abuse. However, for the most part, the effectiveness of these strategies in reducing actual rates of delinquency and drug abuse among high-risk groups remains to be demonstrated. . . . Additional work is needed in this area" (278–79).

In fact, any reasonable reading of their evidence, much of which has already been covered in this and other chapters, leads to the far more reasonable observation that no promising leads have been identified while the professional literature has consistently recommended additional work for itself without accurately addressing the effectiveness of prevention and treatment programs.

Hawkins et al. carry the scuffed baggage of psychotherapy into the delinquency and drug abuse arena. Their credulity is self-serving; their selection of evidence is remarkably incomplete; their presentation of "promising" data is misleading; and they refuse to address the ineffectiveness of current programs except inferentially as a failure to employ appropriate professional insights. Their unsystematic, incomplete coverage of the literature, their biased reporting, and their enthusiasm for counseling recall earlier unsophisticated attempts to bolster partisan stakes in the factional world of program funding. Yet their essay is the most sophisticated and complete statement, at least within the social work literature, of the response of the human services to these problems.

McAuliffe (1990) estimated the effectiveness of a group relapse prevention program. One hundred sixty-eight newly recovering opioid addicts in Hong Kong, Massachusetts, and Rhode Island were randomly assigned to either the experimental group, Recovery Training and Self-Help (RTSH), or to a control condition. Urinalyses were performed as a part of all interviews.

McAuliffe reported a small success for the study's minimal interventions: "subjects who participated in the RTSH program were significantly more likely to remain opioid free or to use opioids less often than were their control group counterparts" (208). In the United States 36 percent of RTSH and 23 percent of the control group remained abstinent for the entire one-year follow-up period, a treatment gain of only 13 percent. Results for abstinence were similar in Hong Kong.

If abstinence, and not just the decrease of drug intake, is the goal of the program, then the relapse rate of the experimental American group was approximately 65 percent. If intermittent use and rare use are also accepted as cure, then relapse was only about 50 percent in this group. Yet *relapse* rates represent failures among the small group of those who have already *successfully* completed an initial course of treatment while this latter group represents a very small fraction of those who either enter treatment or are addicted to drugs. Therefore, even low relapse rates indicate high failure rates. High relapse rates, such as those in McAuliffe, represent enormous failure rates.

The enormous failure rates are associated with very weak interventions. This would seem to be a reasonable outcome. The short-term and shallow interventions of drug treatment programs are inadequate to compensate for the large social and psychological deprivations in addition to the physiological dependencies associated with chronic drug abuse. The theories of professional intervention that predict cure on the basis of these programs are obviously incorrect.

Yet even McAuliffe's small success needs to be adjusted. The control, while probably a true randomized condition, was not a true placebo. The denial of the experimental condition may have itself discouraged or disheartened the fragile desire of former addicts to stay abstinent. The differences between groups were so small that just a few recovering addicts affected in this way would have negated the findings. Furthermore, while urinalyses were taken at each interview (that is, at six months and twelve months), they were not taken consistently throughout the study period. Therefore, opioid use largely depended upon self-report. Finally, the substitution of other drugs, notably alcohol, for opioids was not measured.

Yet for all of its problems, McAuliffe may be the single most credible piece of research in the current drug rehabilitation literature. It is certainly not definitive while it sketches a very bleak picture of addiction and treatment. Among a motivated, mature, and highly screened group of former American addicts, only 31 percent may have remained abstinent for one year after treatment. This represents a much lower cure rate when measured against the far larger number entering treatment or the huge number who abuse drugs. Within the McAuliffe experiment itself, the ability of at least one type of treatment to cure addiction is questionable. Against the broader problem it is insignificant.

Carroll et al. (1991) employed clinical trials to compare the effectiveness of two types of psychotherapy in preventing relapse among cocaine abusers. Even using far more convenient criteria for success (three weeks of abstinence during treatment and three weeks of abstinence afterwards), they found no statistically significant differences between their treatment and control groups. Even though this finding seemed to corroborate MacAuliffe, it was far less credible.

Ignoring the logic of their own research, the authors inventively concluded that "indicators of clinical significance (attrition, proportion of subjects recovered or abstinent) generally supported the effectiveness" of the experimental condition over the control condition, especially for severe cocaine users. But clinical significance depends at a minimum upon statistical significance while the differential attrition between groups invalidates the study itself, raising additional questions about imperfections in its design, namely the absence of blinding. There was nothing in Carroll et al. that contradicted bleak assessments of psychotherapy or psychotherapy outcome research.

Power and Truth

In 1990 the NAS published a heartening overview of drug abuse treatment (Gerstein and Harwood 1990). As one reviewer noted, "most readers of this journal will be relieved to hear that the committee concludes that it is a 'good bet' to put more money into drug treatment" (Gossop, 1163). The NAS committee that was charged to come up with the report, reviewed the current literature, acknowledged a few of the methodological problems of the research, but still concluded that

> treatment reduces the drug consumption and other criminal behaviors of a substantial number of people. . . . There are large variations in effectiveness across programs, which seem to be related to the varying quality of clinical management and competence. . . . The length of time in treatment is a very important correlate of outcome. . . . The benefits of treatment programs on the whole outweigh their costs, but variations in cost-benefit methodologies and results are great. (134–35)

The report failed to put the outcome literature through any sort of skeptical review, accepting self-reports, nonrandomized studies, uncontrolled studies, expectancy biases, and so forth as constituting "a significant controlled observational literature." The committee ignored the possibility that factors outside of treatment—particularly patient creaming, aging, self-motivation, natural remission, and socioeconomic factors—accounted for its limited positive outcomes. It refused to look at the variability in outcomes as a sign that the base of research may be biased, reflecting different program and researcher stakes more than the reality of treatment. TOPS and DARP were accepted as definitive data sets along with other improbable, uncorroborated and unreplicated studies. But none of the studies that the NAS relied upon, not one, provided credible proof of treatment efficacy. A more restrained conclusion would have indicted the quality of research, concluding that treatment for drug abuse is a still experimental procedure of questionable value.

Instead, NAS tilted one of the essential pillars of science—skepticism, the obligation of the intervenor to prove efficacy—in support of unproved conjecture, providing the cachet of science to convenient belief. This report was not a surprise, considering the composition of the study committee.

The report was contracted for by NIDA, the government agency most culpable in producing the current body of misleading drug abuse research and an organization that is deeply committed to treatment. Two of the members of the committee resigned during the course of the study to accept positions in the Office of National Drug Control Policy, Executive Office of the President—the office of the nation's "drug czar." The other NAS committee members had also been deeply involved in producing the treatment literature, including Hubbard, the principal author of TOPS.

More than simply misinterpreting the available outcome data, the NAS process that created this influential report distorted the essential ability of a scientific subcommunity to reach objective assessments by intruding professional and institutional stakes—the pursuit of government contracts, funding success—into the research process. This is the triumph of power over truth. It is the characteristic process by which universities, think tanks, commercial firms, and other scientific organizations eventually learn to conform with the wishes of government.

The Influence of the Research in Delinquency and Drug Abuse

The extended effect of this poor research is to deprive social policy arenas of an accurate view of the resources and conditions that are required to deal with delinquent and drug-abusing youth. If delinquents are to conform to more lawful patterns of behavior, they may need a far greater amount of service than the funded experiments were equipped to deliver or the researchers were willing to acknowledge. Where there seems to be a legitimate change of behavior—usually in elaborate, high-service residential programs—the costs are huge, usually more than the median income for a family of four. These are not promising leads.

Scholarly interests thrive on lengthy consecutive argumentation, the give and take between advocates and critics. Yet the shorter run policy debate is more affected by the initial announcement of positive findings that corroborate contemporary social beliefs than by whether those findings pass a test of time. The apparent failure of deinstitutionalized services for delinquent youth is still resisted by many researchers who stubbornly insist upon both the fact and the potential for socially efficient community-based rehabilitation programs.

The critical tradition in delinquency and drug programs, as in other program areas, has had little impact on public policy. The happy findings and the promising leads of each new generation of rehabilitation programs, although faulty and incomplete, have a greater influence in maintaining the contemporary myths for efficient treatments than later critical analyses have in grounding those enthusiasms in fact.

The "promising leads" for reducing juvenile crime fall into a similar pattern of poor, partisan research. Contemporary proposals for novel policy changes, in particular, Wilson and Herrnstein's fashionable neoconservative thirst for retribution, are stuck with the same weak empirical base. "Definitive" conclusions carry no greater scientific authority than other speculations on the causes and cures for crime.

The legacy of CTP, expressed in its programmatic lineage as well as in other recent social experiments, competes with the tradition of science. These experiments were conducted to test the wisdom of public policies that inspired a variety of approaches to juvenile delinquency and drug abuse. Most of them were similarly flawed, bending to pressures for social compatibility. In spite of their ostensible commitment to scientific tests of program outcomes, few of the research staffs prevented professional stakes from distorting their reported outcomes.

Conclusion: Nothing Has Worked

The heart of the matter is cure—long-term abstinence from drugs and lawful behavior. The best of the relapse studies claimed that they succeeded with perhaps 50 percent of their patients. But these 50 percent were those who had gone through therapy successfully—detoxifying and then remaining abstinent during their treatments. A wildly high estimate would put this figure at 50 percent. But those who entered detoxification and treatment programs were a very small fraction, certainly less than 10 percent of the huge number of addicts. In the end then, a very generous estimate is that curative services are successful with less than 5 percent of the addict population.

But this estimate is far too generous; the truer figure reflects relapse rates that are well above 70 percent and in reference to McAuliffe, probably around 85 percent for even highly amenable populations. Short-term cure rates are certainly less than 50 percent while the population that enters treatment is more motivated toward abstinence than the general addict population. A more realistic estimate would peg cure at less than 1 percent of the addict population and less than ten percent of the population presenting themselves for services.

But even this tiny figure probably overestimates the curative power of services. Without true randomized, placebo controls, the possibility remains that a patient's maturity, not services, accounts for abstinence. This is likely and, in its own convoluted manner, is acknowledged by the literature. Therapists consistently state that the motivation of clients is a necessary precondition for cure while motivation is typically associated with maturity and age. Therapy has had little if any demonstrated ability to motivate patients, that is, to substitute for the life experiences that create maturity.

The researchers have neglected the plausible hypothesis that their interventions may not be necessary or sufficient conditions of cure. Typically, abstinence is achieved only within an immensely structured and controlled environment. When these controls are removed relapse occurs. A small population ages out of addiction and crime. The general prognosis for positive outcomes may be even bleaker for youth. Young people may be less affected by the natural pressures to conform with societal norms that are imposed over time—biologically by age and socially through learning.

The literature occasionally approaches this sort of conclusion. More customarily it publishes misleading and reassuring evidence that socially efficient solutions are possible. The Musto claim—that drug addiction is a periodic phenomenon that has never been successfully handled through social interventions—has not been refuted. Yet there is no rational or empirical basis to accept any of the vast array of socially efficient recommendations to handle drug addiction and juvenile delinquency. Their proofs of effectiveness are flawed from their first assumptions, tendering inadequate substitutes to compensate for the severe deprivations of addicts and delinquents.

The view that delinquency and addiction are chronic problems requiring permanent and expensive solutions may be correct. The proofs for more hopeful alternatives are social propaganda in the service of a low-tax, low-service social philosophy and not the products of science in pursuit of remedies. It is therefore understandable that many of the claims for success—Shapiro's description of the Door is typical—appear in fugitive form, avoiding scrutiny of their claims.

Taken as a whole, the literature may have been more successful in identifying what does not work than what does. They seem to have covered the range of inadequate and superficial interventions. They have also covered a portion of the continuum of rehabilitation that dips into cruelty. Yet they have not tested the effects of providing humane and relatively permanent environments to youngsters deprived of the common conditions of American culture: a personal, long-term special relationship with at least one responsible adult, access to education, supervised social interactions (a formal way to say "community"), and so forth. These conditions cost a lot of money, especially if they are going to be provided to those at risk of delinquency in addition to adjudicated delinquents.

Yet studies that fail to show experimental group improvement frequently claim that their experimental interventions cost less than standard care and are therefore preferable, in the end perversely instituting greater deprivation in the name of altruism. Thus, even failed attempts to demonstrate effectiveness may further the stakes of American society in ever more socially efficient solutions. Yet whatever their actual outcomes—bogus proofs of benefit or the proofs of equivalence—the studies obdurately refuse to measure their long-term effects.

The only position that seems tenable is a "very firm version of 'nothing works.'" In denial, Andrews et al., Palmer, Amatetti and many others continue the true-believer tradition in the human services. The think tanks reinforce it. The federal government funds it.

In spite of the years of activity, the many research projects, and a cloying moralism, the human service professions offer no reliable way to rehabilitate or to prevent juvenile delinquency. The problem seems to be a true dilemma, there is a big price for any choice. Political demands for low-cost social programs will prevent any resolution of the problems of delinquency and drug addiction. Alternative structural solutions, by requiring great resources from wealthier populations will result only from great political turmoil, an unlikely occurrence. The final choice, neglect, is cruel and dangerous.

Nevertheless, public policy still pursues the myth of efficient rehabilitation. Neither OSAP's fanciful approach to prevention nor the Urban Institute's truisms of the need to involve "the school, the home, the media, the community and local government" in solutions are matched with recommendations to provide adequate resources to do so. Each strategy, having consumed millions of dollars to develop, turns away from the needs of the youths and the intractability of their problems.

They also tacitly deny the pervasive failures of programs to achieve even modest levels of success.

Their vacuous recommendations quietly shift the burden of social responsibility from the public sector, that is, from the shoulders of the culture in its collective form, to those least able to afford the solutions. The effect of this hypocrisy is pious neglect, a renewal of hope for a revolution in human consciousness. It implements Musto's insight that addiction is typically modified through the gruesome process by which an abstemious generation learns its lessons from the suffering of its self-indulgent parents and grandparents.

This is not much of a solution; indeed it would seem to be the definition of failure. It may also be a somewhat optimistic view that exaggerates the influence of the family. In contrast, adolescent peer groups may be passing on addictive and criminal patterns unmoderated by parental influence. For many in America the institution of the family simply does not exist.

Without vastly increased funding to handle not only delinquents but those at risk of delinquency and addiction, there is no credible basis to expect the problems to be reduced. Fifteen thousand dollars per year is a very low estimate of the per capita costs for reasonable treatment, that is, to create an environment in which to repair the social deprivations of delinquents and addicts (or to put this in other terms, an environment that reduces the temptations to commit crime and maintain substance abuse, or in other terms still, the only environments in which crime and addiction seem to be reduced). If only one percent of the culture is either addicted or involved in crime or both (a very low estimate) then 37.5 billion dollars—more than the entire AFDC budget for 1990—would be required, half being spent on youngsters. The bill climbs much, much higher for services with any reasonable chance at preventing addiction and delinquency. These are very improbable expenditures.

6

Conclusion: The One-Percent Solution

The myth of social efficiency—that scientific social cures are possible, are cheap, and are consistent with prevailing social arrangements—has warped the social services. Social efficiency and its convenience for a conservative political agenda inspire ineffective social programs. The inadequacy of social services does not stem from the many nostalgic and emotional forms of the myth, powerful as they are; rather, services are inadequate because the myth is not viable for those who are poor, addicted, delinquent, disturbed, or are without families, education, or jobs. The inexpensive, superficial, short, and weak interventions of the social services cannot resolve their problems.

Mental health services do not restore people to mental health nor protect those who are debilitated. Welfare services neither provide adequate welfare nor do they offer solutions to dependency. Juvenile delinquents are not reformed. Addicts are not rehabilitated. Social casework is ineffective, probably across social need. But the literature of the human services does not describe the depth of these failures. It expresses the stakes of practitioners and of the prevailing social ethos in the myth of efficient solutions.

The perfusion of this myth throughout the American culture denies remedy to people without adequate access to social institutions. The myth blots out of the public consciousness the prolonged gravity of its own social problems, the severity of its social needs, and the true bill for approximating solutions.

Compassion, understanding, and insight may indeed be of great value to people in trouble. The standard virtues may cure and prevent. The social service professions may have fractionated, recombined, and applied the milk of human kindness in an especially efficient and powerful form to social problems. But the literature of the social services has not provided any credible basis upon which to accept the effectiveness of psychotherapy, social rehabilitation, or any other inexpensive and non-disruptive intervention to cure and prevent social problems. Even under optimal test conditions, socially efficient interventions have not demonstrated a capacity to achieve even their narrow service goals. In general field situations they have been hopelessly ineffective—one-percent solutions, if even this much—confirming the guileless observation that nothing seems to be working.

The community of social service professionals has made its peace with a political and social process that has assigned to social services the symbolic role of caring without providing resources to fulfill a substantial care giving function. Without those resources, no solution is possible to America's domestic social problems even while they eat away at its economic and cultural viability.

Effectiveness and Political Choice

The scope of this analysis encompassed pressing social problems and central social services. It relied upon the best of the available scholarship and, when possible, the most sophisticated studies. Twenty years after Segal's essay, there has still not been one critical test of any social service program. The effectiveness of the social services is indeterminate at best. More probably, services are ineffective and perhaps even consistently harmful for many people. Rare individual studies—for example, Weisz et al.'s study of the Willie M Program—provided preliminary signs of true outcomes. Even fewer studies provided preliminary evidence for credible and hopeful leads. They were usually not replicated even once. None of the preliminary studies of program outcomes spawned a respectable descendant scholarship. None tested their underlying theories.

If the total number of people that the previously reviewed literature of the social services claimed were helped is reduced by the number of those people who were probably not helped and by the number of those people who did not need to be helped in the first place, then a very small number of people are left who may have been actually helped. Setting this small remainder of true benefits alongside of the substantial number of people who may have actually been harmed while they were being helped brings into very high relief the question of why the social services persist. They are certainly not effective when measured against any reasonable standard of cure, prevention, or rehabilitation. They are provided at such meager levels as to be incapable of giving substantial care.

This summary is largely atheoretical, speaking to the seminal issue of credible outcomes, not to derivative concerns with particular causes and remedies. Yet the social services as practiced constitute a tacit theory of social intervention—socially efficient solutions. The fact of their ineffectiveness implies that the strategy of social efficiency has been ineffective. Superficial, professionally oriented interventions do not prevent or cure social problems.

These observations about social services probably extend also to the education system and the health care system in the United States. The American educational system does not provide probably half of its citizens with adequate preparation for either employment or citizenship. Medical care in particular offers the conundrum of theoretical effectiveness (the efficacy of optimal care) and practical failure, especially as it affects lower income groups. For all of its vaunted sophistication, management science—the essence of health care delivery—has failed to engineer solutions to the problems of access, cost, and quality of medical services for huge numbers of Americans.

The ineffectiveness of social efficiency in the human services generally suggests that if social problems in the United States are to be effectively handled, then either different strategies need to be tried or the problems are inevitable and intractable, a position of radical fatalism. Radical fatalism places the sustaining causes of contemporary social problems so deeply in the nature of mans gene pool, the environment, and the collective human experience that no social intervention can conceivably modify those basic conditions. Two strategic alternatives are possible to radical fatalism: neglect or much greater intervention. Within the broader democratic framework of the United States, greater equality is very expensive to create.

American liberalism has been tied to social efficiency, symbolized by the Pygmalion myth, the belief that the trip out of a cockney underclass involves little more than the good wishes, charity, and avuncular lessons of an effusive and benign wisdom: a few hours, a few dollars, and discipline. It has built the aphorisms, fables, legends, and myths of modern culture onto the architecture of its patrician, Fabian ideals: redemption through education, science as socially curative, functional analysis, social engineering, the special nobility of the human heart and soul. Yet American liberalism as theory has not been supported by the lessons of its social service research. American liberalism as politics has offered only superficial approaches to resolve America's problems, refusing to acknowledge either the relatively permanent effects of social deprivation or the high costs for remedying them.

American liberalism as myth reconciles the nation to the inevitability of its current choices by hiding the deep disparities and inequities of American society behind the mask of social service effectiveness. The myth's decisive tenet and the source of its long-standing grasp on the nation's imagination is personal virtue, the notion of an instinctive preference for civic responsibility. Accordingly, social services offer only the opportunity for redemption; election is the will of God. This is expressed as the ponderous wisdom that social services are effective only when the patient is motivated to change, suggesting that seeking care is a moral act of penitence and excusing otherwise ineffective interventions.

American liberalism is surprisingly similar to American conservatism. The difference may lie largely in the degree to which different political parties reflect different professional constituencies. Engineers do better with Republicans; social service workers do better with Democrats. But the huge number of underserved people do about the same in any administration.

Neither party is willing to invest in costly remedies; the American people refuse to tax themselves sufficient amounts to resolve their social problems. These entrenched preferences are in turn reinforced by the current practice of the social services. Indeed, this mythic function is their principal role, especially in light of their consistent ineffectiveness to resolve their defining social problems.

The failure of liberal social policy has triggered the dilemma of American social welfare. Liberalism is not working. Neglect is morally repugnant if not actually counterproductive. In turn, the programs to achieve greater social equality face the historic parsimony of the American people. The Civil War did not produce a generous Freedmans Bureau. The economic depressions of the late 1800s and the twentieth century gave rise to reforms that still left much of the nation in need.

The reforms of the 1960s seem in retrospect to be a public relations flop; the nation never actually funded its many planning initiatives. The New Frontier and the Great Society stalled on the issue of redistribution.

The problems of poverty and social opportunity were unable to attract a sufficient constituency. Indeed, economic growth itself is a questionable antidote to any but the problem of income poverty for some.

In recent decades, liberal impulses and constituencies have been channeled into procedural reforms that frequently benefitted a largely middle-class constituency. Each reform had its own merits but each reform ignored the deeper social problems of huge numbers of Americans. The anti-Vietnam War movement, the consumer movement, the women's movement, the environmental movement, and the neoconserv-ative and fundamentalist movements marked off greater distances from the problems of poverty, unemployment, fractured communities, poor education, and failing families. Each movement, initially claiming broad social meaning, came to represent in the fact of its agenda, benefits for only a fraction of its members. In this way, the women's movement and the civil rights movement, as two examples, effectively represented the interests of their professional and mobile constituents, largely neglecting the needs of far poorer women and minorities. The paid victors in these movements frequently voiced the comforting belief that their successes would inspire similar benefits for the waiting lists of their less fortunate fellow persons.

Social service agencies are themselves the repositories of these movements. These agencies are the service organizations that deliver care and, broadly conceived, they are also the public and private agencies that plan, administer, and fund those services: voluntary and charitable organizations such as the United Way, philanthropic foundations, state and federal agencies, and legislative bodies and their committees. Staff appointments and decisions about who to serve reinforce the political successes of their constituent groups. Loyalty, but not skill, wisdom, or commitment to service, is the bedrock qualification for hiring, promotion, and care. This political process operates at the price of effective services. Social service agencies that function as political clubhouses prefer to avoid objective scrutiny.

In this way social service has become as narcissistic as American liberalism, serving the mobility aspirations of wealthier constituent groups—their boards, their staffs, their funding sources—at the price of their service populations. Historic attempts to make agency boards accountable to their service populations (e.g., pressure for community control in the poverty programs of the 1960s) failed. The dilemma of

American social welfare dominates the actuarial futures of more than half of its citizens. This is a prescription for immense social disruption: social need may yet give rise to an effective political response. But contrary to Cloward and Piven and the rest of the chop-sockie school of social protest, there is little in American history to nurture the hope that socially and economically marginal groups will press their grievances. They customarily suffer their deprivations silently. The problems they cause are political issues not political acts.

Belief in the effectiveness of any social service is not the judicious result of scientific objectivity and logic. It is not the result of sorting through a paradox of conflicting but still credible evidence. That evidence is nonexistent. Belief in the effectiveness of psychotherapy, corrections, rehabilitation, social work, and the rest is a self-serving act of faith.

The Communal Enterprise of Research: Professional Convenience and Myth

What explains the persistence of social services? They are not effective nor have they ever been. Neither Rothman nor Leiby make claims for their effectiveness. Rothman in discussing prisons and mental institutions argues that asylums were an administrative convenience. Leiby suggests that the persistence of the social services lies in their service to the interests of the business elite. Yet human services are administratively convenient and satisfying to business only because they are socially efficient.

This is their "main effect." The social services sustain the myths of a popular ideology, social efficiency. Service to social efficiency is not a jury-rigged, ad hoc function, but a part of the chassis of modern culture that reconciles large portions of the society to their social and economic fate. This acculturation implies that essentially ineffective services are promoted as effective and that unremedied problems are considered to be fixed or at least to be tolerable.

In a subtle, even sly way, the social context of social problems has been replaced by the individual's intractability as the sustaining explanation of social distress. Teenage promiscuity replaces the neglect of children as the operant cause of the welfare problem; laziness, not the absence of jobs, as the reason for unemployment; stubbornness and inborn intellectual incapacity, not a poor educational system and deficient home life, as the reasons for failure in school; black culture, not social neglect, as the reason for telling ethnic differences. In return for a reasonable income and a professional's social status, the human services have abandoned people in need. This is a Faustian bargain.

Recent innovations in outcome research, particularly an enchantment with single subject designs, are scientific eccentricities that subvert rigorous methods for evaluating services. Credible research—the randomized placebo controlled trial—is feasible. But not one credible and definitive study has emerged from the social service research.

The "practical" accommodations of the social service outcome research have mediated the expectancy biases of the researchers. Faulty studies have become the indexed and alphabetized wisdom of the applied social sciences.[1] The community of social service scholars does not cherish and nurture the scientific spirit of tough skepticism. It is structured for unquestioning belief.

The contract research process, largely financed by the federal government, has undermined the critical tradition in the human services generally. Contracts for outcome research are typically awarded as part the process of justifying an organization's budget. The organization that funds the research is frequently also tied to the organization that is evaluated (sometimes it is the same organization). Funding organizations —Congress, state legislatures, and private and public agencies —are the audience for the research. Budget justifications customarily entail evidence of program effectiveness or at least progress in achieving goals. The culture respects scientific evidence. Social scientists most often reside in universities and private research firms that, whatever their charters may say about nonprofitability, are fixed on accounting sheets. These are the settings for the soap opera of social program evaluation.

Government grants for human services research have customarily been directed toward the faithful and the compliant. Research funded by state government and private sources, most notably by the Rockefeller Foundation and the Ford Foundation, have had the same effect. The poor methodological quality and the biases of the literature are tributes to the influence of the funding sources over the community of social service scholars. But those political motives, centered on proving the effectiveness of socially efficient programs, express the preferences of the culture. They are not the conspiratorial successes of hidden actors and will not be remedied by tinkering with the charters of private foundations or by closer oversight of the federal contracts process.

The peer review process in federal research grants for human service evaluation generally has not withstood the political demands of successive administrations. It has failed to find a cushion of support in either academia or professional organizations. The universities as well as the so-called think tanks—National Academy of Science, Brookings Institution, Rand Corporation, Urban Institute, MDRC, and many others—are professional bounty hunters. Their unremitting pressure on faculty and staff to raise money encourages scholarly concessions to the ambitions of funding sources. In addition, the contract research firms—"the shadow government," "the Beltway bandits"—have no pretense about their function; they are in business to satisfy a client, not an abstract notion of scientific truth.

This degradation of public service has proceeded quickly under recent administrations that invoked the panacea of private enterprise. However, it would not have been possible without the widespread support of the American people. The policies that cheapened public service were popular.

The deep impediment to credible evaluations of outcomes lies in the dominance of popular social values within intellectual community itself and not simply in the narcissism of social scientists. Notably, the statistics discipline, priding itself as the gatekeeper of science, has not guarded the gates. Indeed they have been among the accommodationists, finding excuses in the pilot and preliminary nature of investigations to justify their consultative relationships with patently misleading research. They have not been prominent critics of social service outcome research, the income maintenance experiments being a prominent case. They have been largely silent.

More than simply technical flaws, the failures of method, objectivity and skepticism are failures of a communal enterprise. The community of social service scholars has sidestepped the career risks of applying the spirit of science to the practice of evaluation. It has been dominated by its own social ambitions.

The social "clinic" is demonstrably neither safe nor effective. Social services are delivered without safeguards against harm and, lamentably, without a structure that would produce credible information or even modest accountability for vulnerable target groups. Moreover, the recent fashion of privatization has created a promiscuity of profit-making human service enterprises that all but gut even the thinnest pretense to effectiveness or human concern.

If an accurate picture of American social problems—including assessments of programs to resolve those problems—has value, then the practice of evaluation research needs to be overhauled. Evaluative research is obviously at risk when conducted by practitioners or researchers with a stake in the outcomes.

The critical tradition in the human services has been an ineffective counterweight to the force of the prevailing orthodoxy. Wootton has obviously had little effect on the course of the field's interests. This can also be said of Martinson, the Lipton group, Haveman, Cook and Shadish, the Sechrest group, and the Prioleau group. Even Weisz et al., good soldiers marching under the regimental banner of psychotherapeutics, mute the impact of their findings.

Criticism is an act of faith in rational discourse—the application of scientific method within a scientific community of scholars—and its contribution to a humane civic culture. In light of the contemporary social and economic problems of the United States, the distortions of social service research may not hold for long. But there is no reasonable basis to argue that a failed community of scholars will yield to a more durable and truthful scholarship. The business of the social services is embedded in ineffective but still politically useful and popular programs.

The Business of the Social Services

The human services—medical care and public health, education, and the social services—constitute the largest employment sector in the nation. By themselves the social services are an immense business. But unlike industry or even the other human services, the ideological value of the social services in sustaining the myth of social efficiency dominates their putative production functions in resolving social problems.

American industry has long acknowledged the profitability of a positive image. Advertising budgets are large; corporations play social roles to complement the reveries of their consumers; product packaging is designed to enhance sales. Yet image, advertising, and packaging are tangential to the quality of the product itself. Product quality is the essential function of industry, the single most important characteristic contributing to profit, and the principal playing field of long-term competition. The ideological meaning of a product is secondary; it is important, but still secondary. This relationship is inverted in the social services.

As the mythic vehicles of social efficiency, social services have been quite successful in reconciling the deprived to their fate and in forestalling the prospect of massive redistribution. Social service agencies abet their mythic influence by co-opting the natural dissent of deprived groups. Agencies offer jobs—prestigious opportunities, the noble burden of altruistic service—to the emerging leadership of deprived groups that gives them a personal stake in those organizations and blunts the edge of their opposition. This is an old story in the United States told pointedly by Dollard and by DuBois, and more recently by Marris and Rein.

The business of social efficiency is conducted like any other, except that a political goal is substituted for a true production function and compatibility, not profit, is the bottom line. In this way, the human services create a surreal maze of meaning by using rational terms for largely cultural and political events.

As in any commercial area, a variety of tasks are conducted by many different organizations: innovation, adaptation, marketing, pricing, sales, consumer affairs and government relations. Social service agencies "price" the value of an emerging problem or program novelty in a social "election" of competing target groups and program novelties. The total cost of solutions, that is, the relative amount of the existing service pie or, much less frequently, additional moneys, is set in a marketplace of political factions. Agencies, representing different needs and different services, auction their attractiveness to competitive bidders—funding agencies. It is always a buyers market.

In individual communities, the private sector, largely expressing itself through the United Way, sets the market for benevolence by maintaining an annual competition between agencies that fixes social priorities. The private voluntary sector also typically sets the agendas and budgets of public agencies. It is the very rare community either today or in the past that has experienced a healthy conflict between the United Way and government.

Because the federal budget dominates public financing and because public financing of social services overshadows private and philanthropic giving, the national political arena—courts, administration, Congress, lobbies, and the vague polled presence of the national will—has grown proportionately in influence. Most players in Washington politics have local, organized constituencies. The exceptions are usually the secondary organizations—such as management consultant firms, think tanks, and the like—that service the play of power. The essential component is not cure, prevention, or rehabilitation, but the satisfaction of constituent groups.

Once the value of an emerging issue is fixed, either locally or nationally, the social service business implements the new priority through budget allocations and by influencing existing organizations to reallocate budgets and services and, if necessary, by creating new service organizations. The pressure to conform is applied through representative and interlocking boards of directors and through funding, which is often the same thing. The boards are largely drawn from commerce, the professions, and the moneyed, traditional upper class or their proxies. The minority of board positions are reserved for local leadership, staff and union members, representatives of client groups, and clergy. This selection obviously confirms American values. The grander appointees are usually reserved for grander agencies.

It is very difficult to maintain the position that the influence of these social elites and the popularity of their values is the result of an insider's game and not the result of popular preferences. These board members—and the same can be said of elected and appointed public officials—are icons of American aspirations. They seem to hold their positions by popular consent if not actually by popular election.

The immensely rich, overlapping, complex, and deep organizational structure of social decision making in the United States—politics—has produced a national policy that represents majoritarian values even while it may not be just, equitable, adequate, rational, or wise. These values are deeply embedded in the consciousness of a generation and give coherence to its social experience. They perfuse the entire culture, articulating the rib of social services with the spine of socialization, adaptation, and control. These values must change if the nation's social problems are to be addressed, an unlikely event in light of their long-standing popularity.

With a near annual regularity program novelties such as Rolfing, sleep learning, imaging, GGI, community care, and deinstitutionalization are invented to address emerging priorities as well as to handle older ones more efficiently. At this time, the early 1990s, the needs of children appear to be the rising fashion in benevolence, capturing the curative attention of the nation's "third sector"—its nonprofit, philanthropic community.

The business of the social services, animated by a philosophy of social efficiency will probably determine the fate of the emerging concern with children's needs, starkly measured by the single fact that 20 percent of America's children live in poverty and only half of them are touched by public welfare. Poverty in the United States largely prevents access to those cultural institutions that are necessary to prevent personal and social problems. Attention to children, therefore, is a logical focus of attempts to handle social problems generally. More than simply symbolic, to fail with children is to fail with virtually the core of social distress.

The history of fashions in social philanthropy—the elderly, poverty, women's issues, juvenile delinquency, heart disease, smoking, lung cancer, and prior enthusiasms for the needs of children—suggests that the current push for children will probably also conform to a traditional pattern:

Item: The United Way of America is setting up a nonprofit corporation that will devote at least 20 years—the span of a generation—to helping communities reverse the 'alarming' erosion in the well-being of children.

Item: The nation's Catholic bishops have issued a moral appeal to public officials to "put children first," and the head of Catholic Charities USA said he sometimes feels at his wits' end because "all the soup lines and shelters won't do as much for children as enlightened public policy."

Item: Thirty-two community foundations across the country have formed a loose alliance that will serve children in what, for them, is a daring new way—by engaging in public advocacy, community organizing and media campaigns. "We want to do for children's issues roughly what the designated driver program did for the drunk driving issue—help bring about a fundamental change in society's attitudes," said Jan Kreatmer, president of the Greater Kansas City Community Foundation. (Washington Post 13 January 1992, A1)

Children's needs are vast, entailing immense expenditures for food, clothing, shelter, schooling, supports and substitutes for families, day care, tutoring, and so forth. But the response to those needs is curtailed by the refusal to come up with money. Two days after announcing the new initiatives, the Washington Post reported that the more generous of the current school reform bills in the U.S. Congress "seeks to spend $850 million on several thousand public schools, while part of [the President's] plan asks for $1 million each for 535 new experimental schools nationwide" (Washington Post 15 January 1992, A7). This amount is not sufficient to make a dent in the front fender of education in even a moderate size community.

Valuing the needs of children at a serious funding level requires a proportionately large and serious constituency. This is lacking. Children, particularly those with problems and those deprived of adequate access to social institutions, are not attached to parents or groups that effectively politicize their needs. The cultural reality of children is circular: poorer children, that is, those with unmet needs, tend to be attached to poorer parents who live in marginal communities with an economic status that parallels their political weakness and results in fewer enforceable claims on resources to address, once again, the needs of poorer children. After all, the current situation itself seeped through a political soil that enriched supportive blocks of voters and stunted those without a political voice.

Those proposing a new initiative for children are in reality only proposing that their needs should become the new priority in social services. There is no serious proposal to lift the long-standing fiscal limitations of American social policy. This means simply shifting existing funds toward the needs of children and away from those groups who have not maintained their position in the marketplace of benevolence. In this round, children may edge out offenders, the elderly, the mentally ill, or street people. Moreover, following the example of Headstart, many program beneficiaries will not necessarily be among those for whom the program was initially intended. Professional stakes in assuring successful outcomes and pressures from the better organized of the recipient groups will tend to cream a less deprived group of children for care.

Following traditional patterns, the solutions will tend to be focused on professional care—where the constituency lies—in a way that pays a dividend to socially efficient programs, their agencies, and their boards.

But this kind of care nibbles on the edges of children's needs and in the political economy of national opinion militates against substantial budget allocations. It allows a very credulous public to take comfort in symbolic cures that conform with the socially efficient assumptions of American social welfare: voluntary action instead of institutionalized services; private agencies instead of public organizations, the dominance of commercial, not social definitions of the national interest; psychological explanations of social problems, not attention to the imperfections in the society itself. Overall, the charitable impulse is also tempered by the flavor of moral failure, the hint that the problems of children reflect the promiscuity, sloth, and intemperance of their parents and the caution that taking care of the children in some fashion encourages a libertine disregard of personal responsibility.

The problems of children have always been prominent. Their plight in contemporary America has been annually updated. Their needs are known with an unusual precision. Yet neither the United Way of America, the good bishops, nor the philanthropic foundations are willing to take the courageous step beyond popular values and make claims upon the public treasury.

The business of the social services mediates the dilemma of American social welfare: solutions for social problems must conform with popular cultural values; those values deny a large redistribution of resources; yet social needs require immense expenditures. It will be surprising if the current trend in children's problems produces even a one-percent solution. Nevertheless, there has never been a society as wealthy as the United States nor has the United States ever been as rich as it is now.

Implications

"What we know . . . ," an awful gnomic conceit, is actually very little. This ignorance is painful. There are few hopeful leads, if any at all, that cost a little and do a lot. Social engineering has failed. Social problems have not been successfully analyzed to identify causes that could be controlled. The art of prediction in the social services has not gone much past Delphi and tout sheets.

Measuring the plight of the poor and near poor largely in terms of income and wealth obscures the fact that the principal avenues of exit from poverty depend upon much greater provision of immensely expensive cultural institutions—jobs and job training, supportive services (such as day-care), families and education—and not simply the provision of income, money, or even work by itself. The disparity in average income between the poor and the middle, large as it is, still underestimates the chasm of need that divides their separate cultural experiences.

Small income gains over the past few decades have not had a material impact on the lives of poorer groups, especially as those dollar gains were associated with greater unemployment, awful schools, and deteriorating communities. The profits of a buoyant economy will not address their problems. A social investment needs to be drawn from the deep pool of existing resources, not the margins of new wealth, if their problems are to be addressed.

There is a tendency for income and wealth to be associated with cultural success. But money is frequently associated with cultural failure. Many wealthy people are drunks, addicts, criminals, spouse beaters, lazy, crazy, socially irresponsible, and morally reprehensible. The productivity of the managerial and professional middle class may not justify the enormous resources their training absorbs or the enormous salaries their skills command. Indeed it is not at all clear that income and wealth have been invested in any sort of optimal pattern to derive the highest social benefit for the United States.

Without proofs of effectiveness, the helping professions lack rational authority—expertise. Yet the principal problem in searching for effective solutions to social problems is political. There is little support for the large changes required to create greater social equality. The problem of constituency bedevils progressive change.

Accuracy is a just advocate. Hiding the failures of social services denies the gravity of need. The stratification of American society, that is, the degree to which opportunities and institutional advantages are differentiated by socioeconomic position, is an important topic only if these socioeconomic disparities produce enduring and undesirable consequences. If social rehabilitation could easily remedy these consequences, then it would undercut arguments for more thoroughgoing, structural changes. In this sense, the failure of weak interventions to remedy the problems of American social stratification opens the door to more powerful programs. Denying the reality of current failures reduces the possibility for true remedies.

A Final Word

Although swamped by their mythic function, the social services do have a production function: the provision of food, clothing, care and comfort, shelter, family and community, protective services, and so-called support services—in short the common institutions of American life where they do not naturally exist. Social services as well as many other human services have customarily been designed to fulfill this surrogate role, providing substitutes for failed and absent social institutions, notably the family. Foster care for children is the apotheosis of this role. But these services have been so restricted and poorly financed, the widow's mite, that they patently cannot fulfill even their most modest goals. Social service agencies have been very silent about their failures, a silence that is rarely interrupted by the social sciences. On their part the social sciences have largely ignored the proposition that the gross intensity of simple care, a program's ability to replicate customary social institutions, has the greatest predictive value for cure, prevention, or rehabilitation.

Without an immense infusion of resources, any resolution of America's social problems is hopeless. Yet many poorer Americans consistently vote against greater equality. The dilemma of American social welfare persists because those who stand most to gain hold social values that contradict their basic interests.

The literature of the social services can be read as a denial of greater spending for the basic institutions of a humane civic culture, an attempt through myth to ignore stark cultural failure, supplanting it with the fiction of cure, prevention, and rehabilitation. The imposition of this mean spirited little lie through social service agencies—the insistence that their graphic inadequacies are really scientific experiments in social salvation—subverts their production function in favor of ideological service to more favored groups.

The serious pursuit of greater social equality is by default the only humane alternative to current policy. It will assure many more Americans a similar, adequate experience in the culture's critical institutions: family, school, community, work. These institutions are the vehicles of the American formula for a humane civic culture: security, personal fulfillment, a living wage, social and political participation and responsibility, health, freedom of expression, status, and respect. These observations are almost banal, the aphoristic truths of the American belief in equality. Educate to have educated people. Employ to have employment. Good families produce good people; and good people create good families.

The truisms stop at cost. The common and deep institutional failures of American society have produced an enormous number of people who are problems for their neighbors and for themselves. The provision of more equal experiences with these institutions would cost an amount that would change the social face of the United States. The refusal to do so sets a cruel dilemma for American culture: current conditions are intolerable, reform is inadequate, deep change is improbable.

Note

1. See as examples, The National Association of Social Workers' *The Encyclopedia of Social Work*, the anthology by Specht and Gilbert, Bergin and Garfield's *The Handbook of Psychotherapy and Behavior Change*, Kadushin's *Child Welfare*, and the multitude of behavior therapy textbooks previously cited.

References

Akabas, J., M. Fine, and R. Yasser. 1982. "Putting Secondary Prevention to the Test: A Study of an Early Intervention Strategy with Disabled Workers." *Journal of Primary Prevention* 2(Spring):165-87.

Alden, L. 1989. "Short-Term Structured Treatment for Avoidant Personality Disorder." *Journal of Consulting and Clinical Psychology* 57(6): 756-64.

Alexander, P. C., R. A. Neimeyer, V. M. Follette, M. K. Moore, and S. Harter. 1989. "A Comparison of Group Treatments of Women Sexually Abused as Children." *Journal of Consulting and Clinical Psychology* 57(4): 479-83.

Amatetti, S. K. 1989. *Prevention Plus 2*. Rockville, MD: Office of Substance Abuse Prevention.

Andrews, D.A., I. Zinger, R. D. Hoge, J. Bonta, P. Gendreau and F. T. Cullen. 1990a. "Does Correctional Treatment Work? A Clinically Relevant and Psychologically Informed Meta-analysis." *Criminology* 28(3): 369-04.

_____ 1990b. "A Human Science Approach or More Punishment and Pessimism: A Rejoinder to Lab and Whitehead." *Criminology* 28(3): 419-29.

Andrews, D.A., J.J. Kiessin, D. Robinson, and S. Mickus. 1986. "The Risk Principle of Case Classification: An Outcome Evaluation with Young Adult Probationers." *Canadian Journal of Criminology* 28: 377-96.

Andrews, G., and R. Harvey. 1981. "Does Psychotherapy Benefit Neurotic Patients." *Archives of General Psychiatry* 38 (November): 1203-08.

Annis, H. 1990. "Relapse to Substance Abuse: Empirical Findings within a Cognitive Social Learning Approach." *Journal of Psychoactive Drugs* 22(2): 117-24.

Association for Clinical Research. 1988. *Clinical Trial Procedure: Notes for Doctors*. London.

Atkinson, B. J., and P. N. McKenzie. 1987. "Family Therapy with Adolescent Offenders: A Collaborative Treatment Strategy." *American Journal of Family Therapy* 15 (Winter) 316-25.

Auspos, P. 1988. *Maine: Final Report on the Training Opportunities in the Private Sector Program*. New York:MDRC.

Azrin, N.H., V. A. Besalel, R. Bechtel, A. Michalicek, M. Mancera, D. Carroll, D. Shuford, and J. Cox. 1980. "Comparison of Reciprocity and Discussion-Type Counseling for Marital Problems." *American Journal of Family Therapy* 8: 21-28.

Bagarozzi, D.A., and P. Rauen. 1981. "Premarital Counseling: Appraisal and Status." *American Journal of Family Therapy.* 9(3): 13-30.

Baggs, K., and S.H. Spence. 1990. "Effectiveness of Booster Sessions in the Maintenance and Enhancement of Treatment Gains Following Assertion Training." *Journal of Consulting and Clinical Psychology* 58(6): 845-54.

Barlow, D. H., G. T. Obrien, and C. G. Last. 1984. "Couples Treatment of Agoraphobia." *Behavior Therapy* 15: 41-58.

Barton, C., J. F. Alexander, H. Waldron, C. W. Turner, and J. Warburto. 1985. "Generalizing Treatment Effects of Functional Family Therapy: Three Replications" *American Journal of Family Therapy* 13: 16-26.

Baucom, D.H., and G.W. Lester. 1986. "The Usefulness of Cognitive Restructuring as an Adjunct to Behavioral Marital Therapy." *Behavior Therapy* 17: 385-03.

Baucom, D.H., S. L. Sayers, and T. G. Sher. 1990. "Supplementing Behavioral Marital Therapy with Cognitive Restructuring and Emotional Expressiveness Training: An Outcome Investigation." *Journal of Consulting and Clinical Psychology* 58(5): 636-45.

Beach, S.R.H., and K.D. O'Leary. 1986. "The Treatment of Depression Occurring in the Context of Marital Discord." *Behavior Therapy* 17: 43-49.

Beck, D.F. 1975. "Research Findings on the Outcomes of Marital Counseling." *Social Casework* (March): 153-82.

Becker, E. 1973. *Denial of Death.* New York:Free Press.

Bedlington, M.M., C. J. Braukman, K. A. Ramp, and M. M. Wolf. 1988. "A Comparison of Treatment Environments in Community-Based Group Homes for Adolescent Offenders." *Criminal Justice and Behavior* 15(September): 349-63.

Behrens, B.C., M. K. Sanders, and W. K. Halford. 1990. "Behavioral Marital Therapy: An Evaluation of Treatment Effects Across High and Low Risk Settings." *Behavior Therapy* 21: 423-33.

Bell, C.S. and R. Battjes. eds. 1988. *Prevention Research: Deterring Drug Abuse Among Children and Adolescents.* Rockville, MD:National Institute on Drug Abuse.

Bellack, A.S., M. Hersen, and J. Himmelhoch. 1991. "Social Skills Training Compared with Pharmacotherapy and Psychotherapy in the Treatment of Unipolar Depression." *American Journal of Psychiatry* 138(12) (December): 1562-67.

Bennett, G. 1989. *Treating Drug Abusers.* Tavistock/Routledge: New York.

Berger, R.M. and S.D. Rose. 1977. "Interpersonal Skill Training with Institutionalized Elderly Patients." *Journal of Gerontology* 32: 346-53.

Bergin, A.E. 1980. "Negative Effects Revisited: A Reply." *Professional Psychology* (February): 93-100.

Bergin, A.E. 1975. "Individual Psychotherapy and Behavior Therapy" *Annual Review of Psychotherapy and Behavior Therapy* 26: 509-56.

Bergin, A.E. 1971. "The Evaluation of Therapeutic Outcomes." In *Handbook of Psychotherapy and Behavior Change*, edited by S.L. Garfield and AE Bergin. New York:John Wiley.

Bergin, A.E. and M.J. Lambert. 1978. "The Evaluation of Therapeutic Outcomes." In *Handbook of Psychotherapy and Behavior Change*, edited by S.L. Garfield and A.E. Bergin. New York:John Wiley.

Bergin, A.E., and R.M. Suinn. 1975. "Individual Psychotherapy and Behavior Therapy." *Annual Review of Psychology*. Palo Alto, CA: Annual Reviews.

Berlin, S. 1980 "Cognitive Behavioral Intervention for Problems of Self-Criticism among Women." *Social Research and Abstract* 16(Winter): 19-28.

Berk, R.A., R. F. Boruch, D. L. Chambers, P. H. Rossi, and A. D. White. 1985. "Social Policy Experimentation." *Evaluation Review* 9(4) (August).

Berman, J.S., R. C. Miller, and P. J. Massman. 1985. "Cognitive Therapy Versus Systematic Desensitization: Is One Treatment Superior?" *Psychological Bulletin* 97(3): 451-61. Bernard, B. 1989. "Peer Programs: The Lodestone to Prevention." In *Prevention Plus 2*, edited by S.K. Amatetti. Rockville, MD: Office of Substance Abuse Prevention.

Beschner, G.M., and A.S. Friedman, eds. 1979. *Youth Drug Abuse: Problems, Issues and Treatment*. Lexington, MA:Lexington Books.

Blanchard, E.B., F. Andrasik, T. A. Ahles, S. J. Teders, and D. O'Keefe. 1980. "Migraine and Tension Headaches: A Meta-analytic Review." *Behavior Therapy* 11: 613-31.

Bland, K., and R.S. Hallam. 1981. "Relationship between Response to Graded Exposure and Marital Satisfaction in Agoraphobics." *Behavioral Research and Therapy* 19: 335-38.

Blanchard, E.B. and F. Andrasik. 1982. "Psychological Assessment and Treatment of Headaches: Recent Developments and Emerging Issues." *Journal of Consulting and Clinical Psychology* 50(6): 859-79.

Blenkner, M., M. Bloom, and S. M. Nielsen. 1971. "A Research and Demonstration Project of Protective Services." *Social Casework* 52 (October): 489.

Bloom, M., and J. Fischer. 1982. *Evaluating Practice: Guidelines for the Accountable Professional*. New York:Prentice-Hall.

Boelens, W., P. Emmelkamp, D. Macgilla, and M. Markvoor. 1980. "A Clinical Evaluation of Marital Treatment: Reciprocity Counseling vs. System-theoretic Counseling." *Behavioral Analysis and Modification* 4: 85–96.

Boone, R., C. J. Coulton, and S. M. Keller. 1981. "The Impact of Early and Comprehensive Social Work Services on Length of Stay." *Social Work in Health Care* 7(Fall): 1–9.

Borkovec, T.D. 1982. "Insomnia." *Journal of Consulting and Clinical Psychology* 50(6): 880–95.

Botvin, G.L., E. Baker, L. Dusenblur, S. Tortus, and E. M. Botvin. 1990. "Preventing Adolescent Drug Abuse Through a Mutimodal Cognitive-Behavioral Approach: Results of a 3-Year Study." *Journal of Consulting and Clinical Psychology* 58(4): 437–46.

Brasilevsky, A., and D. Hum. 1984. *Experimental Social Programs*. New York:Academic Press.

Braukman, C.J. 1984. "Bad Apples, Silk Purses, and Birds of a Feather." *Contemporary Psychology* 29(8): 655–57.

Brekke, J.B. 1980. "Scientific Imperatives in Social Work Research." *Social Service Review* 55(4): 538–54.

Brock, G.W. and H. Joanning. 1983. "A Comparison of the Relationship Enhancement Program and the Minnesota Couple Communication Program." *Journal of Marital and Family Therapy* 9(4): 413–21.

Brom, D., R. J. Kleber, and P. B. Defares. 1989. "Brief Psychotherapy for Posttraumatic Stress Disorders." *Journal of Consulting and Clinical Psychology* 57(5): 607–12.

Brounstein, P.J. 1990. *Substance Abuse and Delinquency among Inner City Adolescent Males*. Washington, DC:Urban Institute

Brown, S.S., ed. 1991. *Children and Parental Illicit Drug Use: Research, Clinical, and Policy Issues: Summary of a Workshop*. Washington, DC:National Academy Press.

Bureau of the Census. 1991. Current Population Reports, Series P-60, No.174. *Money Income of Households, Families, and Persons in the United States: 1990*. U.S. Department of Commerce, Washington, DC:Government Printing Office.

———— 1987. *Census of Service Industries*. U.S. Department of Commerce, Washington, DC:Government Printing Office.

Bureau of Labor Statistics. 1991. *Employment and Earnings*. U.S. Department of Commerce, Washington, DC:Government Printing.

Burtless, G. 1990. "The Economist's Lament: Public Assistance in America." *Journal of Economic Perspective* 4(1) (Winter).

Butler, G., M. Funnel, P. Robson, and M. Gelder. 1991. "Comparison of Behavior Therapy and Cognitive Behavior Therapy in the Treatment of Generalized Anxiety Disorder." *Journal of Consulting and Clinical Psychology* 59(1): 167-75.

Carpenter, P.A. 1984 "'Green Stamp Therapy' Revisited: The Evolution of 12 Years of Behavior Modification and Psychoeducational Techniques with Young Delinquent Boys." *Psychological Reports* 54: 99-111.

Carroll, K.M., B. J. Rounsaville, and F. H. Gavin. 1991. "A Comparative Trial of Psychotherapies for Ambulatory Cocaine Abusers: Relapse Prevention and Interpersonal Psychotherapy." *American Journal of Drug and Alcohol Abuse* 17(3): 229-47.

Casey, R.J., and J.S. Berman. 1985. "The Outcome of Psychotherapy with Children." *Psychological Bulletin* 98: 388-400.

Clements, C.B. 1988. "Delinquency Prevention and Treatment: A Community-centered Perspective." *Criminal Justice and Behavior* 15 (September): 286-305.

Cloward, R., and F. Piven. 1971. *Regulating the Poor*. New York:Pantheon Books.

Cobb, J.P., A. M. Mathews, C. M. Blowers, and L. A. Childs. 1984. "The Spouse as Co-Therapist in the Treatment of Agoraphobia." *British Journal of Psychiatry* 144: 282-87.

Committee on Ways and Means. 1991. *Overview of Entitlement Programs* 7 May. U.S. House of Representatives, Washington, DC:Government Printing Office.

Conlisk, J. 1986. "Design Model Issues in Social Experimentation." *Journal of Human Resources* 21(4) (Fall) 563-85.

Cook, T.D., and J.R. Shadish. 1982. "Meta-Evaluation: An Assessment of the Congressionally Mandated Evaluation System for Community Mental Health Centers." In *Innovative Approaches to Mental Health Evaluation*, edited by G.J. Stahler, and W.R. Tash. Rockville, MD:Academic Press.

Cooper, N.A., and G.A. Clum. 1989. "Imaginal Flooding as a Supplementary Treatment for PTSD in Combat Veterans: A Controlled Study." *Behavior Therapy* 20: 381-91.

Cooper, S.E. 1983. "The Influence of Self-Concept on Outcomes of Intensive Alcoholism Treatment." *Journal of Studies on Alcohol* 44(6): 1087-93.

Craighead, W.E. 1976. *Behavior Modification: Principles, Issues, and Applications*. Boston:Houghton Mifflin.

Cross, D.G., P. W. Sheehan, and J. A. Khan. 1980. "Alternative Advice and Counsel in Psychotherapy." *Journal of Consulting and Clinical Psychology* 48(5): 615-25.

Daley, D.C., and M.S. Raskin. eds. 1991. *Treating the Chemically Dependent and Their Families*. Newbury Park, CA:Sage Publications.

Danziger, S., and R. Plotnick. 1981 "Income Maintenance Programs and the Pursuit of Income Security." *Annals of the American Academy of Political and Social Sciences* (January): 130-42.

Davidson, W.S., R. Redner, C. H. Blackely, C. M Mitchell, and J. G. Emshoff. 1987. "Diversion of Juvenile Offenders: An Experimental Comparison." *Journal of Consulting and Clinical Psychology* 55: 68-75.

Decker, S.H. 1985 "A Systematic Analysis of Diversion: Net Widening and Beyond." *Journal of Criminal Justice* 13: 207-16.

DeRubeis, R.J., M. D. Evans, and S. D. Hollon. 1990. "How Does Cognitive Therapy Work? Cognitive Change and Symptom Change in Cognitive Therapy and Pharmacotherapy for Depression." *Journal of Consulting and Clinical Psychology* 58(6): 862-69.

DeWitt, K.N. 1978. "The Effectiveness of Family Therapy." *The Archives of General Psychiatry* 35(May): 549-61.

Dolan, M.P., J. L. Black, W. E. Penk, R. Rabinowitz, and H. A. Deford. 1985. "Contracting for Treatment Termination to Reduce Illicit Drug Use among Methadone Maintenance Treatment Failures." *Journal of Consulting and Clinical Psychology* 53(4): 549-51.

Dollard, J. 1937. *Caste and Class in a Southern Town*. New Haven, CT:Yale University Press.

Dowling, T.H., and T.T. Frantz. 1975. "The Influence of Facilitative Relationship on Initiative Learning." *Journal of Counseling Psychology* 22: 259-63.

Druckman, D., and R. Bjork. 1991. *In the Mind's Eyes*. Washington, DC:National Academy Press.

Druckman, D., and J. Swets, eds. 1988. *Enhancing Human Performance*. Washington, DC:National Academy Press.

DuBois, W.E.B. 1931. *The Souls of the Black Folk*. Chicago:AC McClurg.

Dush, D., M. L. Hirt, and H. Schroede. 1983. "Self-statement Modification with Adults: A Meta-analysis." *Psychological Bulletin* 94(3): 408-22.

Dutton, D.G. 1986. "The Outcome of Court-mandated Treatment for Wife Assault: A Quasi-experimental Evaluation." *Violence and Victims* 1: 163–75.

Edelson, J.L., and M. Syers. 1990. "Relative Effectiveness of Group Treatments for Men who Batter." *Social Work Research and Abstracts* 26(2).

Emmelkamp, P.M.G. 1980. "Agoraphobics' Interpersonal Problems." *Archives of General Psychiatry* 37: 1303–06.

Emmelkamp, P.M.G., and I. deLange. 1983. "Spouse Involvement in the Treatment of Obsessive-Compulsive Patients." *Behavioral Research and Therapy* 21(4): 341–46.

Epstein, W.M. 1992. "Professionalization of Social Work: The American Experience." *Social Science Journal* 29(2): in press.

_____ 1990. "Rational Claims to Effectiveness in Social Work's Critical Literature." *Social Science Journal* 27(2): 111–28.

_____ 1984a. "Technology and Social Work, Part 1: The Effectiveness of Psychotherapy." *The Journal of Applied Social Science* 8(2): 155–75.

_____ 1984b. "Technology and Social Work, Part 2: Psychotherapy, Family Therapy and Implications for Practice." *The Journal of Applied Social Science* 8(2): 175–87.

Eysenck, H.F. 1965. "The Effects of Psychotherapy." *International Journal of Psychiatry* 1: 97.

_____ 1961. "The Effects of Psychotherapy." In *Handbook of Abnormal Psychology*, edited by H.F. Eysenck. New York:Basic Books.

_____ 1952. "The Effects of Psychotherapy: An Evaluation." *Journal of Consulting Psychology* 16: 319.

Falloon, F.R.H. 1982. "Family Management in the Prevention of Exacerbations of Schizophrenia." *New England Journal of Medicine* 306(24): 1437–40.

Feldman, R.A., and T.E. Caplinger. 1977. "Social Work Experience and Client Behavioral Change: A Multivariate Analysis of Process and Outcome." *Journal of Social Service Research* 1(1): 5–32.

Feldman, R.A., and J.S. Wodarski. 1984. "Comments on the Review of a Conundrum." *Social Work Research and Abstracts* 20(4): 27–30.

Feldman, R.A., J. S. Wodarski, and T. E. Caplinger. 1983. *The St. Louis Conundrum.* Englewood Cliffs, NJ:Prentice Hall.

Ferber, R., and W.Z. Hirsch. 1982. *Social Experimentation and Economic Policy.* Cambridge, England: Cambridge University Press.

Fischer, J. 1984."Revolution, Schmevolution: Is Social Work Changing or Not?" *Social Work* 29(January): 71–74.

_____ 1981. "The Social Work Revolution." *Social Work* 26(3): 199–209.

_____ 1978. "Does Anything Work." *Journal of Social Service Research* 1(3): 215-44.

_____ 1976. *The Effectiveness of Social Casework.* Springfield, IL:Charles C. Thomas.

_____ 1973b. "Has Mighty Casework Struck Out?" *Social Work* 18(4): 107-10.

_____ 1973a. "Is Casework Effective: A Review." *Social Work* 18(1): 5-20.

Fleischman, M.J., and S.A. Szykula. 1981. "A Community setting Replication of a Social Learning Treatment for Aggressive Children." *Behavior Therapy* 12: 115-22.

Fleiss, J.H. 1986. *The Design and Analysis of Clinical Experiments.* New York:John Wiley.

Frankel, H. 1988. "Family-Centered Home-Based Services in Child Protection: A Review of the Research." *Social Service Review* 62(1): 137-57.

Franks, C.M., and D.T. Mays. 1980. "Negative Effects Revisited: A Rejoinder." *Professional Psychology* 11: 101-05.

Frazier, C.E., and J.K. Cochran. 1986. "Official Intervention, Diversion from the Juvenile Justice System, and Dynamics of Human Services Work: Effects of a Reform Goal Based on Labeling Theory." *Crime and Delinquency* 32: 157-76.

Friedlander, D. 1988. *Subgroup Impacts and Performance Indicators for Selected Welfare Employment.* New York:MDRC.

Friedlander, D., M. Erickson, G. Hamilton, and V. Knox. 1986. *West Virginia: Final Report on the Community Work Experience Demonstrations.* New York: MDRC.

Friedlander, D., S. Freedman, G. Hamilton, and J. Quint. 1987. *Final Report on Job Search and WORK Experience in Cook County.* New York: MDRC.

Friedlander, D., G. Hoerz, D. Long, and J. Quint. 1985a. *Maryland: Final Report on the Employment Initiatives Evaluation* (December).

Friedlander, D., G. Hoerz, J. Quint, and J. Riccio. 1985b. *Arkansas: Final Report on the Work Program in Two Counties.* New York: MDRC.

Friedman, A.S., and G.M. Beschner. 1985. *Treatment Services for Adolescent Drug Abusers.* Rockville, MD:National Institute on Drug Abuse.

Friedman, L.M. 1985. *Fundamentals of Clinical Trials.* Littleton, MA: PSG Publishing Co.

Gambrill, E.D. 1977. *Behavior Modification: Handbook of Assessment, Intervention, and Evaluation.* San Francisco:Josey-Bass.

Gardner, M. 1989. *Science: Good, Bad and Bogus*. Buffalo, NY:Prometheus Books.

_____ 1988. Review of "Pseudoscience and Society in Nineteenth-Century America." *New York Review of Books*.

_____ 1957. *Fads and Fallacies in the Name of Science*. New York:Dover Publications.

Garrett, C.J. 1985. "Effects of Residential Treatment on Adjudicated Delinquents: A Meta-analysis." *Journal of Research in Crime and Delinquency* 22: 287-308.

Geismar, L.L. 1982. "Comments on 'The Obsolete Scientific Imperative in Social Work Research.'" *Social Service Review* 56(2): 246-58.

Geismar, L., and J. Krisberg. 1966a. "The Family Life Improvement Project: An Experiment in Preventive Intervention: Part I." *Social Casework* 47(November): 563-70.

_____ 1966b. "The Family Life Improvement Project: An Experiment in Preventive Intervention: Part II." *Social Casework* 47(December): 663-67.

Gelder, M. 1979. "Behavior Therapy for Neurotic Disorders." *Behavior Modification* 3(October): 469-95.

Gerstein, D.R., and H.J. Harwood, eds. 1990. *Treating Drug Problems. Vol. 1. A Study of the Evolution, Effectiveness and Financing of Public and Private Drug Treatment Systems*. Washington, DC:National Academy Press.

Giblin, P., and D.H. Sprenkle. 1985. "Enrichment Outcome Research: A Meta-analysis of Premarital, Marital and Family Interventions." *Journal of Marital and Family Therapy* 11(3): 257-71.

Gilbert, N., and H. Specht, eds. 1981. *Handbook of the Social Services*. Englewood Cliffs, NJ:Prentice-Hall.

Ginzberg, E. 1988. *Young People at Risk: Is Prevention Possible*. Boulder, CO:Westview Press.

Girodo, M, S. J. Stein, and S. E. Dotzenro. 1980. "The Effects of Communication Skills Training and Contracting on Marital Relations." *Behavioral Engineering* 6(2): 61-76.

Glaister, B., H. Berliner, and M. Ostrow. 1982. "Muscle Relaxation Training for Fear Reduction of Patients with Psychological Problems: A Review of Controlled Studies." *Behavioral Research Therapy* 20: 493-504.

Gold M., J. Mattlin, and S. W. Osgood. 1989. "Background Characteristics and Responses to Treatment of Two Types of Institutionalized Delinquent Boys." *Criminal Justice and Behavior* 16 (March): 5-33.

Goldman, B., D. Friedlander, J. Gueron, and D. Long. 1985. *Findings from the San Diego Job Search and Work Experience Demonstration.* New York:MDRC.

Gordon, D.A. 1988. "Home-Based Behavioral Systems Family Therapy with Disadvantaged Juvenile Delinquents." Unpublished paper. Ohio University.

Gordon, W.E. 1984. "Gordon Replies: Making Social Work a Science-Based Profession." *Social Work* 29(January): 74–75.

_____ 1983. "Social Work Revolution of Evolution?" *Social Work* 28(May):181–85.

Gorski, T. 1990. "The Cenaps Model of Relapse Prevention: Basic Principles and Procedures." *Journal of Psychoactive Drugs* 22(2): 125.

Gossop, M. 1991. Review of *Treating Drug Problems.* Gerstein and Harwood op. cit. *British Journal of Addiction* 86: 1163–64.

Gottfredson, G.D. 1987. "Peer Group Interventions to Reduce the Risk of Delinquent Behavior: A Selective Review and New Evaluation." *Criminology* 25 (August): 671–714.

Graham, L.R. 1987. *Science, Philosophy and Human Behavior in the Soviet Union.* New York:Columbia University Press.

Greenberg, D., and H. Halsey. 1983. "Systematic Misreporting and Effects of Income-Maintenance Experiments on Work Effort—Evidence from the Seattle-Denver Experiment." *Journal of Labor Economics* 1(4): 380–407.

Greenberg, D., R. Moffitt, and J. Friedman. 1981. "Underreporting and Experimental Effects on Work Effort: Evidence from the Gary Income Maintenance Experiment." *Review of Economics and Statistics* 63(4) (November): 581–90.

Greenberg, N. 1988. "The Discovery Program: A Way to Use Volunteers in the Treatment Process (Massachusetts Program)." *Federal Probation* 52 (December): 39–45.

Gueron J. 1990. "Work and Welfare: Lessons on Employment Programs." *Journal of Economic Perspectives* 4(1): 79–98.

_____ 1987. "Reforming Welfare with Work." *Public Welfare* 45(4) (Fall) (Reprinted from a monograph published by the Ford Foundation that appeared with the same title as Occasional Paper Number Two, Ford Foundation Project of Social Welfare and the American Future, 1987.)

_____ 1986a. *Work Initiatives for Welfare Recipients: Lessons from a Multistate Experiment.* New York:MDRC.

_____ 1986b. "Work for People on Welfare." *Public Welfare* 44(1): 7–12.

Gurman, A.S. 1973. "The Effects and Effectiveness of Marital Therapy: A Review of Outcome Research." *Family Process* 12: 145-70.

_____ 1986. "Research on Marital and Family Therapies." In *Handbook of Psychotherapy and Behavior Change*, edited by S.L. Garfield and A.E. Begin. New York:John Wiley.

Gurman, A.S., and D.P. Kniskern. 1978a. "Behavioral Marriage Therapy: II. Empirical Perspective." *Family Process* 17: 139-48.

_____ 1978b. "Research on Marital and Family Therapy: Progress, Perspective and Prospect." In *Handbook of Psychotherapy and Behavior Change*, edited by S.L. Garfield and A.E. Begin. New York:John Wiley.

_____ 1977. "Enriching Research on Marital Enrichment Programs." *Journal of Marriage and Family Counseling* 3: 3-11.

Haapala, D.A., and J.M. Kinney. 1988. "Avoiding Out-of-Home Placement of High-risk Status Offenders through the Use of Intensive Home-Based Family Preservation Services." *Criminal Justice and Behavior* 15 (September) 334-48.

Hafner, R.J. 1983. "Spouse-Aided Versus Individual Therapy in Persisting Psychiatric Disorders: A Systematic Comparison." *Family Process* 22: 385-99.

Hahlweg, K. 1982. "Treatment of Marital Distress: Comparing Formats and Modalities." *Advances in Behavior Research Therapy* 4: 57-74.

Hahlweg, K., and H.J. Markman. 1988. "Effectiveness of Behavioral Marital Therapy: Empirical Status of Behavioral Techniques in Preventing and Alleviating Marital Distress." *Journal of Consulting and Clinical Psychology* 56(3): 440-47.

Hall, A., and A.H. Crisp. 1987. "Brief Psychotherapy in the Treatment of Anorexia Nervosa: Outcome at One Year." *British Journal of Psychiatry* 151: 185-91.

Hall, J.A., and S.D. Rose. 1987. "Evaluation of Training in Groups for Parent-Adolescent Conflict." *Social Work Research and Abstracts* 23(1): 3-8.

Harris, M., and R. Rosenthal. 1988. "Interpersonal Expectancy Effects and Human Performance Research." In *Background Papers, Enhancing Human Performances: Issues, Theories, and Techniques*. Washington, DC:National Academy Press.

Hausman, J.A. and D.A. Wise. 1985. *Social Experimentation*. Chicago:University of Chicago Press.

Haveman, R.H. 1986. "Social Experimentation" *Journal of Human Resources* 21(4) (Fall): 586-605.

Hawkins, J.D., J.M. Jenson, R.F. Catalano, and D.M. Lishner. 1988. "Delinquency and Drug Abuse: Implications for Social Services." *Social Service Review* (June): 258-85.

Haworth, G.O. 1984. "Social Work Research: Practice and Paradigms." *Social Service Review* 58(3): 343-57.

Heineman, M.B. 1981. "The Obsolete Scientific Imperative in Social Work." *Social Service Review* 55(3): 371-97.

Heineman-Pieper, M. 1989. "The Heuristic Paradigm: A Unifying and Comprehensive Approach to Social Work Research." *Smith College Studies in Social Work* 60(1): 8-34.

_____ 1985. "The Future of Social Work Research." *Social Work Research and Abstracts*: 12-21.

Hill, D. 1989. "The Relationship of Process to Outcome in Brief Experiential Psychotherapy for Chronic Pain." *Journal of Clinical Psychology* 45(6)(November): 951-57.

Hoberman, H.M. 1988. "Group Treatment of Depression: Individual Predictors of Outcome." *Journal of Consulting and Clinical Psychology* 56(3): 393-98.

Hogarty, G.E., S. C. Goldberg, N. R. Schooler, and R. F. Ulrich. 1974. "Drug and Sociotherapy in the Aftercare of Schizophrenic Patients." *Archives of General Psychiatry* 31(November): 603-18.

Hogarty, G.E., N. R. Schooler, R. Ulrich, F. Mussare, P. Ferro and E. Herron. 1979. "Fluphenazine and Social Therapy in the Aftercare of Schizophrenic Patients." *Archives of General Psychiatry* 36(November): 1283-94.

Hollister, W.G., J. W. Edgerton, and R. H. Hunter. 1985. *Alternative Services in Community Mental Health.* Chapel Hill:The University of North Carolina Press.

Holroyd, K.A., and F. Andrasik. 1982. "Do the Effects of Cognitive Therapy Endure? A Two-Year Follow-up of Tension Headache Sufferers Treated with Cognitive Therapy or Biofeedback." *Cognitive Therapy and Research* 6(3): 325-34.

Holtzworth-Munroe, A., N. S. Jacobson, M. Deklyen, and M. A. Whisman. 1989. "Relationship between Behavioral Marital Therapy Outcome and Process Variables." *Journal of Consulting and Clinical Psychology* 57(5): 658-62.

Howard, K.I., S. M. Kopta, M. S. Krause, and D. E. Orlinsky. 1986. "The Dose-Effect Relationship in Psychotherapy." *American Psychologist* (February): 159-64.

Hsu, L.K.G. 1980. "Outcome of Anorexia Nervosa." *Archives of General Psychiatry* 37 (September): 1041–46.

Hubbard, R.L. 1989. *Drug Abuse Treatment: A National Study of Effectiveness.* Chapel Hill:The University of North Carolina Press.

_____ 1985. "Characteristics, Behaviors, and Outcomes for Youth in the TOPS." In *Treatment Services*, by Friedman and Beschner. Rockville, MD:National Institute on Drug Abuse.

Hudson, W.W. 1982. "Comments on 'The Obsolete Scientific Imperative in Social Work Research.'" *Social Service Review* 56(2): 246–58.

Iber, F.L. 1987. *Conducting Clinical Trials.* New York:Plenum Medical Book Co.

Imber, S.D., P. A. Pilkonis, S. M. Sotsky, I. Elkin, J. T. Watkins, M. T. Shea, D. K. Glass, F. F. Collins, and W. R. Leber. 1990. "Mode-Specific Effects Among Three Treatments for Depression." *Journal of Consulting and Clinical Psychology* 58(3): 352–59.

Irgens, E.M. 1936. "Must Parent's Attitudes become Modified in Order to Bring about Adjustment to Problem Children." *Smith College Studies in Social Work* 7(September):14–45.

Iverson, A., and D.H. Baucom. 1990, "Behavioral Marital Therapy Outcomes: Alternate Interpretations of the Data." *Behavioral Therapy* 21: 129–38.

Izzo, R.L., and R.R. Ross. 1990. "Meta-analysis of Rehabilitation Programs for Juvenile Delinquents—A Brief Report. *Criminal Justice and Behavior* 17(1): 134–42.

Jacobson, N.S. 1989. "Research-Structured vs. Clinically Flexible Versions of Social Learning-Based Marital Therapy." *Behavioral Research and Therapy* 27(2): 173–80.

Jacobson, N.S., W. C. Follette, D. Revensto, D. H. Baucom, K. Hahlweg, and G. Margolin. 1984. "Variability in Outcome and Clinical Significance of Behavioral Marital Therapy: A Re-analysis of Outcome Data." *Journal of Consulting and Clinical Psychology* 52(4): 497–504.

Jarrett, R.B., and R.O. Nelson. 1987. "Mechanisms of Change in Cognitive Therapy of Depression." *Behavioral Therapy* 18: 227–41.

Jaynes, G.D., and R.M. Williams. 1989. *A Common Destiny: Blacks and American Society.* Washington, DC:National Academy Press.

Jaynes, J.H., and C.A. Rugg. 1988. *Adolescents, Alcohol and Drugs.* Springfield, IL:Charles C. Thomas.

Joanning, H. 1982. "The Long-Term Effects of the Couple Communication Program." *Journal of Marital and Family Therapy* (October): 463–68.

Johnson, F.N., and S. Johnson, eds. 1977. *Clinical Trials* Blackwell Scientific Publication, Oxford E.J. Mullen 55(3).

Johnson, S.M., and L.S. Greenberg. 1985. "Emotionally Focused Couples Therapy: An Outcome Study." *Journal of Marital and Family Therapy* 11(3): 313-17.

Jones, J.A., R. Neuman, and A. Shyne. 1976. *A Second Chance for Families: Evaluation of a Program to Reduce Foster Care.* New York:Child Welfare League.

Kadushin, A., and J.A. Martin. 1988. *Child Welfare Services* New York:Macmillan.

Kagan, R. M, W. J. Reid, and S. E. Roberts. 1987. "Engaging Families of Court-mandated Youths in an Alternative to Institutional Placement." *Child Welfare* 66: 365-76.

Kane, M.T., and P.C. Kendall. 1989. "Anxiety Disorders in Children: A Multiple-Baseline Evaluation of a Cognitive-Behavioral Treatment" *Behavior Therapy* 20: 499-508.

Kazdin, A.E. 1977. *The Token Economy.* New York:Plenum Press.

1975. *Behavior Modification in Applied Settings.* Homewood, IL:Dorsey Press.

Kazdin, A.E., D. Bass, T. Siegel, and C. Thomas. 1989. "Cognitive-Behavioral Therapy and Relationship Therapy in the Treatment of Children Referred for Antisocial Behavior." *Journal of Consulting and Clinical Psychology* 57(4): 522-35.

Keane, T.M., J. A. Fairbank, J. M. Caddell, and R. T. Zimering. 1989. "Implosive (Flooding) Therapy Reduces Symptoms of PTSD in Vietnam Veterans." *Behavior Therapy* 20: 245-60.

Keeley, M.C. 1987. "The Effects of Experimental NIT Programs on Marital Dissolution: Evidence from the Seattle and Denver Income Maintenance Experiments." *International Economic Review* 28(1) (February).

Kirigin, K.A. 1982. "An Evaluation of Teaching-family (Achievement Place) Group Homes for Juvenile Offenders." *Journal of Behavior Analysis* 15: 1-16.

Kirkham, M.A., and R.F. Schilling II. 1989. "Life Skills Training with Mothers of Handicapped Children." *Journal of Social Service Research* 13(2):67-87.

Klein, M.W. 1986. "Labeling Theory and Delinquency Policy: An Experimental Test." *Criminal Justice and Behavior* 17(March):47-79.

Klosko, J.S., D. H. Barlow, R. Tassinar, and J. A. Cerny. 1990. "A Comparison of Alprazolam and Behavior Therapy in Treatment of Panic Disorder." *Journal of Consulting and Clinical Psychology* 58(1): 77-84.

Kovacs, M. 1979. "Treating Depressive Disorders." *Behavior Modification* 3(October): 496–517.

Krasnegor, N. 1980. "Analysis and Modification of Substance Abuse: A Behavioral Overview." *Behavior Modification* 4(January): 35–55.

Kratochwill, T.R. 1978. *Single Subject Research*. New York:Academic Press.

Lab, S.P., and J.T. Whitehead. 1990. "From 'Nothing Works' to 'The Appropriate Works': The Latest Stop on the Search for the Secular Grail." *Criminology* 28(3): 405–18.

_____ 1988. "An Analysis of Juvenile Correctional Treatment." *Crime and Delinquency* 24 (January): 60–83.

Lambert, M. J. 1976. "Spontaneous Remission in Adult Neurotic Disorders: A Revision and Summary." *Psychological Bulletin* 83(1): 107–19.

Lambert, M.J., D. A. Shapiro, and A. E. Bergin. 1986. "The Effectiveness of Psychotherapy." In *Handbook of Psychotherapy and Behavior Change*, edited by S.L. Garfield and A.E. Bergin. New York:John Wiley.

Landman, J.T., and R.M. Dawes. 1982. "Psychotherapy Outcome: Smith and Glass' Conclusions Stand Up Under Scrutiny." *American Psychologist* 37(5): 504–16.

Lasch, C. 1978. *The Culture of Narcissism*. New York:Norton.

Leiby, J. 1978. *A History of Social Work and Social Welfare*. New York:Columbia University Press.

Leff, J., L Kuipers, R. Berkowitz, R. Eberlein, and D. Sturgeon. 1982. "A Controlled Trial of Social Intervention in the Families of Schizophrenic Patients." *British Journal of Psychiatry* 141: 121–34.

Lerman, P. 1984. "Child Welfare, the Private Sector, and Community-based Corrections." *Crime and Delinquency* 30: 5–38.

Lester, M.E., and W.J. Doherty. 1983. "Couples' Long-Term Evaluations of Their Marriage Encounter Experience." *Journal of Marital and Family Therapy* 9(2): 183–88.

Leukefeld, C.G. 1990. *Aids and Intravenous Drug Use: Future Directions for Community Based Prevention Programs*. Rockville, MD:National Institute on Drug Abuse.

Levine, K.A. 1975. "How and Why the Experiments Came About." In *Work Incentives and Income Guarantees: The New Jersey Income Tax Experiment*, edited by J. Pechman and P.M. Timpane. Washington, DC: Brookings Institution.

Lewinsohn, P.M., G.N. Clarke, H. Hops, and J. Andrews. 1990. "Cognitive-Behavioral Treatment for Depressed Adolescents" *Behavior Therapy* 21: 385–401.

Liddle, H.A., and R.J. Halpin. 1978. "Family Therapy Training and Supervision Literature: A Comparative Review." *Journal of Marriage and Family Counseling* 4:77–98.

Linn, M.W., E.M. Caffey, C.J. Klett, G.E. Hogarty, and H.R. Lamb. 1979. "Day Treatment and Psychotropic Drugs in the Aftercare of Schizophrenic Patients." *Archives of General Psychiatry* 38(October):1055–66.

Lipton, D., R. Martinson, and J. Wilks. 1975. *The Effectiveness of Correctional Treatment*. New York:Praeger.

Luborsky, L. and B. Singer. 1975. "Comparative Studies of Psychotherapies: Is It True that 'Everybody has Won and All Must have Prizes.'" *Archives of General Psychiatry* 32(August): 995–1008.

Lundman, R.J., P.T. McFarlane, and F.R. Scarpitti. 1976. "Delinquency Prevention: Description and Assessment of Projects Reported in Professional Literature." *Crime and Delinquency* 22(3):297–308.

McAuliffe, W.E. 1990. "A Randomized Controlled Trial of Recovery Training and Self-help for Opioid Addicts in New England and Hong Kong." *Journal of Psychoactive Drugs* 22(2): 197–208.

McClean, P.D., and A.R. Hakstian. 1990. "Relative Endurance of Unipolar Depression Treatment Effects: Longitudinal Follow-up." *Journal of Consulting and Clinical Psychology* 58(4): 482–88.

McCord, W., and J. Sanchez. 1983. "The Treatment of Deviant Children: A Twenty-five Year Follow-up Study." *Crime and Delinquency* 29:238–53.

Magura, S., C. Casriel, and D.S. Goldsmith. 1987. "Contracting with Clients in Methadone Treatment." *Social Casework* 68(October):485–93.

Mann, B.J., C.M. Borduin, S.W. Henggeler, and D.M. Blaske. 1990. "An Investigation of Systemic Conceptualizations of Parent-Child Coalitions and Symptom Change." *Journal of Consulting and Clinical Psychology* 58(3): 336–344.

Manne, S.L., W.H. Redd, and P.P. Jacobson. 1990. "Behavioral Intervention to Reduce Child and Parent Distress During Venipuncture." *Journal of Consulting and Clinical Psychology* 58(5):565–72.

Marchine, K.E. 1987. "Cognitive Behavioral Treatment of Agoraphobia." *Behavioral Research and Therapy* 255:319–28.

Marmor, R.R., J.L. Mace, and P.L. Harvey. 1990. *America's Misunderstood Welfare State*. New York:Basic Books.

Marris, P., and M. Rein. 1973. *Dilemmas of Social Reform: Poverty and Community Action in the United States.* Chicago:Aldine.

Martinson, R. 1976. "California Research at the Crossroads." *Crime and Delinquency* (April):180-91.

———— 1974. "What Works—Questions and Answers about Prison Reform." *Public Interest* (Spring):22-54.

Masten, A.S. 1979. "Family Therapy as a Treatment for Children: A Critical Review of Outcome Research." *Family Process* 18:303-35.

Matson, J.L. and V. Senatore. 1981. "A Comparison of Traditional Psychotherapy and Social Skills Training for Improving Interpersonal Functioning of Mentally Retarded Adults." *Behavior Therapy* 12:369-82.

Mattick, R.P., and L. Peters. 1988. "Treatment of Severe Social Phobia: Effects of Guided Exposure With and Without Cognitive Restructuring." *Journal of Consulting and Clinical Psychology* 56(2): 251-60.

May, P.R.A. 1971. "For Better or for Worse? Psychotherapy and Variance Change: A Critical Review of the Literature." *Journal of Nervous and Mental Disease* 152:184-92.

Mays, D.T., and C.M. Franks. 1980. "Getting Worse: Psychotherapy or No Treatment—The Jury Should Still be Out." *Professional Psychology* 11: 78-92.

Mehlman, S.K., D.H. Baucom, and D. Anderson. 1983. "Effectiveness of Cotherapists Versus Single Therapists and Immediate Versus Delayed Treatment in Behavioral Marital Therapy." *Journal of Consulting and Clinical Psychology* 51(2):258-66.

Meinert, C.L. 1986. *Clinical Trials: Design, Conduct, and Analysis.* Oxford:Oxford University Press.

Meltzoff, J., and M. Kornreich. 1970. *Research in Psychotherapy.* New York:Atherton.

Mickelson, D.J., and R.R. Stevic. 1971. "Differential Effects of Facilitative and Non-facilitative Behavioral Counselors." *Journal of Counseling Psychology* 18:314-19.

Miller, I.W., W.H. Norman, and G.I. Keitner. 1989. "Cognitive-Behavioral Treatment of Depressed Inpatients." *Behavior Therapy* 20:25-47.

Miller, R.C., and J.S. Berman. 1983. "The Efficacy of Cognitive Behavioral Therapies: A Quantitative Review of the Research Evidence." *Psychological Bulletin* (1): 39-53.

Miller, W.R. 1980. "Focused versus Broad-Spectrum Behavior Therapy for Problem Drinkers." *Journal of Consulting and Clinical Psychology* 48(5):590-01.

Mitchell, J., and C.K. Varley. 1990. "Isolation and Restraint in Juvenile Correctional Facilities." *Journal of the American Academy of Child and Adolescent Psychiatry* 29: 251-55.

Morris, J.B. 1987. "Group Psychotherapy for Prolonged Postnatal Depression." *British Journal of Medical Psychology* 60: 279-81.

Morris, R.J., and K.R. Suckerman. 1974. "Therapist Warmth as a Factor in Automated Systematic Desensitization." *Journal of Consulting and Clinical Psychology* 21: 244-50.

Munnell, A.H. 1987. *Lessons from the Income Maintenance Experiments,* Boston: Federal Reserve Bank of Boston.

Musto, D. F. 1973. *The American Disease: Origins of Narcotic Control* New Haven, CT: Yale University Press.

Namenek, A.A., and W.J. Schuldt. 1971. Differential Effects of Experimenters' Personality and Instructional Sets on Verbal Conditioning." *Journal of Counseling Psychology* 18: 170-73.

National Association of Social Workers. 1987. *Encyclopedia of Social Work.* Silver Spring, MD:NASW.

National Institute on Alcohol Abuse and Alcoholism. 1990. *National Directory of Drug and Alcoholism Treatment and Prevention Programs.* Rockville, MD:US Department of Health and Human Services, Public Health Service, Alcohol, Drug Abuse and Mental Health Administration.

National Institute on Drug Abuse. 1988, 1989, 1990. *National Household Survey on Drug Abuse.* Rockville, MD:US Department of Health and Human Services, Public Health Service, Alcohol, Drug Abuse and Mental Health Administration.

Neubeck, K.J., and J.L. Roach. 1981. "Income Maintenance Experiments, Politics and the Perpetuation of Poverty." *Social Problems* 28(3)(February): 308-20.

Nezu, A.M., and M.G. Perri. 1989. "Social Problem-Solving Therapy for Unipolar Depression: An Initial Dismantling Investigation." *Journal for Consulting and Clinical Psychology* 57(3):408-13.

Nirenberg, T.D., and S.A. Maisto. 1990. "The Relationship between Assessment and Alcohol Treatment." *International Journal of the Addictions* 25(11): 1275-85.

Nirenberg, T.D. and S.A. Maisto, eds. 1987. *Developments in the Assessment and Treatment of Addictive Behaviors.* Norwood, NJ:Alex Publishing.

O'Farrell, T.J., H.S.G. Cutter, and F.J. Floyd. 1985. "Evaluating Behavioral Marital Therapy for Male Alcoholics: Effects on Marital Adjustment and Communication from Before to After Treatment." *Behavior Therapy* 16: 147-67.

Office of Technology Assessment. 1980. *The Implications of Cost-Effectiveness Analysis of Medical Technology Background Paper #3: The Efficacy and Cost-Effectiveness of Psychotherapy.* United States Congress, Washington, DC.

O'Leary, K.D. 1981. "A Comparative Outcome Study of Behavioral Marital Therapy and Communication Therapy." *Journal of Marital and Family Therapy* 7: 159-69.

O'Leary, K.D., and S.R.H. Beach. 1990. "Marital Therapy: A Viable Treatment for Depression and Marital Discord." *American Journal of Psychiatry* 147(2):183-86.

O'Leary, K.D., and G.T. Wilson. 1980. *Behavior Therapy: Application and Outcome.* Englewood Cliffs, NJ:Prentice-Hall.

_____ 1975. *Behavior Therapy: Application and Outcome.* Englewood Cliffs, NJ:Prentice-Hall

Olson, I. 1970. "Some Effects of Increased Aid in Money and Social Services to Families Getting AFDC Grants." *Child Welfare* 49(February): 94-104.

Olson, D.H., C. S. Russell, and D. H. Sprenkle. 1980. "Marital and Family Therapy: A Decade Review." *Journal of Marriage and the Family* 42:973-94.

Ozawa, M. 1982. *Income Maintenance and Work Incentives.* New York:Praeger Publishers.

Palmer, J.L., and J.A. Pechman, eds. 1978. *Welfare In Rural Areas: The North Carolina-Iowa Income Maintenance Experiment.* Washington, DC:Brookings Institution.

Palmer, T. 1991. "The Effectiveness of Intervention: Recent Trends and Current Issues." *Crime and Delinquency* 37(3): 369-404.

_____ 1975. "Martinson Revisited." *Journal of Research in Crime and Delinquency.* (July):133-52.

_____ 1974. "The Youth Authority's Community Treatment Program." *Federal Probation.* 38(1):3-14.

Parloff, M.B. 1978. "Assessment of Psychosocial Treatment of Mental Health Disorders." Report to the National Academy of Sciences, Institute of Medicine. Washington, DC.

Patterson, C.H. 1984. "Empathy, Warmth, and Genuineness in Psychotherapy: A Review of Reviews." *Psychotherapy* 21(4): 431–38.

Petersilia, J., and S. Turner. 1986. *Prison versus Probation in California: Implications for Crime and Offender Recidivism.* Santa Monica, CA:Rand.

Phillips, J., and R. Ray. 1980. "Behavioral Approaches to Childhood Disorders." *Behavior Modification* 4(January):3–34.

Piele, C. 1988. "Research Paradigms in Social Work: From Stalemate to Creative Synthesis." *Social Service Review* 62(1)

Pieper, M.H., and W.J. Pieper. 1990. *Intrapsychic Humanism: an Introduction to a Comprehensive Psychology and Philosophy of the Mind.* Chicago:Falcon 11 Press.

Piliavin, I., and A.E. Gross. 1977. "The Effects of Separation of Services and Income Maintenance on AFDC Recipients." *Social Service Review* 51(September):389–406.

Pilkonis, P.A. 1984. "A Comparative Outcome Study of Individual, Group, and Conjoint Psychotherapy." *Archives of General Psychiatry* 41(May): 431–37.

Piper, W.E., H.F.A. Azim, M. McCallum, and A.S. Joyce. 1990. "Patient Suitability and Outcome in Short-Term Individual Psychotherapy." *Journal of Consulting and Clinical Psychology* 58(4): 475–81.

Pisterman, S., P. McGrath, P. Firestone, J.T. Goodman, I. Webster, and R. Mallory. 1989. "Outcome of Parent-Mediated Treatment of Preschoolers with Attention Deficit Disorder with Hyperactivity." *Journal of Consulting and Clinical Psychology* 57(5):628–35.

Polster, R.A. 1986. "Research in Behavioral Parent Training in Social Work: A Review." *Journal of Social Service Research* 10(2,3,4): 37–52.

Prioleau, L., M. Murdock, and N. Brady. 1983. "An Analysis of Psychotherapy versus Placebo Studies." *Behavioral and Brain Sciences* 6:275–310.

Proctor, E.K. 1990. "Evaluating Clinical Practice: Issues of Purpose and Design." *Social Work Research and Abstracts* 26(1)(March): 32–40.

Rabkin, Y.M. 1988. *Science Between the Superpowers.* NY:Priority Press.

Rachman, S. 1971. *The Effects of Psychological Treatment.* Oxford:Perragon Press.

Ratcliff, K.S. 1984. Book Review of *The St. Louis Conundrum. Contemporary Sociology* 13(1): 50–1.

Rausch, S. 1983. "Court Processing versus Diversion of Status Offenders: A Test of Deterrence and Labeling Theories." *Journal of Research in Crime and Delinquency* 20: 39–54.

Ravetz, J.R. 1990. *The Merger of Knowledge with Power*. London:Mansell Publishing Ltd.

Ravetz, J.R. 1971. *Scientific Knowledge and its Social Problems*. Oxford:Clarendon Press.

Raz-Duvshani, A. 1986. "Cognitive Structure Changes with Psychotherapy in Neurosis." *British Journal of Medical Psychology* 59:341–50.

Rehm, L.P., N. J. Kaslow, and A. S. Rabin. 1987. "Cognitive and Behavioral Targets in a Self-Control Therapy Program for Depression." *Journal of Consulting and Clinical Psychology* 55(1): 60–67.

Rehm, L.P., S.J. Kornblit, M.W. Ottara, D.M. Lamparski, J.M. Romano, and J.I. Volkin. 1981. "An Evaluation of Major Components in a Self-Control Therapy Program for Depression. *Behavior Modification* 5(4) 459–89.

Reid, W.J. 1978. *The Task Centered System*. New York:Columbia University Press.

Reid, W.J., L. Epstein, L. B. Brown, E. Tolson, and r. H Rodney. 1980. "Task Centered Social Work." *Social Work in Education* 2(January):7–24.

Reid, W.J., and P. Hanrahan. 1982. "Recent Evaluations of Social Work: Grounds for Optimism." *Social Work* 27(4):328–40.

Rezmovic, E.L. In Sechrest op. cit:163–209.

Riccio, J. 1986. *Final Report on the Virginia Employment Services Program*. New York:MDRC.

Rimm, D.C., and J.C. Masters. 1974. *Behavior Therapy: Techniques and Empirical Findings*. New York:Academic Press.

Robin, A.L. 1976. "Behavioral Instruction in the College Classroom." *Review of Educational Research* 46:313–54.

Robins, P.K., ed. 1980. *Guaranteed Annual Income: Evidence from a Social Experiment*. NY:Academic Press.

Rodwell, M.K. 1987. "Naturalistic Inquiry: An Alternative Model for Social Work Assessment." *Social Service Review* 61(2): 231–46.

Rose, G., and I.M. Marshall. 1974. *Counseling and School Social Work: An Experimental Study*. London: John Wiley.

Rosenthal, R. 1983. "Assessing the Statistical and Social Importance of the Effects of Psychotherapy." *Journal of Consulting and Clinical Psychology* 51(1):4–13.

Rosenthal, R., and R. Rosnow. 1984. *Essentials of Behavior Research*. NY:Mc-Graw Hill.

Rosenthal, R., and D.B. Rubin. 1978. "Interpersonal Expectancy Effects: The First 345 Studies." *Behavioral and Brain Sciences* 3:379–86.

Roskin, M. 1982. "Coping with Life Changes—A Preventative Social Work Approach." *American Journal of Community Psychology* 10(Fall): 331–39.

Ross, R.R., and E.A. Fabiano. 1988. "Reasoning and Rehabilitation." *International Journal of Offender Therapy and Comparative Criminology* 32: 29–35.

Rothman, R. 1980. *Conscience and Convenience*. Boston:Little, Brown.

Rounsaville, B.J., E.S. Chevron, B.A. Prusoff, I. Elkin, S. Imbers, S. Sotsky, and J. Watkins. 1987. "The Relation Between Specific and General Dimensions of the Psychotherapy Process in Interpersonal Psychotherapy of Depression." *Journal of Consulting and Clinical Psychology* 55(3):379–84.

Rubin, A. 1985. "Practice Effectiveness: More Grounds for Optimism." *Social Work* 30(6).

Ruckdeschel, R.A. 1985. "Qualitative Research as a Perspective." *Social Work Research and Abstracts* 21(2):17–22.

Russell, C.S., S.A. Anderson, R.B. Atilano, A.P. Jurich, and L.P. Bergen. 1984. "Intervention Strategies: Predicting Family Therapy Outcome." *Journal of Marital and Family Therapy* 10(3): 241–51.

Russell, G.F.M., G.I. Szmukler, C. Dare, and I Eisler. 1987. "An Evaluation of Family Therapy in Anorexia Nervosa and Bulimia Nervosa." *Archives of General Psychiatry* 44(December):1047–56.

Rutter, M., and H. Giller. 1984. *Juvenile Delinquency*. New York: Guilford Press.

San, L., G. Pomarol, J.M. Peri, J.M. Ollie, and J. Cami. 1991. "Follow-up after a Six-month Maintenance Period on Naltrexone versus Placebo in Heroin Addicts." *British Journal Of Addiction* 86:983–90.

Schneider, A.L., and P.R. Schneider. 1984. "A Comparison of Programmatic and Ad Hoc Restitution in Juvenile Court." *Justice Quarterly* 1: 529–47.

Schwartz, D. 1980. *Clinical Trials*. New York:Academic Press.

Schwartz, E.E., and W.C. Sample. 1967a. "First Findings from Midway." *Social Service Review* 41(June): 113–51.

_____ 1967b. *The Midway Office*. New York:National Association of Social Workers.

Scogin, F., C. Jamison, and K. Gochneau. 1989. "Comparative Efficacy of Cognitive and Behavioral Bibliotherapy for Mildly and Moderately Depressed Older Adults." *Journal of Consulting and Clinical Psychology* 57(3):403-07.

Sechrest, D.K. 1989. "Prison 'Boot Camps" Do Not Measure Up." *Federal Probation* (September):15-20.

Sechrest, L., S.O. White, and E.D. Brown, eds. 1979 *The Rehabilitation of Criminal Offenders*. Washington, DC:National Academy of Sciences.

Segal, S. 1972. "Research on the Outcome of Social Work Therapeutic Interventions: A Review of the Literature." *Journal of Health and Social Behavior* 13(March): 3-17.

Select Committee on Narcotics Abuse and Control. United States House of Representatives. July 1989.

Selke, W.L. 1982. "Diversion and Crime Prevention: A Time-Series Analysis." *Criminology* 20:395-406.

Sells, S.B., and D.D. Simpson. 1979. "Evaluation of Treatment Outcome for Youths in the Drug Abuse Reporting Program (DARP): A Follow-up Study." In *Youth Drug Abuse*, edited by Beschner and Friedman. Lexington, MA:Lexington Books.

Senatore, V. 1983. "A Comparison of Behavioral Methods to Train Social Skills to Mentally Retarded Adults." *Behavior Therapy* 13:313-24.

Shapiro, D.A. 1985. "Recent Applications of Meta-analyses in Clinical Research." *Clinical Psychology Review* 5:13-34.

Shapiro, D.A., M. Barkam, G.E. Hardy, and L.A. Morrison. 1990. "The Second Sheffield Psychotherapy Project: Rationale, Design and Preliminary Outcome Data." *British Journal of Medical Psychology* 63: 97-108.

Shapiro, D.A., and D. Shapiro. 1983. "Comparative Therapy Outcome Research: Methodological Implications of Meta-analysis." *Journal of Consulting and Clinical Psychology* 51(1):42-53.

_____ 1982a. "Meta-analysis of Comparative Therapy Outcome Research: a Critical Review." *Behavioral Psychotherapy* 10:4-25.

_____ 1982b. "Meta-analysis of Comparative Therapy Outcome Studies: A Replication and Refinement." *Psychological Bulletin* 93(3): 581-604.

Shapiro, S.H., and T.A. Louis. 1983. *Clinical Trials: Issues and Approaches*. New York:Marcel Dekker.

Sheldon, B. 1986. "Social Work Effectiveness Experiments: Review and Implications." *British Journal of Social Work* 16(2): 223-42.

Shipley, R.H., and P.A. Boudewyns. 1980. "Flooding and Implosive Therapy: Are They Harmful?" *Behavior Therapy* 11: 503–08.

Shivrattan, J.L. 1988. "Social Interactional Training and Incarcerated Juvenile Delinquents." *Canadian Journal of Criminology* 30(April):145–63.

Shorts, I.D. 1986. "Delinquency by Association." *British Journal of Criminology* 26: 156–63.

Sidney, S. 1990. "Discrepant Data Regarding Trends in Marijuana Use and Supply, 1985-1988." *Journal of Psychoactive Drugs* 22(3).

Siegel, L.J., and J.J. Senna. 1991. *Juvenile Delinquency.* St. Paul:West Publishing.

Silverman, J.S., J.A. Silverman, and D.A. Eardley. 1984. "Do Maladaptive Attitudes Cause Depression." *Archives of General Psychiatry* 41(January):28–30.

Simons, A.D., G.E. Murphy, J.L. Levine, and R.D. Wetzel. 1986. "Cognitive Therapy and Parmacotherapy for Depression." *Archives of General Psychiatry* 43(January):43–8.

Smith, D. 1979. "Treatment Services for Youthful Drug Users." In *Youth Drug Abuse,* edited by Beschner and Friedman. Lexington, MA:Lexington Books.

Smith, J.W., and P.J. Frawley. 1990. "Long Term Abstinence from Alcohol in Patients Receiving Aversion Therapy as Part of a Multimodal Inpatient Program." *Journal of Substance Abuse* 7(2): 77–82.

Smith, M.L., and G.V. Glass. 1977. "Meta-analysis of Psychotherapy Outcome Studies." *American Psychologist* 32(September):752–60.

Smith, M.L., G.V. Glass, and T.I. Miller. 1980. *The Benefits of Psychotherapy.* Baltimore MD:Johns Hopkins Press.

Snyder, D.K., and R.M. Wills. 1989. "Behavioral Versus Insight-Oriented Marital Therapy: Effects on Individual and Interspousal Functioning." *Journal of Consulting and Clinical Psychology* 57(1):39–46.

Snyder, D.K., R.M. Wills, and A. Gradyfle. 1991. "Long-Term Effectiveness of Behavioral Versus Insight-Oriented Marital Therapy: A 4-Year Follow-Up Study." *Journal of Consulting and Clinical Psychology* 59(1):138–41.

Sokol, L. 1989. "Cognitive Therapy of Panic Disorder." *Journal of Nervous and Mental Disease* 177(12)(December):711–16.

Specht, H. 1990. "Social Work and the Popular Therapies." *Social Service Review* 64(3): 345–57.

Spergel, I.A. 1984a. Book Review of *The St. Louis Conundrum. Social Work and Research Abstracts* 20(2):3–7.

_____ 1984b. Comment on the Review of *Conundrum Social Work Research and Abstracts* 20(4):30–1.

Sprenkle, D.H., and C.L. Storm. 1983. "Divorce Therapy Outcome Research: A Substantive and Methodological Review." *Journal of Marital and Family Therapy* 9(3):239–58.

Spriet, A., and P. Simon. 1985. *Methodology of Clinical Drug Trials.* Basel, Switzerland: Karger.

Stanton, M.D. 1979."Family Treatment Approaches to Drug Abuse Problems: A Review." *Family Process* 18:251–80.

Stanton, M.D., F. Steier, and T.C. Todd. 1982. "Paying Families for Attending Sessions: Counteracting the Dropout Problem." *Journal of Marital and Family Therapy* 8:371–73.

Stanton, M.D., and T.C. Todd. 1982. *The Family Therapy of Drug Abuse and Addiction.* New York:Guilford Press.

Statistical Abstract of the United States. 1990. Washington, DC: U.S. Department of Commerce

Stein, J. 1976. "Early Intervention in Foster Care." *Public Welfare* 34(Spring): 38–44.

Stein, J. 1978. *Children in Foster Homes.* New York:Praeger Publishers.

Stein, J., and E. Gambrill. 1977. "Facilitating Decision Making in Foster Care." *Social Service Review* 51(September): 502–11.

Stein, L.I., and M.A. Test. 1980. "Alternatives to Mental Hospital Treatment." *Archives of General Psychiatry* 37(April): 392–412.

Steinbach, C. 1991 *Innovations in State and Local Government 1991* New York: Ford Foundation

Steinbrueck, S.M., S.E. Maxwell, and G.S. Howard. 1983. "A Meta-analysis of Psychotherapy and Drug Therapy in the Treatment of Unipolar Depression with Adults." *Journal of Consulting and Clinical Psychology* 51(6):856–63.

Strube, M.J., and D.P. Hartmann. 1983. "Meta-analysis: Techniques, Applications, and Functions." *Journal of Consulting and Clinical Psychology* 21(1):14–27.

_____ 1982. "A Critical Appraisal of Meta-analysis." *British Journal of Clinical Psychology* 21:129–39.

Stryker, R. 1990. "Science, Class and the Welfare State." *American Journal of Sociology* 96(3).

Stunkard, A., and M. Mahoney. 1976. In *Handbook of Behavior Modification and Behavior Therapy*, edited by H. Leitenberg. Englewood Cliffs, NJ:Prentice-Hall.

Subcommittee on Long Term Care, Select Committee on Aging. United States House of Representatives. 1981. Quackery: A $10 Billion Scandal. Washington, DC: Government Printing Office.

Swift, W.J. 1982. "The Long-term Outcome of Early Onset Anorexia Nervosa." *Journal of the American Academy of Child Psychiatry* 21:38–46.

Szapocznik, J., W.M. Kurtines, F.H. Foote, A. Perezvid, and O. Hervis. 1983. "Conjoint Versus One-Person Family Therapy: Some Evidence for the Effectiveness of Conducting Family Therapy Through One Person." *Journal of Consulting and Clinical Psychology* 51(6): 889–99.

Szapocznik, J., E. Murray, M. Scopetta, O. Hervis, A. Rio, and R. Cohen. 1989. "Structural Family Versus Psychodynamic Child Therapy for Problematic Hispanic Boys." *Journal of Consulting and Clinical Psychology* 57(5):571–78.

Tableman, B., D. Marchiniak, D. Johnson, and R. Rodgers. 1980. "Stress Management Training for Women on Public Assistance." *American Journal of Community Psychiatry* 10(Fall):357–67.

Telch, C.F., W.S. Agras, E.M. Rossiter, D. Wilfley, and J.Kenardy. 1990. "Group Cognitive-Behavioral Treatment for the Nonpurging Bulimic: An Initial Evaluation." *Journal of Consulting and Clinical Psychiatry* 58(5):629–35.

Thomlison, R.J. 1984. "Something Works: Evidence from Practice Effectiveness Studies." *Social Work* 29(1): 51–6. Thomlison, R.J. 1972. "A Behavioral Model for Social Work Intervention with the Marital Dyad." Ph.D. diss., University of Toronto.

Thompson, L.W., D. Gallegher, J.S. Breckenridge. 1987. "Comparative Effectiveness of Psychotherapies for Depressed Elders." *Journal of Counseling and Clinical Psychology* 55(3): 385–90.

Tobler, N.S. 1986. "Meta-analysis of 143 Adolescent Drug Prevention Programs—Quantitative Outcome Results of Program Participants Compared to a Control or Comparison Group."*Journal of Drug Issues* 16(4):537–67.

Tolman, R.M., and S.D. Rose. 1989. "Teaching Clients to Cope with Stress: The Effectiveness of Structured Group Stress Management Training." *Journal of Social Service Research* 13(2): 45–66.

Toseland, R.W. 1990. "Long-Term Effectiveness of Peer-Led and Professionally Led Support Groups for Caregivers." *Social Service Review* 64(2):308–27.

Toseland, R.W., C.M. Rossiter, and M.S. Labrecqu. 1989. " The Effectiveness of two Kinds of Support Groups for Caregivers." *Social Service Review* 63(3):415-32.

Toseland, R., E. Sherman, and S. Bliven. 1981. "The Comparative Effectiveness of Two Group Work Approaches for the Development of Mental Support Groups among the Elderly." *Social Work with Groups* 4(Spring-Summer):137-53.

United States Department of Justice. 1989. *Correctional Populations in the United States. 1986.* Washington, DC: Government Printing Office.

Velasquez, S., and H.I. McCubbin. 1980. "Towards Establishing the Effectiveness of Community Based Residential Treatment Program Evaluation by Experimental Research." *Journal of Social Service Research* (Summer):337-59.

Videka-Sherman, L. 1988. "Meta-analysis of Research on Social Work Practice in Mental Health." *Social Work* 33(4): 325-38.

Vitalo, R.L. 1970. "Effects of Facilitative Interpersonal Functioning in a Conditioning Paradigm." *Journal of Counseling Psychology* 17:141-44.

Wakefield, J.C. 1988a. "Psychotherapy, Distributive Justice and Social Work Part I." *Social Service Review* 62(2):186-210.

_____ 1988b. "Psychotherapy, Distributive Justice and Social Work Part II." *Social Service Review* 62(3):353-81.

Wampler, K.S. 1982a. "The Effectiveness of the Minnesota Couple Communication Program: A Review of Research." *Journal of Marital and Family Therapy* 8:345-56.

_____ 1982b. "Bringing the Review of Literature into the Age of Quantification: Meta-analysis as a strategy for Integrating Research Findings in Family Studies." *Journal of Marriage and the Family* 44:1009-23.

Weidman, J.C., R.N. White, and B.K. Swartz. 1988. "Training Women on Welfare for 'High-Tech' Jobs." *Evaluation and Program Planning* 11(2): 105-15.

Weisz, J.R., B. R. Walter, and B. Weiss. 1990. "Arrests among Emotionally Disturbed Violent and Assaultive Individuals Following Minimal versus Lengthy Intervention through North Carolina's Willie M. Program." *Journal of Consulting and Clinical Psychology* 58(6):720-28.

Weisz, J.R., B. Weiss, M.D. Alicke, and M.L. Klotz. 1987. "Effectiveness of Psychotherapy with Children and Adolescents: A Meta-analysis for Clinicians." *Journal of Consulting and Clinical Psychology* 55:542-49.

Wellisch, D.K., and G.K. Ro-Trock. 1980. "A Three-Year Follow-up of Family Therapy." *International Journal of Family Therapy* 2(3): 169–75.

Wells, R.A., and A.E. Dezen. 1978. "The Results of Family Therapy Revisited: The Nonbehavioral Methods." *Family Process* 17:251–74.

Whitaker, J.M. 1984. "A Comprehensive Community-Based Youth Diversion Program." *Child Welfare* 63:175–81.

Whitehead, J.T., and S.P. Lab. 1989. "A Meta-analysis of Juvenile Correctional Treatment." *Journal of Research in Crime and Delinquency* 26:276–95.

Whitney, D., and S.D. Rose. 1989. "The Effect of Process and Structured Content on Outcome in Stress Management Groups." *Journal of Social Service Research* 13(2):89–104.

Williams, S.L., P.J. Kinney, and J. Falbo. 1989. "Generalization of Therapeutic Changes in Agoraphobia: The Role of Perceived Self-Efficacy." *Journal of Consulting and Clinical Psychology* 57(3):436–42.

Wilson, J.Q. 1980. "'What Works' Revisited: New Findings on Criminal Rehabilitation." *Public Interest* 61(Fall):3–17.

Wilson, J. Q., and R. J. Herrnstein. 1985. *Crime and Human Nature* New York: Simon and Schuster.

Wilson, R.A. 1967. "An Evaluation of Intensive Casework Impact." *Public Welfare* 25(October):301–6.

Witkin, S.L. 1991. "Empirical Clinical Practice: A Critical Analysis." *Social Work* 26(2):158–62.

Wood, K. M. 1978 "Casework Effectiveness: A New Look at the Research Evidence." *Social Work* 23(November): 437–58.

Woody, G.E., A.T. McLellan, L. Luborsky, and C.P. O'Brien. 1987. "Twelve-Month Follow-Up of Psychotherapy for Opiate Dependence." *American Journal of Psychiatry* 144(5)(May):590–96.

Wootton, B. 1959. *Social Science and Social Pathology*. London:George Allen and Unwin.

Wrobel, A. 1987. *Pseudo-science and Society in Nineteenth-Century America*. Lexington, KY:University Press of Kentucky.

Yohman, J.R., K.W. Schaeffe, and D.A. Parsons. 1988. "Cognitive Training in Alcoholic Men." *Journal of Consulting and Clinical Psychology* 56(1):67–72.

Zimmerman, J. 1989. "Determinism, Science and Social Work." *Social Service Review* 63(1):52–62.

Author Index

235

Subject Index

AIDS, 140-141
Aid to Families with Dependent Children (AFDC), 3, 101-102, 104, 113
Aid to Families with Dependent Children of Unemployed Parents (AFDC-U), 113
Anti-Graffiti Network (project), 116
Appropriate treatment, 70-74, 91-92; social work and 70
Arkansas (project), 122-125
Attrition, 24, 54, 56

Battered mates (project), 94
Behavior modification, 73-77; and eating disorders, 91; and neurotic disorders, 91
Blinding, 25, 26, 56
Boot camps, 155
Box scores, 152

Censoring 24, 54
Chicago (project), 131-132
Collegefields (project), 150
Community Treatment Program (CTP), 141-145, 152, 154, 185
Conspiracy theory, 13
Contracting, 138-140
Corrections, 145-148
Counseling, 163, 172, 180
Critical tests, 31
Critical tradition, 9; in corrections, 188, 184; in psychotherapy, 47; in social work, 96
Cultural equality, 67

Deinstitutionalization (project in mental health), 87-88
Deinstitutionalization of Status Offenders (project), 161
Dilemma of social welfare, 96, 187; defined, 7
Door (project), 172-173, 186
Drunk driving, 96

Drug abuse, 1, 6-8, 11, 17, 23, 42, 139, 168-182; and social work, 63, 90, 96; and treatment, 6, 140-141, 168-182
Drug Abuse Reporting Program (DARP), 173-175, 183
Drug addiction. See Drug abuse

Economic poverty, 2-4
Essexfields (project), 150, 152
Expectancy bias, 6, 9, 55, 65

Family therapy, 177
Field experiments, 102
Ford Foundation, 21, 116, 195
Foster care (project), 85-86
Freedom of expression, 57
Friends of the Family (project), 116
Fugitive research, 148-149, 168, 170, 172, 186
Functional family therapy, 158-159

Grey Area Projects, 116
Guided Group Interaction (GGI), 149-153, 155

Highfields Project, 150
Home-based counseling, 159
Human services, 6, 8-13, 15; research methods in, 17-19, 22-31. See also Social services

Innovations in State and Local Government, 113-136
Institute of Behavioral Research, 174
Intensive case management, 166-167
Intensive community treatment. See Community Treatment Program
Interpersonal Skills Training (project), 84

Juvenile crime. See Juvenile delinquency
Juvenile delinquency, 1, 7-8, 17, 51-52, 78-83, 91, 100, 139-168, 184-185, 186-188, 189, 200

Printed in the United States
by Baker & Taylor Publisher Services